Empty Nurseries, Queer Occupants

Who is the proper occupant of the nursery? The obvious answer is the child, and not an archive, a seductive troll-princess, or poor fosterlings. Nevertheless, characters in *Hedda Gabler*, *The Master Builder*, and *Little Eyolf* intend to host these improper occupants in their children's rooms. Dr. Gunn calls these dramas "the empty nursery plays" because they all describe rooms intended for offspring, as well as characters' plans for refilling that space. One might expect nurseries to provide an ideal setting for a realist playwright to dramatize contemporary problems. Rather than mattering to Ibsen in terms of naturalist detail or explicit social critique, however, they are reserved for the maintenance of characters' fears and expectations concerning the future. *Empty Nurseries, Queer Occupants* intervenes in scholarly debates in child studies by arguing that the empty bourgeois nursery is a better symbol for innocence than the child. Here, "emptiness" refers to the common construction of the child as blank and latent. In Ibsen, the child is also doomed or deceased, and thus essentially absent, but nurseries persist as spaces of memorialization and potential alike. Nurseries also gesture toward the domains of childhood and women's labor, from birth to domestic service. "Bourgeois nursery" points to the classed construction of innocence and to the more materialist aspects of this book, which inform our understanding of domesticity and family in the West and uncover a set of reproductive connotations broader than "the innocent child" can convey.

Olivia Noble Gunn is Assistant Professor and Sverre Arestad Endowed Chair in Norwegian Studies at the University of Washington, Seattle. She completed her PhD in comparative literature at the University of California, Irvine, in 2012. Gunn has been a fellow of the Society of Scholars at the Simpson Center for the Humanities and received a Royalty Research Fund grant to support archival research in Norway. She has published research on adaptations of Ibsen and on constructions of the family, class, gender, and racialization in Norwegian literature and film. Her teaching interests range from the modern novel to representations of sexuality in the Nordic countries. Gunn currently serves as the President of the Ibsen Society of America.

Studies in Childhood, 1700 to the Present

This series recognizes and supports innovative work on the child and on literature for children and adolescents that informs teaching and engages with current and emerging debates in the field. Proposals are welcome for interdisciplinary and comparative studies by humanities scholars working in a variety of fields, including literature; book history, periodicals history, and print culture and the sociology of texts; theater, film, musicology, and performance studies; history, including the history of education; gender studies; art history and visual culture; cultural studies; and religion.

Recent titles in this series:

Transdisciplinary Perspectives on Childhood in Contemporary Britain
Edited by Ralf Schneider and Sandra Dinter

Children's Play in Literature
Investigating the Strengths and the Subversions of the Playing Child
Edited by Joyce Kelley

Gaming Empire in Children's British Board Games, 1836–1860
Megan A. Norcia

Childhood in the Contemporary English Novel
Sandra Dinter

Victorian Coral Islands of Empire, Mission, and the Boys' Adventure Novel
Michelle Elleray

Empty Nurseries, Queer Occupants
Reproduction and the Future in Ibsen's Late Plays
Olivia Noble Gunn

For more information about this series, please visit: https://www.routledge.com

Empty Nurseries, Queer Occupants

Reproduction and the Future in Ibsen's Late Plays

Olivia Noble Gunn

Routledge
Taylor & Francis Group

NEW YORK AND LONDON

First published 2020
by Routledge
605 Third Avenue, New York, NY 10017

and by Routledge
2 Park Square, Milton Park, Abingdon, Oxon, OX14 4RN

First issued in paperback 2022

Routledge is an imprint of the Taylor & Francis Group, an informa business

Library of Congress Cataloging-in-Publication Data
Names: Gunn, Olivia Noble, author.
Title: Empty nurseries, queer occupants : reproduction and the future in Ibsen's late plays / Olivia Noble Gunn.
Description: New York, NY : Routledge, 2020.
Identifiers: LCCN 2019055686 (print) I LCCN 2019055687 (ebook) I ISBN 9780367330477 (hardback) I ISBN 9780367330484 (ebook) I ISBN 9781000764253 (adobe pdf) I ISBN 9781000764444 (mobi) I ISBN 9781000764635 (epub)
Subjects: LCSH: Ibsen, Henrik, 1828–1906—Criticism and interpretation. I Nurseries in literature.
Classification: LCC PT8897.N87 G86 2020 (print) I LCC PT8897.N87 (ebook) I DDC 839.822/6—dc23
LC record available at https://lccn.loc.gov/2019055686
LC ebook record available at https://lccn.loc.gov/2019055687

ISBN: 978-1-03-240081-5 (pbk)
ISBN: 978-0-367-33047-7 (hbk)
ISBN: 978-0-367-33048-4 (ebk)

DOI: 10.4324/9780367330484

Typeset in Sabon
by codeMantra

This book is dedicated to
two moms (Herbjørg and Ingrid)
two babies (Levi and Roland)
and Adam

Contents

Acknowledgments

I am obliged to many institutions, friends, and colleagues for their generous support during the writing of this book. Its completion was made possible by a Society of Scholars fellowship from the Walter Chapin Simpson Center for the Humanities at the University of Washington (UW). Thanks are due to the Center, its staff, and other fellows for intellectual (and edible) sustenance and time to write. A grant from the Royalty Research Fund at the Office of Research Central at UW provided the means to reside in Oslo while completing archival research at the National Library, as well as the opportunity to visit and connect with colleagues at the Norsk Folkemuseum and the Centre for Ibsen Studies at the University of Oslo. I especially thank Kari Telste and Ellen Rees.

A thousand thanks are due to my colleagues in the Department of Scandinavian Studies at UW, especially my encouraging chair, Andrew K. Nestingen, and the other new kid on the block, Amanda Doxtater. I also thank our indispensable administrator, Tina Swenson; the graduate students, especially those who took my seminar on "Ibsen and the Future"; the members of the Performance Studies Reading Group at UW for emboldening feedback and inspiration; colleagues from other institutions and fields who read and commented on drafts or provided support in other ways, including Jenny James, Dean Krouk, Joan Templeton, Pål Bjørby, Leonardo F. Lisi, and Victoria Dickman-Burnett; the friendly baristas at Milstead & Co. in Fremont; friends, advisors, and mentors from my time as a graduate student at the University of California, Irvine; colleagues at Pacific Lutheran University, where I held my first position; and the donor of the Sverre Arestad Endowed Chair in Norwegian Studies, which enables the Norwegian program at UW to thrive. Last but never least, thanks and thanks and thanks again to my family and friends for their love and patience, especially when this project was all-consuming.

Chapter 3 includes already published material from an essay titled "Lost Boys in *Little Eyolf*" (my copyright) in *On Replacement: Cultural, Social and Psychological Representations*, edited by Jean Owen and Naomi Segal (Palgrave MacMillan 2019).

A Note on Abbreviations

I have abbreviated Ibsen's titles in in-text citations (based on the original Norwegian) as follows:

A Doll House: *Du*
The Wild Duck: *Vi*
Hedda Gabler: *HG*
The Master Builder: *BS*
Little Eyolf: *LE*
John Gabriel Borkman: *JGB*
When We Dead Awaken: *Nvdv*

Prologue

A Nursery at the Museum

In the summer of 2017, I occupied an empty nursery at the Norsk Folkemuseum (the Norwegian Museum of Cultural History) on the peninsula of Bygdøy in Oslo. I walked into the space accessible to visitors, which constitutes about a third or so of the room. A transparent plastic wall prevented me from approaching or touching the small bed or cradle, taking a closer look at the wall decorations and dollhouse, or playing with the toys left out on the floor. When I turned my back on these furnishings and decorations, I encountered a doorway and another transparent plastic wall, through which I could see a dining room. These rooms are part of an installation called "Et dukkehjem—1879" (A Doll House—1879), which is intended to be both a "faithful reconstruction of a home from the second half of 1800s Norway" and an instantiation of the fictional Helmer family home from Ibsen's *A Doll House* (Sverdrup Ugelstad 129).[1] In an article summarizing the aims and historical context of the apartment-installation, Janike Sverdrup Ugelstad writes, "One family is a fiction that appears on a stage, the other appears in real life. There are two stagings, two entry points for creating a lived-environment—the stage of the theater and the culturally correct apartment" (129). Two families, two appearances (or performances), and two stagings as entry points for a third staging: reconstitution in the museum. And that old familiar odd-couple: the theater and the so-called real or unfeigned world.

The curators at the folk museum have reconstructed something that resembles a realistic lived-environment. Of course, the only living human occupation of the nursery at the museum involves museumgoers. We—those of us who visit—are the only surviving progenies in this empty room. Whether or not we have read *A Doll House*, our presence demonstrates that we are the descendants of domestic, museal, and dramatic practices from the late nineteenth century. This prologue begins at the museum and tries to find its way back to fiction, in the form of the dramatic text.[2] I also occupy the empty nursery at the museum as a means of working my way back to the future, or to what it might mean to reconsider the family and gender in conversation with Ibsen's late dramas today. By defining the distinct characteristics of nursery space at the museum and in the dramas, I aim to create space for the primary work of this book: putting Ibsen's empty children's rooms in dialogue with some major claims from queer and critical child studies.

"A Doll House—1879" is part of *OBOS-gården Wessels gate 15* (OBOS-apartment Wessels Street 15), a condemned building gifted to the museum by the Oslo Cooperative Housing Corporation in 1998, then relocated to Bygdøy in 2001 and restored and fully furnished by 2009.[3] In one of his articles for *Forstenet tid* (*Time Turned to Stone*), a special issue of the museum's yearly journal, *By og Bygd* (*Town and Country*), Chief Curator Morten Bing calls the building "A time machine of stone" ("En Tidsmaskin" 11). This phrase suggests solidity (stone), transport (travel), and immersion (access to the past). "Every front door," Bing writes, "is intended to be the way into a surprising journey through time" (Bing 12). On the museum's website, the building is described as "an old three-storey brick building from down town [sic] Oslo. Wessels gate [street] 15 was built in 1865, and was very typical for the residential quarters in the older parts of Oslo."[4] In total, there are eight apartment-installations in the building, including an apartment for "a modern woman with modern ideas and a modern life" from 1935; a "Cleaning Lady's Home" from 1950; and a "Pakistani Home in Norway" from 2002. These staged homes express changes in lifestyle and material culture and, perhaps more implicitly, the shifting class-landscape of the city of Oslo. "A Doll House—1879," which was opened to the public in 2005, offers access to the oldest time period and original petit bourgeois class context of Wessels Street 15.

The nursery at the Norsk Folkemuseum is probably the only concrete manifestation of an Ibsenien nursery outside of the imagination of readers and theatergoers. The practicalities of staging, the explicit world of many of Ibsen's plays—semi-private domestic spaces and the fourth wall—and Ibsen's primary focus on marriage, husband and wife, mean that nursery rooms are both offstage and un-staged. Although the character list for *A Doll House* tells us that Torvald and Nora Helmer have three children and employ a maid and a nanny, nursery rooms are not mentioned by name. The children are sent "*into the room to the left*," but their destination is not described (*Du* 27). Thus, the curators at the museum had to assemble their nursery space despite the absence or lack of description—a kind of negative space—in the play. Their faithful mise-en-scène relied on other sources and on a realist-naturalist reading of Ibsen's play, which assumes embedded-ness in, and continuity with, the contemporary world outside the text. This reading allows one to envision and add other spaces to the Helmer home, because they were common to bourgeois dwellings in the late nineteenth century. Of course, such faithfulness also represents a form of faithlessness, or a break with the bounds of the text.

This claim of faithlessness is not intended as a critique of the exhibition, as if it had failed in some sense, or as if staging and adaptation should not transgress the bounds of a given drama. Nevertheless, I did ask myself when visiting the museum, What am I doing here, in this space that conflicts so strongly with the central interests of my book, which include the literary-theoretical significance of rooms left *un-staged*; the role of emptiness and absence (specifically the absence of children, which is not uniquely communicated by the apartment-installation); and the peripheral status of women's labor in the plays? I also wondered, How many visitors think about Nora's decision to leave her children at the end of the play while standing in the empty nursery?[5] Or about Nora's conversation with the nanny, Anne-Marie, which offers readers a brief glimpse into a working-class understanding of motherhood and survival? Or about the fact that private and mixed-class spaces are exposed in the museum, while they remain offstage in Ibsen's plays? The mimetic characteristics of the nursery in "A Doll House—1879," its historically accurate decorations, as well as the museumgoer's relationship to such a staging, can fulfill the postmodern spectator's curiosity, their longing to know what such rooms "were really like." But Ibsen does not offer detailed naturalist portraits of nurseries, as he does with drawing rooms and other semi-private spaces. Thus, another kind of curiosity must be cultivated if one is to approach Ibsen's plays *from a more private room in the house.*

Although nursery rooms are not named in *A Doll House*, they do show up later in Ibsen's oeuvre—still not staged or described in detail, but in dialogue. Characters mention offstage children's rooms in *Hedda Gabler* (1890), *Bygmester Solness* (*The Master Builder*) (1892), and *Lille Eyolf* (*Little Eyolf*) (1894). In each case, the rooms are empty or emptied under the course of action, and characters make plans for repurposing, refilling, or recreating them. As I argue throughout this book, these rooms are significant threads in the warp of Ibsen's treatment of reproduction in its broad sense: from origin story to dreaded mortality, from procreativity to creativity, from the (dream of the) masterpiece to the derivative and degraded copy, from baby-making to capital. Ibsen's children's rooms are most certainly mimetic—again, in the sense that they are typical features of the bourgeois home. Nonetheless, they matter to Ibsen not in terms of realistic detail, but as spaces reserved for the maintenance of characters' expectations, dreams, hopes, and fears. They also matter to our relationship to an imagined future—or, perhaps more precisely, to futurisms involving no small amount of projection, repetition, and deferral. Ibsen is uninterested in detailed portraits of children and their spaces because he is more interested in the emptiness that dead children leave behind, and in his character's desire to fill that emptiness up.

I linger in the museum for a while to consider how children's rooms, emptiness, and occupation manifest differently in the apartment-installation and in *Hedda Gabler, The Master Builder*, and *Little Eyolf.* In *Living Pictures, Missing Persons* (2003), Mark Sandberg names a correspondence between Scandinavian folk museum practices, theatrical realism, and Scandinavian cinema: "a profound respect for the integrity of original space" (12).[6] He continues, "Ibsen's and Strindberg's dramaturgy of minutely realistic illusionism is perhaps best known in this regard" (Sandberg 12).[7] Although Ibsen's empty nurseries in no way demonstrate *disrespect* for "the integrity of original space," one major difference between the museum's empty nursery and Ibsen's children's rooms is that the latter are located beyond the limits of any "minutely realistic illusionism."

The apartment-installation "A Doll House—1879" can offer a neat point of distinction and dissolve for a concept such as realism. It can lead one to re-ask familiar questions, such as What does realism have to do with faithfulness, cultural correctness, and illusionism? How does realism imply continuity and/or break with the world outside the text? How does realism reconfirm and/or help us to problematize the distinction between actuality, fiction, and figure? As Sandberg notes, both the folk museum and realist drama seek to re-create forms of immersive experience that hold out promises of authenticity (*Living Pictures* 12). Bing refers to all of Wessel Street 15's various reconstructed homes as "story-telling about dwelling customs and daily life in diverse periods and diverse social classes" ("Tidsmaskin" 27). While the telling has much in common in each case—because the finished installations share similar techniques of display—the curating and composing of each story involved distinct primary sources and connections with historical occupation. Bing differentiates the earlier installations from those on the third floor, which were all completed between 2005 and 2008, asserting that the latter involved a higher degree—indeed the highest degree—of "diktning" (fiction), a term implying the creation of poetry, invention, and fabrication (including lies and tall tales): "While the furnishings in the previous phase of the project had been based, to various degrees, on a combination of building-archaeology and cooperation with living people, the stories on the third floor were totally and completely a result of fiction" ("Tidsmaskin" 19). Bing immediately tempers his claim that the third floor is a total and complete result of fiction, stating that "color investigations"—"to be sure"—were conducted in Wessels Street 15 and other buildings of the period for the creation of "A Doll House—1879." His somewhat sweeping rhetoric concerning *diktning* thus appears to rely not only on the fact that a work of dramatic fiction was used as a primary source but also on the fact that living people were not (and could not be) consulted in the case of the third-floor installations.

Bing's acknowledgment of the significance of storytelling, fiction, and fantasy for the furnishing of the third floor does not disrupt the museum's pursuit of a relatively straightforward form of mimetic representation, which is part and parcel of the desire for authenticity—or for faithful and correct representations of the past—at the museum. Significantly, my own questions about the installation and its relationship to drama are less about revisiting and rethinking realist aesthetics and ideologies, and more about the distinct silences and non-appearances at the museum and in the plays.[8] What gets fleshed out, what is missing, and why might this matter?

The visitor to "A Doll House—1879" is asked to imagine a doubled absent-presence, based on both historical-material and textual-fictional sources. That is, the rooms and material objects of the apartment-installation are as if reserved for an historical family, absented by time. They are also as if reserved for a fictional family, which was never really present in such a dwelling. Sandberg opens *Living Pictures, Missing Persons* by describing an analogous empty space: "Just inside the entrance at the Grand Café on the central boulevard of present-day Oslo, there is a table reserved for a missing person" (1). The missing person in this case is Henrik Ibsen (1828–1906),

> who for most of the 1890s came punctually to the Grand every noon and late afternoon, always sitting at the same table for an aperitif and a newspaper. The restaurant has been waiting for Ibsen to return since 1978, when the management of the restaurant reenshrined his reserved table in a museum-like display. (Sandberg 1)

Sandberg uses Ibsen's empty chair to exemplify an unoccupied but highly productive space created by the "placeholder techniques of spatial effigy" found in modern spectator culture, including wax, folk, open-air and natural history museums (*Living Pictures* 15). These techniques were used to replace the older "[principles of] taxonomic display" with "living, contextualized scenes" (7). Sandberg calls this practice of creating "living" or productive empty space "the missing person display" (15). Although "collection, preservation, and authentication" remained central ideals and practices, operations of collection and classification were erased through naturalization of the scene (Sandberg 11). Eventually, even mannequins were removed, making possible a particularly compelling and uncanny form of spectatorship, which relies on the play of absence and presence. This modern form of display asks people to engage their sophisticated skills for threshold spectatorship, wherein they "perform the imaginary substitution of bodies," mentally placing themselves in a vacant space, or imagining other bodies there (Sandberg 2).

The empty nursery at the Norsk Folkemuseum is also a kind of "effigy" or "trace space," evoking both "missing persons" and concrete historical spaces (Sandberg 4). The toys—a tea set, a doll's bed, a horse figurine, and more—are out on the floor, as if a (very neat) child left them there moments before and might return to play at any moment. At the same time, the museumgoer is acutely aware that this room represents a past. Although not so distant—about 140 years ago, at the time of writing—this past is certainly distinct in particular ways. Many middle-class families still reserve space for young children and decorate that space with stimulation, education, care, and discipline in mind; yet the materials (e.g., no plastic), toys (e.g., no battery-operated or electronic gadgets), cultural objects (e.g., the handmade display dollhouse), and the location of the space (in close proximity to rooms for domestic servants/ service) probably feel outmoded to most visitors. The transparent barrier between spectatorial and display spaces also breaks the "promise of unlimited access" found in other spaces in the folk museum, while the nursery room remains "visually available" to visitors (Sandberg 11). As Sandberg emphasizes, Ibsen's table at the Grand Café demands a greater degree of normative control from café-goers, who are asked not to touch the artifacts, but could simply reach out, becoming "transgressors" rather than spectators (3). Still, and despite the barrier to touch in "A Doll House—1879," the person behind the Plexiglass is also both "inside and outside the display," in familiar yet curious (uncanny) relationship to the space and its presentation of another time (the 1870s) and another dimension (the fictional text) (Sandberg 3). The museum captions and Plexiglass are telling signs of our desire for authenticity, a desire that is arguably central to the production of dramatic realism. The captions assure the museumgoer that an appropriate, contemporaneous archive has been consulted; the Plexiglass at once protects and offers visual access to bona fide and appropriately displayed artifacts. At the same time, the captions and Plexiglass are the clearest signs that we are entering spaces of representation and spectatorship.

"A Doll House—1879" allows museumgoers to walk into a (representation of a) home, a staging inspired by a realist work of literature. But what remains of theater and of Ibsen's dramatic text here? For some readers, this question might evoke theorizations of performance as disappearance and/or remains in the work of scholars such as Peggy Phelan and Rebecca Schneider.[9] And it is certainly fascinating to consider how issues including spectatorship, experiential time, memory, and embodiment work in this kind of space. Above, I insisted that my questions about what gets fleshed out and what is missing are not really about realist aesthetics. Nor are they directed at performance, as a happening or occurrence that can be understood as opposing a certain kind of archive (the documents and objects at the museum).[10] I am wondering, instead, about the ways in which the apartment-installation is, and is not, reminiscent of *A Doll House*. I want to allow the fictional text its limits, so as to acknowledge its *discontinuity* with the world when it comes to the nursery and other mixed-class spaces. In a sense, "A Doll House—1879" is over-real and ahistorical (or otherwise historical), taking the part of material culture against both theater and drama. That is, it presents minimal access to histories of reception, interpretation, and staging.[11] It breaks with the fourth wall, which creates a differently voyeuristic experience than the Plexiglass barrier between the museumgoer and the rooms as action-less stages for artifacts. Most significantly for my interest in empty nurseries, "A Doll House—1879" breaks with Ibsen's text by (faithfully unfaithfully) exceeding it. It offers access to spaces that are offstage and un-described in the stage directions (not only the nursery but also the kitchen and servants' bedroom) and makes visible what readers like me can no longer picture when reading the drama. Conversely, many of Ibsen's contemporary readers would have had intimate knowledge of such spaces, given that they returned home from the theater to similar rooms, read Ibsen's plays under a "måneskinnslampe" (moonlight lamp) (Sverdrup Ugelstad 138) or by the warmth of a "stentøjsovn" (ceramic oven) (Ibsen, *Du* 5) when they were released just before Christmas, had grown up with nannies like Anne-Marie, or put their own children to sleep in such nurseries.

While addressing philosophical and aesthetic concerns about personhood, mastery, and calling—and, especially in the later plays, failure and mortality—Ibsen both uses and neglects aspects of a specifically classed and gendered world that exceeds the drawing room. The staging at the museum suggests that Ibsen's dramas ask us to imagine a complete bourgeois home, including rooms for children and servants. Do we? The Introduction and first three chapters of this book focus on rooms located at the very edge of the playwright's line of sight. They focus on what might be called the absent-presence of children's rooms in *Hedda Gabler*, *The Master Builder*, and *Little Eyolf*. The significance of Ibsen's empty nurseries does not depend on detailed naturalistic descriptions, because Ibsen's understanding of reproduction and his dramatization of visions of the future are not staged but evoked by means of peripheral spaces. In Ibsen, the nursery is primarily a space of desire, pointing to the emptiness at the heart of reproduction, or indicating that reproduction involves both repetition and loss, that only death guarantees survival, and that the future itself never arrives. Nonetheless, as Nora's "playroom" metaphor in *A Doll House* suggests, both women's labor and childhood remain essential to Ibsen's understanding of the bourgeois family's inauthenticity and bankruptcy: "our home has been nothing more than a playroom" (*Du* 87). The line between the real world and literature (like the discontinuity between real and performed or real and figurative) can be drawn for strategic purposes in specific contexts, but it cannot be rigorously maintained, and Ibsen's children's rooms cannot be fully stripped of their gendered and classed identities. Thus, even as I consider the significance of figurative emptiness, I insist that the treatment of childhood and innocence in the empty nursery plays is, in fact, classed and culturally specific, rather than universal. Even in its suggestive, rather de-materialized form, the nursery remains a sign of worlds that can only partially give way to absence, including those of motherhood and domestic labor. In the fourth and final chapter of this book, I turn to these worlds by returning to the museum, and by looking at archival materials on the nursery and nanny available in Norwegian at the turn of the century, showing how the empty nursery remains a fitting figure for innocence, full of anxious expectations, in dramatic literature and advice manuals alike.

Unlike the children's rooms mentioned in Ibsen's late plays, the nursery at the Norsk Folkemuseum was never empty when I visited. Of course, it is always devoid of the proper, historical occupation of children, nannies, and mothers, but this is a different kind of emptiness than the one that dead children leave behind in Ibsen's plays. Other museumgoers occupied the museum's nursery when I was there, but this is a very different occupation than the endless books of *Hedda Gabler*, the adolescent seductress of *The Master Builder*, or the poor boys in *Little Eyolf*. When it comes to children's rooms and refilling emptiness in Ibsen, queerer forms of (mostly) futural occupation matter more than what more commonly passes as cultural correctness and the past. This might seem like a strange thing to say about a realist, analytical playwright. It is true that Ibsen is renowned for his realism, for his early-feminist characterizations of (Western European and mostly bourgeois) women's experiences of marriage and family, and for his disclosures of the past. His last dramas depict the ends of family lines, the aftereffects of failed projects, and the end of life. What, then, does Ibsen have to say about and to the future, including our queer and postfeminist era?

As I will address in the Introduction, this book is inspired both by antisocial queer theory and by scholarship that treats the child as an ideologically fraught category rather than as the issue of a natural process that, in Judge Brack's words, confronts "most women" with the "solemn demands of responsibility" (*HG* 47). Together with Ibsen, I will displace the innocent child and center the empty bourgeois nursery, while rejecting the erasure of class and other concrete and embodied modes of life that sometimes takes place when seemingly natural categories such as childhood and motherhood are given center stage. In "When We Dead Awaken: Writing as Re-Vision" (1971), Adrienne Rich defines re-vision as "the act of looking back, of seeing with fresh eyes, of entering an old text from a new critical direction" (35). Rich opens her essay by telling readers that Ibsen's last play (the work from which she borrows her title) is "about the use that the male artist and thinker—in the process of creating culture as we know it—has made of women, in his life and in his work" (34). She then insists that feminism serves the slowly waking "sleepwalkers" who "have drawn connections between our sexual lives and our political institutions" (34–35). I continue, in this book, to make use of the use that Ibsen has made of women characters and domestic spaces in his considerations of vision and vocation, (pro)creativity, survival, and mortality. I hope that my insights and readings are renewed by means of queer theory and child studies' critical (and sometimes pessimistic) stance toward innocence, the family, and the future—a stance that might even be described as another attempt to awaken to the deadness at the heart of our ideologies of survival.

Notes

1 Unless otherwise noted, translations from Norwegian are my own. When translating Ibsen, I have sometimes referred to Rolf Fjelde's translations.
2 My description of the work of this prologue is inspired, in part, by Rebecca Schneider's description of the trajectory of her chapter, "Finding Faux Fathers," in *Performing Remains*: "If this chapter begins in the theater, it does not end in the theater. But it never leaves the theater either, though the theater ceases to be 'just pretend' when explored as a vehicle for collective reconstitution of the so-called real" (61).
3 In "En Tidsmaskin," Bing offers a timeline of construction and curation. Some highlights: the building was torn down in 1999. Reconstruction began in 2000 in *Gamlebyen*, or the old city section of the museum (displaying urban dwelling customs as well as peasant culture has been a goal since the founding of the museum in 1894) (Bing 11). The "pilot project," or the first installation-apartment, was underway by spring 2001. Furnishing of the third floor, which includes "A Doll House—1879," took place between 2005 and 2008 (Bing 19).
4 See https://norskfolkemuseum.no/en/the-apartment-building.
5 The captions inside the front door refer to Nora and her departure at the end of the play. First, they contextualize her character—"the depiction of the woman as a childish songbird"—as reflecting "a widespread attitude to women held by many authors in the 19th century." Then, they briefly contrast Nora with Dora from Charles Dickens's *David Copperfield*. Whereas Dora dies, Nora "matures into a woman. She leaves her dollhouse and the door slams shut."
6 Sandberg pays careful attention throughout his study to points of divergence and overlap between missing person display, with its "allegiance to the object and original space," and "more simulative" contemporaneous media, including film (*Living Pictures* 7). By considering wax museums and open-air and folk museums in relationship to other forms of spectatorship, he acknowledges Europe's turn of the century culture as one of disruption *and* continuity (a paradox apparent in recording and transportation technologies, and in the cultivation of the illusions of immersion and authenticity). Sandberg also follows the particularly Scandinavian development of modern display practices, which can be explained in large part by "comparatively belated modernization on the northern periphery of Europe" and by the significance of folk culture and rural traditions for the developing national identities in northern Europe: "Scandinavian spectators consistently imagined themselves in threshold positions, voyeurs of both the old and the new" (11).
7 Sandberg continues, "but the early Scandinavian cinema's innovative use of deep staging and early bias against editing and reversal of field was equally indebted to this tradition. To borrow some filmic terms, this was broadly speaking more a culture of mise-en-scène than of montage" (12). Sandberg's

clever analogy relies on a good deal of historical and regional cultural knowledge. I assume that today's museumgoers recognize the methods of reconstruction at Wessels Street 15 as a global mode of museal display. Moreover, the uniquely Scandinavian aspects of "A Doll House—1879" are rather diffuse, because they represent pan-European middle-class cultural practices rather than something markedly "Norwegian."

8 Realism signals a variety of complex and contested aesthetic practices and philosophies. I have no desire to simplify its resonances and possible meanings or applications here. The philosophical-aesthetic principles of both realism and naturalism are rich and fascinating and remain relevant modes for considering many aspects of Ibsen's late plays.

9 In her chapter, "In the Meantime: Performance Remains," Schneider offers a useful literature review of major interventions, including Phelan's *Unmarked: the Politics of Performance*, into the debate surrounding performance and the character of liveness (often as opposed to theater) within the field of performance studies.

10 In *Performing Remains*, Schneider is critiquing the ideology that always opposes performance and the archive, and thereby reifies a certain conception of the archive/archival as the privileged space of enduring, and therefore surviving, objects. She writes,

> The definition of performance as that which disappears, which is continually lost in time, is a definition well suited to the concerns of art history and the curatorial pressure to understand performance in the museal context where performance appeared to challenge object status and seemed to refuse the archive its privileged 'savable' original. Arguably even more than in the theatre, it is in the context of the museum, gallery, and art market that performance appears to *primarily* offer disappearance. (98)

11 The first set of captions inside the door of the installation focus on the play and its performance: a photograph of Ibsen, taken in Munich in 1878, is captioned with a brief publication history; a photograph of Jane Fonda performing Nora's tarantella in 1973 is captioned with the claim that "A Doll's House has been performed numberless times all over the world and has also been filmed several times"; a reproduced xylograph from *Ny Illustrert Tidene* (*The New Illustrated Times*) by painter Olaf Jørgensen shows the tarantella scene from the first performance of *A Doll House* in Norway at the Christiania Theatre (20 January 1880), staring Johanne Juell.

Introduction

Ibsen's Empty Nurseries

Who is the proper occupant of the nursery room? The obvious answer is the child, and not a boring and ever-expanding archive, a seductive adolescent troll-princess, or a mischief of poor and naughty fosterlings. Ibsen's characters nonetheless mean to host these improper occupants in their empty nurseries in *Hedda Gabler* (1890), *Bygmester Solness* (*The Master Builder*) (1892), and *Lille Eyolf* (*Little Eyolf*) (1894). I call these dramas the "empty nursery plays" because they all mention rooms originally intended for children, as well as characters' plans for refilling, repurposing, or re-creating the space. In each play, the rooms are off-stage, more or less peripheral to the action, yet central to the characters' experiences of failure and unfinished projects, to their attitudes toward meaning and mortality, and to their hopes for the future. This introduction tells the stories of failure and false starts that explain the absence of children in each play, explores scholarly sources that wield and/ or critique the concept of innocence, and considers the proposed occupants that signify Ibsen's dramatization of non-procreative futurism: his characters dreams of continuation beyond the deaths of children. Taken together, Ibsen's nurseries can exemplify the claim, much discussed in critical child studies, that innocence itself is a form of emptiness and deferral. I intervene in this conversation by offering the empty bourgeois nursery as a better symbol for innocence than the child.

By nursery, I mean a room intended for children. What I do not mean by nursery is the room managed by the Victorian Nanny, a figure that emerged in England.[1] This specific version of the nursery, according to Jonathon Gathorne-Hardy, was "[a]ustere and remote—situated at the top or in far-flung parts of the house, among the servants" (Gathorne-Hardy 58). Although fascinating, the Victorian Nanny, her role, training, and influence on English (and to some extent European) society, and the rooms over which she ruled, are not immediately relevant to a study of Ibsen's empty nursery plays.[2] Nonetheless, factors such as class, ideologies of childhood and child-rearing, and the cultural influence of the private home are surely relevant for thinking about these (mostly) empty dramatic rooms. I touch on some of these factors briefly as I introduce and describe Ibsen's nurseries, their peripheral place in terms of dramatic action, and their centrality to the concepts of reproduction and originality that are evoked in the plays and reproduced in criticism. The word "nursery" admittedly carries a lot of cultural baggage, but it remains the best word in English for describing the major figure of this book.[3]

In a certain sense, Ibsen's nurseries are little more than traces. They are mentioned, offstage spaces in the dramas, not described in detail. They are also un-staged spaces in the theater, given that no action takes place in them. The nursery itself is often contingent, a shifting use of space dependent on a phase of life in a specific class context rather than on necessary architectural or reproductive-familial characteristics.[4] One might expect that such rooms would provide an ideal setting for a realist playwright to dramatize contemporary social problems, but Ibsen is clearly not interested in the specific features and functions of these rooms, and so they remain obscure, not unlike his characters' offspring, who, with the exception of Eyolf, all die as un-staged babies. In "Ibsen's Paradoxical Attitudes Toward *Kindermord*" (1989), Terry Otten claims,

> The late eighteenth and nineteenth centuries produced a gallery of [martyred and suffering children], beginning most dramatically perhaps with Blake's 'suffering children of Generation.' Among subsequent writers, none, not even Dickens, has created more striking portraits of disenfranchised, orphaned or maimed children than Ibsen. (117)

One could counter that there are no portraits of children in Ibsen's oeuvre. This would not mean that *Kindermord*, innocence, and child abuse are not significant themes, but rather that there are no fleshed-out child characters in Ibsen's major works, with the possible exception of Hedvig in *The Wild Duck* (1884) and Hilde in *The Lady from the Sea* (1888)— although Hedvig and Hilde are both adolescents, just at or just passed the threshold of puberty. Otten's claim and the counter-claim that there are no portraits of children in Ibsen are both possible because childhood is a highly imprecise and flexible category. Otten, for example, treats Osvald's death in *Ghosts* as child-murder, although Osvald is a grown man. Robin Young makes a similarly flexible use of childhood (as concept and identity category) in *Time's Disinherited Children* (1989) by insisting that Ibsen's retrospection always enables discernment of "the child within the adult" (15). It seems that one remains a child forever if one has parents, and this permanent state of (ruined) innocence is particularly persistent when one has "bad" parents.

In another sense, it is the nurseries' trace-like qualities that make them significant to Ibsen's treatment of reproduction in the late plays. Forever empty, Ibsen's children's rooms are preserved for possibility; they are spaces for imagination, where one can envision collecting quantities of objects or creatures or temporalities that exceed both in-dividual readings and stagings and the normative story of generational survival—even as they often appear to suggest more of the same. In *Ib-sen's Houses* (2015), Mark Sandberg describes the unoccupied nurseries of *The Master Builder* as a "useless architectural feature" (162). I do not disagree with Sandberg's description but spend more time lingering in uselessness in order to argue that it is the very lack of occupation that makes these rooms figures for unfinished business and failure, as well as placeholders for replacement projects and possible futures in an oeuvre better known for conjuring (to exorcise?) the ghosts of the past.

Ultimately, the figure of the nursery brings together the aspects of Ib-sen's oeuvre that are more frequently opposed: the "universalizing 'cover story'" *and* the "concrete, gendered reality" of reproduction, existen-tial concerns *and* the material, political world (Fuchs 59). Ibsen's empty nurseries invoke both the foundational void of innocence and the divi-sion of women's reproductive labor—which enables me to deploy strate-gically, while also problematizing, the (admittedly unstable) distinction between figures and the real or actual thing.[5] The empty nursery is a better symbol for innocence than the child both because innocence is frequently treated as a kind of emptiness—a structure to be filled, the starting and gathering point of all loss, an interiority that contains the depths of "tainted" authenticity (adulteration) (Goldman 69)[6]—and be-cause the innocent child turns out to be a highly bourgeois and white or race normative idea that conjures a certain kind of child rather than standing for a natural-universal human experience.[7] What really inter-ests Ibsen in the empty nursery plays is not the child but *uninterest* in children, absence or absenting, the emptiness left behind, and the desire to fill that emptiness up. Essential to this desire, in this case, is tempo-ral and material wealth, or the ability to plan for the future and afford unutilized space.

In addition to exploring the dramas, this book offers theoretical and literary-critical contextualization for the distinct manner in which I ap-proach reproduction and the future in Ibsen: not through the child alone, primarily through the empty nursery. A major task is observing habits of thinking about innocence in criticism on Ibsen from the decades sur-rounding our own turn of the century and considering the extent to which the dramas can aid us in resisting current modes of reproducing the child as "the center of fantasy" (Goldman 75). Critics who have fo-cused on the child in Ibsen's dramas have tended either to exempt this figure from Ibsen's skepticism, re-idealizing it by rendering it in norma-tive or romantic ways, or to reproduce it as an empty or otherwise vague space for housing anxieties, including (rhetorical) concerns for the very future of civilization.[8]

In *No Future* (2004), queer theorist defines "reproductive futurism" through the Child as a fetish that "figures our identification with an always about-to-be-realized identity" (13). The Child and the future, in other words, are collapsed *and* deferred, which means that the Child is understood to guarantee social survival through a reproduction of the past—as if the "father of the Man" (Edelman alludes to Wordsworth)—and in this sense can threaten "a life," or the freedom of the individual now, in the name of that survival (Edelman 10, 29–30).[9] The rhetoric of reproductive futurism, which Edelman both mocks and mimics in *No Future*, often takes place as an accumulation of fears and hopes concerning threats to "social organization, collective reality, and, inevitably, life itself" (13). Although *No Future* has been subject to a good deal of criticism for abstraction and false universalism, among other things, it remains a good source of inspiration for critiquing reproductive futurism in Ibsen studies and for understanding Ibsen's own pessimistic critique of the bourgeois family. Like Edelman, Ibsen insists that the future means death, regardless of reproduction (because reproduction is the sign of survival *and* demise); he depicts time as threatening rather than guaranteeing identity; and he doubts his characters' faith that meaning will become whole (or unbroken by the past) in time. In the empty nursery plays, Ibsen gets rid of children and asks, if no child, what future? With the help of Edelman, James R. Kincaid, and others, I ask, in turn, whether the empty, childless space left behind still houses innocence.

After introducing the shared pattern of emptying and (dreaming about) refilling nurseries in the dramas, I reflect on the emptiness and flexibility of the concept of the innocent child. I then explore each of the empty nursery plays in succession—considering the past (failure, backstory, and retrospection), the present state of non-procreative reproduction, and the stories that empty nurseries appear to tell about the future—and briefly introduce the moves and claims of subsequent chapters. Finally, I conclude by addressing why Ibsen's pessimism might make him a good ally for the project of queer antisocial critique.

Empty Rooms, Queer Occupants

When Sandberg claims that the nursery rooms of *The Master Builder* are "useless," he refers to lack of occupation by the intended, proper persons, that is, children. In Act Two, we learn that the Solness's twin babies died some eleven years before the action begins, just after his wife's childhood home burnt to the ground. Yet Solness has built three nursery rooms in his current house, and is building three more in the new house, for "the children who will never come" (Sandberg, *Ibsen's Houses* 162). Concerning this new house, the one under construction "on the same spot as the one lost in the fire," Sandberg writes, "Since this house is a completely new construction on a razed lot, it could have been designed to suit its inhabitant's future needs. The nurseries are thus vestigial in the purest sense of the word: the needs of the past continue to haunt the new structure" (161–162). Sandberg associates the future with change and practical, domestic "needs" (a more precise term might be wants or normative requirements, given that no baby needs a room of its own). The present is always haunted by the past in Ibsen's oeuvre—a circumstance made explicit in plays such as *Brand* (1865) and *Ghosts* (1881) by means of dialogue about inheritance and fates understood to be determined by the "sins of the father," among other factors. The term "vestigial" can suggest a mere remnant of something bigger or more noticeable. As Sandberg knows, however, in the empty nursery plays the supposed liveliness of children pales in comparison with the "lively" presence of the (un)dead (as *genganger* or *revenant*) and the considerable staying power of architecture. Again, it is precisely the *lack of proper occupation* that interests me here. This interest emerges, in large part, from a queerly inspired wariness of—a desire to understand, denude, and perhaps revalue—the association of children, child-rearing, and the reproductive family with properness, timeliness, and suitability. It emerges from a desire to think the future as otherwise reproduced.

Does Sandberg's claim of uselessness apply equally in *Hedda Gabler* and *Little Eyolf*? When *Hedda Gabler* opens, Jørgen and Hedda Tesman have just returned from a long honeymoon abroad. In Act One, Tesman and his aunt discuss "the two empty rooms between the back parlor and Hedda's bedroom" (*HG* 10–11). Tesman is not sure which purpose these empty rooms will serve. Miss Juliane Tesman assures him that they will certainly find some use "as time goes on" (*HG* 10). Tesman and Aunt Julie do not seem to know it yet, but Hedda is pregnant.[10] Nonetheless, the nursery rooms of *Hedda Gabler* are not (explicitly) employed or occupied under the course of action. Moreover, they will never house Hedda's child, because she kills herself at the end of the play. In *Little Eyolf*, the only son's rooms aren't quite so "useless": they belong to the living, eight-year-old child when the play begins. They are emptied almost immediately, at the end of Act One. Eyolf, who is lame and cannot swim, wanders down to the shore and drowns, apparently lured there by the Ratmaid, a Pied Piper/werewolf figure. His rooms stay empty throughout the remaining acts. Significantly, Eyolf's rooms are not named until the final moments of the play, when we learn all we know about them: there is more than one, they are referred to as "stuer" (rooms or parlors) (*LE* 77), they contain Eyolf's books and toys, and they are spacious enough to house several children.

The pairing of dead or doomed, mostly absent children with dialogue concerning specific rooms in the home, intended for children but empty or emptied under the course of action, is unique to *Hedda Gabler*, *The Master Builder*, and *Little Eyolf*. The dead or doomed child is a theme and spur to dramatic and psychological action in other plays, most notably *Brand* and *The Lady from the Sea*. There is no mention, however, of separate rooms intended primarily for Brand and Ellida's dying and dead (respectively) sons. In *The Wild Duck*, Hedvig has a room of her own offstage, and her dead body is placed in that room in the fifth and final act; but Hedvig is an adolescent and a highly developed character, and no planning for future occupation takes place in this drama. In *A Doll House* (1879), Nora and Helmer's three children—who are alive and presumably go on living after Nora slams the door—are often sent to be with the nanny, Anne-Marie, who was also Nora's nanny. Ibsen depicts Nora as a beloved playmate who can entrust her children to their caretaker whenever necessary, but no specific mention is made of children's rooms. While *A Doll House* includes both a nanny and a parlor maid in its character list, in the empty nursery plays there is only one servant: Berte, the maid in *Hedda Gabler*, who also performed some unspecified nanny duties for Tesman when he was a boy. In the Prologue, I argued that Ibsen's nurseries are located beyond the limits of the "minutely realistic illusionism" that we might associate with Ibsen's earlier dramas (Sandberg, *Living Pictures* 12). The absence of domestic laborers in *The Master Builder* and *Little Eyolf* represents a curious mimetic minimalism, or another form of absence in the late plays. Both the shortage of nannies and the obscured nurseries indicate that Ibsen's decision to include children's rooms in the dialogue of three late plays is not simply a matter of including naturalist detail, that is, of portraying typical spaces and practices in the bourgeois home. Nurseries are named because the pairing of dead children and empty socio-architectural space is relevant to each play's retrospection, characterization, and thematic or figurative schemes.

Ibsen's characters not only dwell on the past and the proper functions of nursery rooms but also imagine future occupations of improper varieties.[11] In *Hedda Gabler*, the imagined occupants are endless documents, books, and transcripts, which will form an academic archive that Tesman proposes to house in the empty nurseries of the Falk town house. In *The Master Builder*, one of the nursery rooms—"The middle one" (*BS* 41)—is occupied under the course of dramatic action, by Hilde, who is not a child, but in whose figure childhood, youth, desire, vitality, and mortality (among other things) are collapsed. This occupation is the primary exception to the more general rule of emptiness in the empty nursery plays—although the remaining five, extant nurseries are empty during this drama too. In *Little Eyolf*, a bereaved mother plans to fill her drowned son's empty rooms with a group of poor children (all boys?), who will play with the son's toys and take turns sitting in his chair. By improper occupants, I mean the proposed and longed-for inhabitants that are not the children of the family, not the offspring of the dramas' husbands and wives, but rather creatures (or, in *Hedda Gabler*, objects) that represent reproduction other than the child as carrier of the future.

Emptiness and/as Innocence

In common with Jacqueline Rose and other scholars invested in analyzing and resisting sentimental and idealist understandings of childhood, I aim with this book "to make some contribution to the dismantling of [...] the ongoing sexual and political mystification of the child" (11). Although children are of the past and primarily un-staged in the empty nursery plays, one could argue that loss of innocence—what might be called the death as well as the sustaining fantasy of the child—remains primary in the empty nursery plays. Both Robin Young and Michael Goldman have argued that forms of arrested development and child abuse constitute chief motivations for Ibsen. Young insists that childhood never stops (negatively) determining the present: "the true 'disinherited children' are adults who are sealed by environment, heredity, chance or self-will into childish roles which they are incapable of outgrowing" (15). In *Ibsen: the Dramaturgy of Fear* (1999), Goldman argues that child abuse is an "exemplary" dramatic effect in Ibsen and then asks, "If every adult is a wounded or tainted child, who tends to see things with the wounded and tainted eyes of those who initially abused him, what kind of revealing or redeeming vision is possible?" (69, 93). Neither Young nor Goldman use the word "child" to mean a person under the age of twelve or thirteen, a boundary that could render the figure more specific, restraining its applicability.

Of course, categories such as childhood and adolescence are historically contingent and can overlap and even merge. What is the difference, one might ask in this context, between Ibsen's interest in wounded innocence and his interest in adolescence and the threshold of sexual awakening in *The Wild Duck* and *The Master Builder*? Kincaid uses the term "child," as well as pedophile, to point not "to things but to roles, functions necessary for our cultural life" (5). He sometimes defines the "child"—not capitalized as the ultimate symbol of the heteronormativity of politics, as in Edelman, but set apart with scare quotes—as "not, in itself, anything. Any image, body, or being we can hollow out, purify, exalt, abuse, and locate sneakily in a field of desire will do for us as a 'child'" (Kincaid 5). The very flexibility of the concept of the child can result in a voiding of anything concrete and identifiable, in favor of a self-evident wielding that sustains an emptiness filled with hopes and fears concerning survival.

Such emptiness, as well as the notion that innocence is an adult construct rather than a description of childhood, has been described, dissected, and reestablished (with difference) in Kincaid's *Child Loving* (1992) and other examples of deconstructive, critical, and queer child studies.[12] Both Young and Goldman depend on innocence and childhood as concepts that can obliterate boundaries and expand into (or lurk in) all ages, all human experiences. They do not always bring the dynamics of obliteration and expansion under explicit critique. In his readings of *The Wild Duck* and *Little Eyolf*, Goldman recognizes that the child, as Kathryn Bond Stockton also reminds us, is "a fond fantasy held by adults" (*The Queer Child* 505); yet he expresses less critical resistance to, and more faith in, that fantasy. For example, he writes,

> The point is that, regularly, wound round the figure of the wounded child we find an anxiety about history, society, and the self that rises from the traumas of the French revolution and anticipates some of the central questions of modern culture. The child functions as a center of fantasy in which we are all implicated, all betrayed.
>
> We can, then, usefully distinguish two aspects of child abuse in nineteenth-century thought (and indeed in the thought of our own century) that will figure in our exploration of Ibsen. First, the figure of the wounded child as the intersection of many strands of social investigation. Second, this child as a peculiarly empowering figure, whose wound speaks for us and to us not simply of guilt and/or desire but of a power to engage, even to change the secret life of our times. (75–76)

Here, Goldman associates the abused child with "anxiety about history" and with a specific history of thought, that is, developments in the nine-teenth century and their influence on "our own century" (meaning the twentieth). He also differentiates childhood and history by associating the former with some deeper place apart: "Coming up from childhood we enter history" (91). His rhetoric makes the child into the intersec-tion of all the strands of human loss and agency, a kind of endless knot (wound round a wound) that empowers us to address wrongs as well as rights. Although a certain kind of childhood is extra-historical for Goldman (presumably because it is natural and/or naïve), we nonethe-less cannot leave childhood behind—for better or worse: "For if it is true that we all come up injured from the depths of childhood, we also retain something of childhood's magic—something of its wildness, ex-pansiveness, mystery, authenticity, though in wounded or tainted form" (Goldman 90). Goldman's child might remind us of the accumulation and collapse that also characterizes reproductive futurism. That is, his child is an alternating conviction and exoneration mechanism that manages to gather together history, society, the self, modernity, desire, agency, trauma, and "our times"—even as it becomes, as Kincaid sug-gests, nothing specific in itself.

There is no doubt that Ibsen dramatizes wounded and lost innocence, or that this is what the figure of the child often signifies in his oeuvre. I am simply insisting that it is important to notice how this dramatization depends more on absenting and voiding and less on centering and spec-ifying childhood and child characters. Goldman claims that when Ibsen "extensively presents [a damaged child's] suffering" in *The Wild Duck* and *Little Eyolf*, he "links the subject to an equally extensive imagery of sight and seeing" (76). There are no seeing children's eyes unfiltered through adult perspectives in the empty nursery plays, however—with the exception of a few moments in the first act of *Little Eyolf*, when Eyolf "*looks loyally up*" at his father before looking into the eyes of the Ratmaid's dog, who helps to seduce him down to the water, like a rat (*LE* 9). Queer theory and child studies aid me in taking another step away from the idealization and centering of the child as a means through which we "see," as the (fragile) linchpin or (faulty) foundation of enlightenment, trauma, and humanity. These fields enable me to acknowledge both the desired child and what often amounts to its nothingness, or its status as an empty place to invest with longing. In their introduction to *Curiouser* (2004), editors Steven Bruhm and Natasha Hurley write,

> The contributors to this volume agree that there is no constituency in Western culture as susceptible to narratives of simplification as children. They also agree that the seemingly invisible processes that distill the child into an image and a story are anything but simple [...] the children who populate the stories our culture tells about them are, in fact, curiouser than they've been given credit for. (xiv)

Note the specification of Western culture here and the tension proposed between simplifying stories, "anything but simple" processes, and child characters, who are "curiouser" than such stories allow. This approach to the child aims to resist an earlier tendency simply to oppose the child to queerness and to trace the collapse of the child into/as simplified narratives without taking counter-narratives or counter-figuration into consideration. Significantly, Ibsen offers up a series of empty rooms rather than dramatizing a series of child characters. In this book, I ask how innocence becomes an empty room; what is distilled in these invisible, not only Western but also bourgeois, spaces; and whether their proposed occupants are also "curiouser" (not more real but less normative and self-evident in their figuration) "than they've been given credit for."

The figure of the empty nursery—a chamber or series of chambers reserved for dwelling in the aftereffects of false starts and dreams of the future—resonates with other forms of emptiness that contribute to the general imagery, mood, and treatment of idealism in Ibsen's late plays. In *Ibsens Samtidsskuespill* (*Ibsen's Contemporary Plays*) (1999), Asbjørn Aarseth titles his chapter on *Little Eyolf* "Emptiness after a drowned pest." The compound word that Aarseth uses for emptiness—*tomrom*—combines "tom" (empty) and "rom" (space or room) and means void or gap. It is not a reference to a room in a house, but to the fact that the whole play is about dealing with the void that a child's death leaves behind, especially when that child was already a sign of nagging loss.[13] In *Little Eyolf*, the poor families' homes are referred to as "rønner" (shacks or shanties) (*LE* 76). It seems unlikely that such dwellings contain separate spaces for either the keeping or the memorialization of a small number of children—much less Eyolf's rooms, which are reserved for the books and toys of the only, lame son. Perhaps empty space, and the wealth that enables maintenance of such space, is needed for dwelling on ideals like "vine leaves in one's hair" (Hedda's dream of will and beauty) (*HG* 67); the artist's troll-like will and "castles in the air" (Solness's rationalization for any and all acts and his final building scheme with Hilde) (*BS* 89); and "Human responsibility" and higher duties to one's offspring (the subject of Alfred's book and his reason for abandoning it) (*LE* 19). We might go so far as to insist that idealism itself is a form of emptiness in Ibsen—sometimes empty rhetoric, sometimes a space of hope and possibility, or sometimes a willingness to heed the call of impossibility, which is the reason Solness gives Hilde for continuing to build empty nurseries in *The Master Builder*. Often, it is difficult to tell which is which.

In her analysis of *Peter Pan* and its afterlives, Rose describes innocence as a fantasy of "origins—the belief that each one represents an ultimate beginning where everything is perfect or can at least be made good" (138). While some of Ibsen's characters and many of his critics persist in their belief in innocent origins and are on the lookout for ways to "make good," the dramas show us that innocence is never an "ultimate beginning." Although the death of a child is obviously an important motivator, retrospection always destabilizes the child's status as origin story and primary ground. Characters' revelations and reconsiderations of the past offer glimpses of other losses, other failures that came *before* or otherwise trump the death of children. Such losses and failures can make children look like compensatory replacement projects, doomed aftereffects, or secondary considerations rather than new beginnings. At the same time, Ibsen's dramas offer evidence that life does, indeed, go on after the deaths of children.

I now turn to each of the empty nursery plays in succession, showing how they dwell on dissatisfaction, replacement projects, and troubled relationships with vision, vocation, and creativity. Ibsen also extends the problem of reproduction and failure beyond the biological or generational—his treatment of dead or doomed offspring—in part through more and less explicit reproductive metaphors and references to plans that do not come to fruition. Given that all of the main characters either are or have been procreative, the emptiness of nurseries figures not failure to procreate as such, but rather the aftereffects of apparently unviable starts. Barrenness is either metaphorical or the result of age and other, unexplained factors.[14] The degree to which characters purposefully enable or attempt to execute the (impossible) ends of reproduction varies; but in every case, Ibsen, his characters, and his critics take a profound interest in blame, guilt, and uncertain accountability. We are tempted to evaluate characters' fitness, asking whether they are good mothers and fathers, whether they are capable of positive procreativity or creative mastery. If not, who or what (past encounter, trauma, or obsession) is to blame? Can we be sure? Although there are significant differences between the dramas when it comes to their nurseries and their improper occupants, each also involves accumulation, uncertain numbers, and replacement projects that exist in tension with supposedly singular (precious and one-and-only) creatures. Each is poised between characters' mourning of the loss of originality and mastery and the suggestion that faith in, or longing for, this kind of control and originality might be the problem to begin with.

Hedda Gabler

Hedda Gabler is about a father's daughter who refuses to become her husband's wife and mother to his children. Hedda is the daughter of a General (a daughter of the civil class), who is extremely dissatisfied with her husband's petty bourgeois credentials. When the drama opens, Jørgen and Hedda Tesman have no deceased offspring, and so the unfinished business of biological reproduction entails the suicide-conterminous abortion that takes place just moments before curtain. The present action of the drama is concerned with the destruction of another "child," an allegedly visionary book manuscript about the future, dictated by Hedda's former companion, Ejlert Løvborg, and transcribed by Hedda's former schoolmate, Thea Elvsted. In Act Three, we learn that Løvborg believes he lost the manuscript after a night of revelry with Tesman and Judge Brack. The truth is that it has come into Hedda's possession through her husband, who found it on a street corner. Because Løvborg does not know into whose hands the manuscript has fallen and believes that losing a child is worse than killing a child, he lies to Thea, telling her he destroyed the manuscript. Thea responds, "Do you know Ejlert, this thing you've done with the book—for the rest of my life it will seem to me as if you'd killed a little child" (*HG* 85; 286). He agrees,

> You're right. It is like a kind of child murder.
>
> MRS. ELVSTED   But how could you do it—! It was my child too.
>
> HEDDA (*almost inaudible*)
> Ah, the child—(*HG* 85)

As the drama comes to its climax, Hedda again confirms Thea and Løvborg's reproductive metaphor while burning the manuscript, although (or because) she has been told that it is precious and irreplaceable: "Now I'm burning,—now I'm burning the child" (*HG* 88). This outrageous moment brands Hedda a destroyer and enemy of the (literary) family. She wittingly burns the "unborn" book and then kills herself, resulting in the death of her unborn child. Her motivations continue to fascinate and elude us: Is she a victim or a perpetrator, heroic or pathetic, hysterical or calculating?

Some scholars understand Hedda to be a woman of the future, born too early, denied the freedom to take power and follow her desire (e.g., Joan Templeton and Toril Moi). Others see the future not in the character but in the drama, or in the continued reincarnation of the role in the theater (e.g., Arnold Weinstein and Julia Jarcho). Hedda has also been labeled as an enemy of the future, or as embodying an abstract form of barrenness because she refuses to be a mother. In *Ibsen the Romantic* (1982), for example, Errol Durbach incorporates a version of the reading of Hedda as enemy of the future into an otherwise sympathetic portrait. He asserts, "The future history of civilization perishes twice in Ibsen's play. And in this act of perverse negation, Hedda's Romantic selfhood stands condemned in its barrenness" (52). Durbach's double perishing refers to Løvborg's burned manuscript and to the death of Hedda's baby, "the living counterpart of the symbolic 'child'" (52). His phrase "future history" refers to Ibsen's handling of the academic discipline of history in *Hedda Gabler*. This phrase shares a teleology with reproductive futurism, in which the only conceivable future involves a projection of the (idealized) past and its offspring (civilization) into a forever-deferred arrival at freedom and/as innocence (Edelman's capital-C Child). According to Durbach's rhetoric, Hedda destroys *what will have been, twice*, thus threatening the future in its recursive, future anterior form. The passively voiced phrase "stands condemned" leaves open the question of who, exactly, does the condemning—although we know what is condemned: Hedda's perverse negation, and therefore her "Romantic selfhood," for its barrenness.

Hedda manages to kill both "children," book and baby, but nonetheless fails to fulfill her own projects. First, she wants to regain power and influence over Løvborg and to play some part in his triumph. When that fails, she wants him to kill himself "beautifully" (*HG* 87), so that she can know that "something brave and freely willed can really still happen in the world" (*HG* 100). When that fails—because Løvborg shoots himself in the groin, by accident—and Thea and Tesman state that they will attempt to rewrite Løvborg's manuscript from the dictation notes that Thea has kept in her pockets, Hedda shoots herself in the temple, seemingly committing a beautiful suicide. But there are no spectators left in the world of *Hedda Gabler* (and in the theater?) to appreciate this apparent triumph. Even Brack, Hedda's blackmailer/seducer, is rendered impotent following her suicide. Slumping down in the armchair after Tesman announces that Hedda has shot herself, he exclaims, "But good God! People don't *do* such things!" (*HG* 107). Despite Brack's suggestion that Hedda disrupts the category of "people" by means of her act, her suicide does not stand alone. Its triumph depends on iteration (fixing Løvborg's failure to get it right), and it is framed by a world that both misunderstands her and is prepared to get along without her.

The tension between the supposedly singular and precious work and the notion of copies in *Hedda Gabler* involves the disparity between Løvborg's book manuscript about the future and the proposed occupants of nurseries: the texts of Tesman's ever-expanding academic archive. At first, it appears that Løvborg's manuscript is diametrically opposed to Tesman's regime of specialization, his never-ending collection of texts relevant to his discipline, and his own book project on the "domestic handicrafts of medieval Brabant," which can only be completed through archival toil (*HG* 12). While Løvborg has written at a rapid pace, using Thea to transcribe his visionary or future-oriented ideas to the page, Tesman has been collecting the writings of others with the aim of accurately describing the past. Aunt Julie is aware that the empty nurseries in the Falk town house are intended for offspring, but Tesman suggests in passing that they might serve to house his "book collection" (*HG* 10). Although these nurseries remain empty under the course of action, there are references to various forms of text, their collection, creation, and copying, throughout *Hedda Gabler*. In Act Two, Tesman assures Hedda that one can never have too many academic journals. Thus, the proposed occupants of empty nurseries in *Hedda Gabler* evoke continual accumulation. Unlike Løvborg's manuscript, these occupants are not referred to as children. They are rather anonymous and detached from Tesman's/the father's (lack of) vision.

As I will show in Chapter 1, Hedda will ultimately fail to put a stop to her husband's archival progression by burning Løvborg's manuscript-child. Toward the end of Act Three, Tesman and Thea begin the work of rewriting the manuscript. This rewriting is described as a memorial project for Løvborg; but it might also represent a professional boon for Tesman, or yet another example of accumulation, continuing to archive a future of deferral by continuing to collect texts fit for empty nurseries. *Hedda Gabler* asks us to consider whether Hedda and her unborn child are precious and irreplaceable, whether their deaths put a hole in the Tesman family by terminating its expectations. At the same time, the drama suggests that even the burning of the manuscript-child cannot halt the expansion of the specialist's collection. If something precious and irreplaceable is lost, there is no guarantee that this loss will have a noticeable or enduring effect on the future.

Chapter 1 follows Eve Kosofsky Sedgwick's advice to "Forget the Name of the Father," thinking instead about aunts, which leads me to argue that *Hedda Gabler* uses its father's daughter to produce a pessimistic and at once feminist and sexist critique of the patriarchal family (59). By tracing instances of ersatz parentage and text–offspring associations, the chapter draws attention to the ways in which *Hedda Gabler* creates a link between reproduction and degradation, proffering the maiden aunt and other secondhand mothers as guarantors of corrupted survival. The drama's empty nurseries and failed or suspended projects ultimately confirm that the future relies on neither inspiration nor vision nor precious children, but instead on *tantified* or auntly collection, organization, and persistence. Although Hedda is a "baby-killer," she does not kill the future. Instead, it is the limited horizons of the future according to *Hedda Gabler* that drive Hedda to commit suicide.

The Master Builder

The Master Builder dramatizes Halvard Solness' final days, when fear of usurpation threatens to overwhelm him. In Act One, Solness reencounters Hilde Wangel, a young woman from his past. She urges him to climb the tower of his new house in order to dedicate it, although he suffers from acrophobia. In the final moments of the drama, he reaches the top, only to plunge head first to his death. As mentioned, Halvard and Aline Solness once had twin boys, but they were belated victims of the fire, which caused Aline's grief and illness, a fever that she supposedly passed on via her milk. Solness, a paranoid and magical thinker, suspects that his will to succeed professionally caused the fire (the crack in the chimney, which he chose not to fix, was not the cause, but he did not fix it because he was ambitious and wanted the old house to burn, making way for subdivision). In the years since the fire and the death of their babies, Aline and Halvard Solness have been competing for the role of principle martyr in their marriage: Whose guilt is primary?

The explicit reproductive metaphor in *The Master Builder* involves Solness's suggestion that good mothers are builders too, not of houses or churches but of "the souls of little children" (*BS* 82). This metaphor is entangled with Solness's stories of luck, happiness, loss, and guilt, because he believes he had to sacrifice his own chances for a happy family life in order to achieve success as a builder. Hilde questions his claim to permanent and irredeemable loss, but Solness assures her that there is no way to begin again:

> SOLNESS   No. In order to build homes for others, I had to give up,—give up having a home for myself for all time. I mean a home for a flock of children. And for a father and mother too. (*BS* 59)

One of the problems with Solness's sacrifice—what he "had to give up"—is that others had to sacrifice more. After all, the price he paid did have a return: "the luck that people are always talking about" (*BS* 59). Aline too paid a price, with no return. What bothers Solness the most, he tells Hilde, is that the cost of his "kunstnerplads" (position as an artist) also involves the sacrifice of his wife's calling to be a mother/ metaphorical builder (*BS* 60). He suffers, in other words, because he has to live with the knowledge that "the price is paid anew" for his sake, "every single day" (*BS* 81). Significantly, Solness is also denying his sub-ordinates opportunities for success and familial well-being, by refusing to give references for his draftsmen, Ragnar, the son of his former boss and current assistant, architect Knut Brovik, and by seducing Ragnar's fiancée, Kaja. Solness does not respond to Brovik's pleas for his son in the same mournful and self-accusing manner in which he discusses his wife with Hilde. Instead, he tells Brovik, "*almost desperately,*" "Yes, because I can't do otherwise, you understand! I am what I am!" (*BS* 15). Solness's belief that his longing was sufficient to start the fire, as well as his insistence on the existence of magical helpers and demons, compli-cates questions of guilt and blame, regardless of his claim that he is to blame for his wife's wasted "calling" (*BS* 82). Is having longed for some-thing sufficient evidence for assignation of guilt? And what difference does it make if you are guided by destiny and unalterable personality (or narcissism) rather than free will?

Several elements in *The Master Builder* suggest that Solness's claims about home, happiness, (pro)creativity, and (especially Aline's) calling are just stories, a kind of acceptable way of describing desires and pre-occupations that are rather less normatively acceptable. That is, behind the Solness's melancholic relationship to lost twins and lost chances for familial bliss are weirder (and perhaps more fundamentally anti-social and melancholic)[15] fantasies about power, magic, domination, and creativity, about being a master un-mastered, not fully subject to guilt, grief, or old age. A question that haunts all the empty nursery plays—are new projects signs of renewal and hope, or simply variations on imperfection and failure?—pertains especially to Solness's building projects, from his days of home building to the proposed castles in the air that he and Hilde are planning to build together. Solness feels that his dream of building happy dwellings for families has failed because people do not want, or cannot manage to dwell successfully in, hap-piness, which means that the homes that he has built also fail when it comes to "proper occupation." There is also a hint, given in the stage directions for Act Three, that his houses might not be so wonderful to live in anyway: "Beyond the fence, a street with low, dilapidated row houses" (*BS* 78). As for Aline, we learn in Act Three that she grieves the loss of her nine dolls, burned up in the fire, more deeply even than the death of her twin babies, whom she assures Hilde are in a better place. Although one might insist that Aline's fixation results from un-processed grief, it also gives us reason to doubt Solness's insistence that she has missed her life's calling to be a metaphorical builder of children's souls.

In *The Master Builder*, it is the nurseries themselves that are of uncertain number and multiplying—there might be six or nine or some other number—while the tension between originality and replacement exists primarily between building projects that fall short of their construction-motivating ideals and a dream of unending domination and potency, of perfect and impossible construction: the castle in the air "with a foundation underneath" (*BS* 89). Hilde, Solness's co-conspirator in castle building, is more singular than the other proposed occupants of empty nurseries because she is a known and staged character, because she spends the night and fulfills the occupation, and because, as I will argue in Chapter 2, she represents the extension or sustainment of adolescence, a kind of permanent youth or a promise of revitalization. At the same time, Hilde is a figure of collapse and multiplication, a young woman who plays at being a child while sleeping in a nursery. After Aline prepares the middle nursery for her, Solness tells her, "*you* can be the child for as long as you are here" (*BS* 28), and the next morning, she reports that she slept, "Marvelously well! Like in a cradle" (*BS* 48). Later, when Hilde confesses to Solness why she finds him to be just a little bit crazy, she describes her experience as multiplied: she has been thinking of "*all the empty nurseries* that I lay and slept in" (*BS* 55, emphasis added). Hilde also moves between vital, robust certainty—making demands with bright eyes—and vague, romantic withdrawal, with "*an indefinable expression in her eyes*" (*BS* 65). She appears to be an unusual or unique personality, and yet she serves as Solness's inspiration and his (almost) mirror image. He has "made" her, and she reflects his desire and self-understanding (*BS* 99). Hilde is a figure of vitality who invites death onto the scene, a powerfully seductive adolescent girl.

Perhaps most importantly, Hilde serves as a strange reminder, bringing back an uncertain past that Solness has either chosen to forget or now chooses to remember. Shortly after arriving at his house in Act One, Hilde tells Solness that ten years ago to the day, after he climbed the new church tower to dedicate it, he kissed her "many times" in her father's house (*BS* 34). He also promised, she claims, to return for her in order to give her a kingdom. It is possible that this seduction never took place—we cannot know for certain; Solness suggests both that he might have willed it and that he "should have" done it (*BS* 77). In any case, whether real, imagined, or invented, the tale enables the seduced to seduce her seducer in turn. It is Hilde who convinces Solness to recreate the climb that so impressed her when she was twelve or thirteen years old. Bringing back the uncertain past in an improper figure of the future leads, perhaps unsurprisingly, to Solness' death.

In Chapter 2, I consider Ibsen's distinct interest in adolescence, arguing that Hilde's uncertain relationship to childhood demonstrates another version of the voiding and emptiness of the figure of the child. After exploring the drama's interest in quantities that do not add up, as well as Hilde's occupation of "all the empty nurseries" and the ages of youth (childhood and adolescence), I analyze a tendency in late twentieth-century criticism to read Hilde as the victim of molestation (*BS* 55). My aims in this chapter are to get some critical distance on what I call pedophilic (dis)empowerment—or an anti-pedophilic stance that appears to locate a strange and dangerous power in erotic innocence—while also resisting the conceptualization of childhood as faulty foundation, permanently traumatized by violations of innocence.

Little Eyolf

Like *The Master Builder*, *Little Eyolf* depicts bereaved parents. Alfred and Rita Allmers lose their only son in the first act, and then must try to come to terms with their grief and with one another. Unlike Solness and Aline, and in the context of substantially fresher grief, they mostly cast rather than contend for blame. *Little Eyolf* also depicts a series of replacement projects and people, the first of which to be introduced involves Alfred Allmers's more implicit reproductive metaphor: he calls his book and son alike "opgaver" (assignments or tasks) (*LE* 21). The first assignment is academic, the other practical (and quick); both pose the question of duty. In Act One, Allmers announces that he has made a decision to give up the book project in favor of the boy project, to be a better father to his son (*LE* 19). His half-sister Asta asks him whether he cannot be both a good father and a writer, but he insists, "No, never, Asta. I tell you, I can't divide myself between two assignments. But I'll follow human responsibility through—in my own life" (*LE* 21). Allmers insists, in other words, that doing his duty involves choosing between creativity and procreativity (or writing and parenting). As always, Ibsen plants seeds of doubt. An open question emerges over the course of the drama as to whether Allmers gives up the book because he loves his son, or because he wants to complete unfinished business before giving into the lure of going back up to the heights, where he might reclaim a satisfying sense of detachment from duty, family, and calling alike.

When *Little Eyolf* opens, Allmers has just returned to the estate near the fjord from a walking tour in the mountains. Ibsen thus returns to a familiar landscape in this play: lowlands are juxtaposed with heights, and this topography mirrors Allmers's internal landscape. In many of Ibsen's works, verticality figures hard choices and isolation from others, tensions between vocation and relationships, between spiritual and mundane (or earthly, embodied, gendered) forms of existence.[16] Allmers asserts that his time in the mountains helped him to choose interpersonal connection, to give up his life's work (which had begun to feel like a waste of time anyway) for the sake of another person: "My thoughts rose, more and more, to the higher duties that claimed me" (*LE* 19). These "higher duties" involve the son, whom we later learn was lamed when left alone as an infant while his parents were having sex: "Poor little Eyolf has taken his place, deeper and deeper within me. Ever since that awful fall from the table. And particularly since we've known it was incurable" (*LE* 20; Fjelde 881–882). The vertical inversion—higher and deeper (but which is which?)—in *Little Eyolf* is dizzying. Having fallen, the son becomes a higher demand. Allmers's decision to give up the elevated work of philosophy for the low romanticism of parenting means at once coming down (physically) and raising oneself (figuratively) to the task at hand. And as the play closes, the son who disappeared in the depths is reconceived as Rita and Alfred's demanding guide on high. Of course, because Eyolf drowns shortly after Allmers announces his change in plans, his decision to begin a more ethical mode of living by replacing the book with the boy never really gets under way.

Eyolf's incurable lameness, caused by his first fall from the table, appears to be the source of his parents' anticipatory, melancholic mourning. Even before Eyolf drowns at the end of Act One, the adults of *Little Eyolf* are desperate to "make good" (Rose). As we have seen, Allmers conceives of a plan to prioritize Eyolf by giving up his own work. Asta attempts to protect her nephew from his father's grief by distracting him with stories of the Ratmaid. Rita appears resigned concerning the child but idealizes the early days of her marriage. Although he once forced Eyolf to study and study, Allmers instructs him to go down to play with the poor (but able-bodied) boys who live by the shore—*before* the Ratmaid arrives on the scene. Goldman insists, "The careless cruelty is breathtaking" (100). Who is to blame for Eyolf's death? Does the Ratmaid lure him into the water, or do his parents send him there because they cannot bear to look at his disability?

After Eyolf dies, Asta stays on for a while to help the parents grieve, and her conversations with Allmers in Act Two reveal both the truth that she has recently uncovered and her primacy: she is an illegitimate child (she and Allmers share neither a mother nor a father), and she is the original Eyolf, who once played at being a little brother, dressing in Allmers's old clothes and going by the nickname Eyolf when they were alone together after her mother and his father died, when she was still a child, and he was a student at university. In Act Two, Asta momentarily disables the memorialization of Eyolf as lost ideal by helping Allmers to forget, and to his back on the fjord, remembering a past as lost ideal that came before the child. Allmers insists on the purity and unchanging nature of brother–sister love and imagines, at, first that he can be healed and perfected by returning to a life with Asta. However, Asta's illegitimacy, announced toward the end of the act, opens the possibility of another kind of relationship. Allmers is interested in re-creating what he describes as a holy union between siblings, in returning to their isolated world of idiosyncratic behaviors and pleasures, but the removal of incestual impediment also serves to seal off the future in this case.

In both *The Master Builder* and *Little Eyolf*, the past is a fantasyland, a place where suggestive and potentially risky intergenerational games are played. It is tempting to think of Eyolf/Asta as contained in the past, but Allmers and Asta's "lovely time" might be more accurately described as taking place in the future anterior, which Bruhm and Hurley define as a kind of queer time (*LE* 38). Stories of childhood queerness, they argue, are generally displaced "from the present to the future or the past (that is, the future anterior)" (xix). Whether or not Ibsen was "intent on making childhood queerness into a story that will not *be*, but will only *have been*" (Bruhm and Hurley xix), Eyolf/Asta came *before*, and so would seem to threaten Eyolf's embodiment of the innocent child as an "ultimate beginning" (Rose).

In Act Three, both Allmers and Rita ask Asta to remain with them in order to take Eyolf's place, *before* Rita conceives of the plan to host all the poor children in Eyolf's empty rooms. Asta was already a replacement child, asked to act out the lost hopes and desires of her big brother (who is not really her brother) for a little brother. Allmers suggests to Asta's suitor, Borghejm, that he now regards Asta as the true, lost companion of his life: "Yes, because you never know who you might meet afterward. During the voyage [...] The true travel companion. When it's too late. Too late" (*LE* 67). Alfred's words—"bagefter" (afterward), "undervejs" (on the journey), and "for sent" (too late)—suggest both deferral and the impossibility of a fresh start once the journey has begun. Significantly, Asta now chooses to escape, running downhill with Borghejm to catch the approaching steamship, which will head south to the city (*LE* 68–69). Thus, Asta—the first lost boy of *Little Eyolf*—also counters and complicates the verticality of the isolated Allmers estate, indicating the existence of a wider, multidirectional world.

The primary mode of *Little Eyolf* is replacement and the recommencement of life's projects. When both Eyolfs have escaped the estate by means of water—by drowning and steamship, respectively—Rita and Alfred Allmers must invent other means of coping. Travel, parties, and a vengeful demolition project, where the homes of the boys who failed to save Eyolf will be razed, are suggested and rejected in turn. Finally, Rita comes up with her own replacement project: the one and only son, once the proposed replacement for the book on human responsibility, is to be replaced by a group of poor children of uncertain number. Rita tells Allmers, who is skeptical at first, "From the day that you have left, they will be here, all of them,—as if they were my own" (*LE* 77). In some ways, these are the least queer occupants of the empty nursery plays, given that they are children who are supposed to enable Rita and Alfred Allmers' to achieve a kind of redemption, a reconnection with and eventual forgiveness from spirits on high. This is why *Little Eyolf* is sometimes read as a drama with a positive ending—an exception to Ibsen's pessimism in the other late plays.

These poor children are anonymous. We hear them and we hear stories about them, but they do not appear on stage. We do know that they have teased Eyolf (for his dreams of becoming a soldier and for his fancy clothes), that they live in shacks down by the shore and cannot afford shoes, that they witnessed Eyolf's second fall (from the end of the wharf, while staring out across the water after the Ratmaid and her dog), and that their fathers come home drunk and beat them. Sometimes these poor replacements are referred to as a group of children, but girls or sisters are never mentioned in *Little Eyolf*. When Rita describes their imagined future as occupants of Eyolf's empty rooms, she says, "They'll get to live in Eyolf's rooms. They'll get to read his books. Get to play with his toys. They'll take turns sitting in his chair at the table" (*LE* 77). In my estimation, this description evokes too many questions to be read as predominantly positive: Where have the parents gone? Will they still live by the shore, or will they be removed, as Allmers has suggested? How many children are there in total? Are some of them too old to play with toys? How long will each child have to wait before taking his turn sitting in Eyolf's chair?

In Chapter 3, I argue that this replacement project represents another turning upside down of the dramatic world of *Little Eyolf*, a figurative drowning that tempts us to continue spinning around the pivot of innocence. Thus, I contribute to the long tradition of pessimistic readings of the conclusion of this drama. Unlike other readers suspicious of *Little Eyolf*'s happy ending, however, I do not question the plausibility of the final replacement project or denounce Rita and Allmers for inauthentic grief. Instead, I use the figure of the lost boy to show how Ibsen's antepenultimate play enables a critique of the ideology of innocence and a reconsideration of the ethics of mourning, despite its apparently redemptive conclusion. As in *Peter Pan*, the lost boys of *Little Eyolf* are produced through loss, neglect, and (sometimes) failure to grow up; but the boys in Ibsen's play also counter Alfred's privileged, vertical understanding of progress and ethical action by their alternative trajectories through the landscape of the play. Unlike Rita and Allmers, Eyolf, Eyolf/Asta, and the poor boys who are to take Eyolf's place do not go up or look up at the end of the play. And unlike the poor boys, Eyolf escapes the circularity of reproduction, or the dream of a charitable refilling of the nursery, by disappearing under the surface of the water. Irretrievable, unseeing, and disengaged from the stories that his parents continue to tell about him, Eyolf embodies indefinite singularity (he is a dead child rather than *the child*), which can help us to think about the alterity of the dead.

Ibsen as Antisocial Ally?

Failure and emptiness reveal attachments to the past and provoke forms of memorialization in Ibsen's empty nursery plays, but characters also make plans for repurposing or recreating empty rooms. This pattern,

shared by *Hedda Gabler, The Master Builder*, and *Little Eyolf*, raises
the question of the future. At the same time, Ibsen's implied futures often appear to promise nothing but more of the same, further degradation
of ideals, another stab at achieving the impossible, another proposed yet
unfulfilled project.[17] Thus, one might ask whether they really represent
an exception to Ibsen's retrospective rule. Together with Aline Solness,
who insists that, no matter how much Solness builds, he can never build
"up any proper home again," audiences might also insist that non- or
post-procreative futures are always deficient and derivative, paling in
comparison with life before the fire (when the dolls had yet to burn and
the twins were still living) (*BS* 45). As I have tried to show, however,
Ibsen both asks us to doubt the completeness of the past, its truths and
traumas, and disallows the child as a symbol of making good. One of the
reasons I call the suggested future occupants of Ibsen's empty nurseries
queer is that they are not the offspring of the family. If nurseries are
"curiouser" than any specific scheme for repurposing them, it is because
they leave space open for undefined events and experiences to come.
Their occupation is mostly in a state of proposal rather than fulfillment,
un-commenced or incomplete.

Finally, neither Aline's fixated resistance to the idea of a better future nor faith in futures full of good possibilities is the right fit for Ibsen's late plays.[18] It is true that Ibsen's characters sometimes express
utopian wishes, even after *Hedda Gabler*, but these plays certainly do
not express more faith than skepticism. Some of Ibsen's contemporaries
classified the taste for "morbid pessimism" among his enthusiasts as a
form of hysteria, a "needless self-torture": "It is difficult to explain on
any other hypothesis [women's] craving for the literature of hysteria"
(Stutfield 12). *Empty Nurseries, Queer Occupants* takes place between
just such a craving—I choose this supposedly hysterical position because
I have a taste for Ibsen's "doleful squalor" (Stutfield 12)—and a form of
resistance to claims made on Ibsen in the mode of reproductive futurism,
which continue to insist that no child means no future.

From the earliest days of Ibsen's reception, critics have referred to him
as a skeptic and nihilist, a "Master Razer" rather than a master builder
(Sandberg, *Ibsen's Houses* 6). In *Ibsen's Houses*, Sandberg quotes several examples of Ibsen's contemporaries lamenting or puzzling over the
purpose such destruction might serve. Sandberg himself recognizes the
"[severity]" of "Ibsen's socio-architectural skepticism," arguing that his
was "an unusually lively architectural imagination [...] poised on the
threshold to the void" (2–3). Sandberg also notes that the architectural
aspects of Ibsen's dramas link him to the well-made play—re-created as
"the retrospective, analytic, interior conversation drama"—and to the
turn of the century European imagination, which was saturated with architectural and domestic metaphors (7–8). He then professes that these
links are both Ibsen's "strength and his liability," or that they might be
responsible for the now "dated" feel of his oeuvre (7–8). For Sandberg,

dated features can be an historical boon, allowing us to observe differences between Ibsen's contemporary moment and our own. Whether or not Ibsen's dramas feel dated or remain universally relevant—both claims are frequently made—the question of what to do with pessimism has been renewed in recent times. The dangerous and seductive powers of skepticism, negativity, and the lengths and limits of the critical mode continue to be debated. It is thus perennial rather than old-fashioned to claim that pessimism, however admirable or seductive it might be, cannot speak to or for the future.

For some queer theorists, the future itself is queer and should not be confused or conflated with what Edelman has called reproductive futurism. In *Cruising Utopia* (2009), José Esteban Muñoz argues that the present is a straight and oppressive category for queer folks. The past, on the other hand, can be creatively reimagined, or made to perform (to *do* things), in the name of a truly queer temporal category, the future: "if queerness is to have any value whatsoever, it must be viewed as being visible only in the horizon" (Muñoz 11). The distinction between queer futures and heteronormative futurism emerges from debates internal to queer studies concerning pessimism and optimism, the shape of privilege and politics, the very meaning and function of the term queer (as identity category or anti-identity concept), and what is known as the antisocial thesis or antirelationality, a lineage of theory often described as commencing with the work of Leo Bersani and ending, according to some, with Edelman.[19] Although this reduces the complexity and diversity of the scholarship that shares or otherwise engages this lineage, a broad definition of the antisocial thesis emerges from an understanding of queerness as that which undoes identity and/or opposes, or represents the necessary negation of, social formations and institutions.

One critique of Edelman and his version of antisocial queer theory is that his concept of reproductive futurism makes queer kids invisible and de-queers possible futures. Muñoz and Tim Dean, for example, worry about real children and the ethics of Edelman's abstraction and polemical style.[20] They both insist that he cannot and should not draw such an easy boundary between "the lived experience of any historical children" and the image or fetish of the Child (Edelman 11).[21] Muñoz writes,

> Theories of queer temporality that fail to factor in the relational relevance of race or class merely reproduce a crypto-universal white gay subject that is weirdly atemporal—which is to say a subject whose time is a restricting hollowed-out present free of the need for the challenge of imagining a futurity that exists beyond the self or the here and now. (94)

Although I do not think Edelman is completely uninterested in the need to change the "here and now"—he frequently refers to "imaginary

Children" as threatening "the lives, the speech, and the freedoms of adults," for example (Edelman 19)—Muñoz's opposition to the reproduction of a "crypto-universal white" (and, in the case of this book, straight) subject is well taken. Unsurprisingly, the extent to which such a subject is perpetuated in Ibsen studies is high. This is one of the reasons why I continue to insist on the situated-ness of his nurseries in terms of class (middle) and place (northern Europe), and why I keep insisting that the empty bourgeois nursery is a better symbol for innocence (and its reproduction) than the child.

The debate concerning the political and ethical viability of the antisocial thesis and the limits of dwelling in the mode of critique probably evokes a few basic questions for some of my readers. First, how relevant is this recent turn of the century (twentieth to twenty-first) debate for a study of Ibsen's dramas? In 2006, the *PMLA* published a series of commentaries on the 2005 conference panel, "The Antisocial Thesis in Queer Theory." Robert L. Caserio opens the commentaries, which include responses from Muñoz, Dean, Jack Halberstam, and Edelman, by insisting on the broad significance of Edelman's critique of the Child and on the generally antirelational character of both aesthetics and eros. Referring to Halberstam's call to extend the archive of queer studies beyond "those elite white boys Gide and Proust," he insists, "what will become clear [if one heeds Halberstam's call], is that homosexual eros is not more arelational than its alternative" (820). Whether written by "homos" or "heteros," he concludes,

> Most literary writing from 1890–1945 does not hold a brief for defenses against time and death. An influential popular archive of fictions thus suggests an undeclared straight-gay alliance, founded in agreement about the inaptitude of all eros for sociality [...] By invoking this alliance, I mean to suggest that what is at stake in the antisocial thesis in queer theory is of interest not only to homos. (820–821)

From this perspective, Ibsen might be read as a kind of antisocial ally, which is not to say that his dramas cannot be adapted or reimagined for utopian purposes, but simply that they most certainly do not "hold a brief for defenses against time and death." His late plays are part of the long turn of the century's "unparalleled assault on heterosexual institutions—on marriage and children and their insurance of futures—by heterosexuals" (Caserio 820). The debate over antirelationality in queer theory is thus more relevant to Ibsen than one might at first assume.

In addition to the question of relevance, one might ask, what can we do with Ibsen's pessimism concerning the future? In *Henrik Ibsen and the Birth of Modernism* (2006), Toril Moi claims that in his "late phase," Ibsen

> shows what the world looks like when we truly have to 'live life without ideals,' as Ulrik Brendel [from *Rosmersholm* (1886)] puts it.

Without the utopian energy of radical idealism, everyday life in modernity becomes incapable of generating meaning, energy, passion, or hope. (319)

I agree that some of the fascination of Ibsen's earlier dramas—*A Doll House*, for example—emerges from their claims on both "utopia and critique" (319). Nevertheless, and although hope might remain the prerogative of utopia, forms of anti-idealism and anti-redemption, radical critique, and skepticism *can* generate meaning, energy, and passion (although they might be of the gloomy, perverse, and resistant sort). One answer to the question about what one can do with Ibsen's pessimism is that one can use it to show how perceptions of the child continue to reproduce an empty place for our fears and desires, while recognizing that the story of innocence is very often a story about the *absence or absenting* of children.

The empty nursery plays depict innocence by means of empty rooms. Ibsen leaves us with emptiness at curtain, which means that he leaves us with his characters'—and our own—desire to fill things up. In Chapter 4, I give in to this desire in a different way, motivated in part by questions about what these rooms "were really like." I begin the chapter by returning to where I started in the Prologue: "A Doll House—1879," the apartment-installation at the Norwegian Museum of Cultural History. This installation enables me to consider the theatricality of the bourgeois household, while moving from the frontstage to the backstage, from the parlor and other semi-private spaces to the more private, yet mixed-class domain of the nursery. The primary materials for analysis in Chapter 4 include not only the limited descriptions of children's rooms and women's labor (and the ways in which these limited descriptions echo with reproductive significance) in the dramas, but also Norwegian scholarship on domestic history and archival sources from the period 1890–1920 that address child-rearing and nannies. The historical world of the turn of the century nursery in Norway might appear to be at odds with Ibsen's children's rooms, or with the ways in which I have described their figurative significance. In this final chapter, however, I show that the nursery remains a fitting figure for innocence in both its empty, offstage dramatic form and its evocation in advice manuals—because it is a space of potential, filled with anxious expectations concerning proper development, housing fears about the threat of the nanny, and the absence of a mother.

Before moving on to Chapter 1, I must make a confession: I do not really believe that plays have futures. That is, the world of a play ends when and where the text ends, on the final page. The future of a text is thus one of repetition and reinterpretation. Characters will say the same things and commit the same crimes and die the same deaths over and over again. Except by means of the reader, director, actor, or storyteller, they do not move into a future, but only go back to the beginning or recommence where interpreters, stagers, and adapters choose to begin. Moreover, while certain aspects of a play can suggest possible futures, in a realist sense the same radical uncertainty that applies to my life would apply to characters' lives. Perhaps I will die today and never finish writing this book on Ibsen, reproduction, and the future. Perhaps Tesman, to take one example, will fail to rewrite Løvborg's book about the future. Perhaps his debts or the scandal following Hedda's suicide will force him to move out of the Falk townhouse and into a living space without extra empty rooms for housing babies or books. To ponder the future can be a violation of the bounds of a text, in formal, narrative, and mimetic senses. Although I am not terribly concerned about textual violations and sometimes give in to the temptation to speculate, I do not seek to pin down what happens after the last page of any of Ibsen's plays. Instead, I pay attention to patterns, repetition, characters' hopes, plans, and expectations, and broader reproductive ideologies found in criticism.

Notes

1 According to "an old ex-Nanny called Mrs. Wake," who wrote an "extremely sharp letter" regarding the subject to Gathorne-Hardy, author of *The Unnatural History of the Nanny*, the Victorian nanny had already disappeared by 1914 (20). The conditions under which she came to rule over her "kingdom" involved, among other complex factors, greater wealth and growth in population, specializations in domestic service, and a parenting culture in which mothers and fathers from the upper (and eventually middle) classes turned the rearing of their children over to women from the working class (Gathorne-Hardy 20, 58–59, 65). Of course, women continued to work in domestic service and childcare after 1914, although institutions and cultural expectations changed dramatically in the twentieth century. I touch on some cultural expectations for late nineteenth-century and early twentieth-century childcare in Norway in Chapter 4 (expectations that do overlap in several ways with those found in the English context).

2 I write "to some extent European" society because English nannies became fashionable to hire in other parts of Europe, including Russia and France.

3 According to the *Oxford English Dictionary*, nursery is "[f]ormed within English, by derivation; modeled on a French lexical item" (related words are *nourrice* and *nourrir*). Relevant definitions from this dictionary include "A place for nursing or fostering"; "A room or area of a house set aside for babies and young children, esp. for those in the care of a nursemaid"; and "a child's bedroom or playroom." Norwegian does not have a similar word, but instead attaches *barn* (child) to various words for room, as in *barneværelse* (child's room). Ibsen uses a compound word, *barnekammers* (a child's bedroom; *kammer* referring specifically to a small chamber in this case), in only *The Master Builder*. In *Hedda Gabler* and *Little Eyolf*, he indicates by other means that empty rooms have been occupied by or intended for children.

4 In *Child Loving*, Kincaid argues that "the species 'child'" has "monolithic power, so much so that even large differences, like class, could sometimes be explained as environmental effects on children, the fundamental 'child' in

these cases being the same across class lines" (83). When he makes this claim, he has in mind the "worrisome" national child, the creation of which takes place in "*all* nurseries [...] even the most humble or, more likely, squalid" (82). Kincaid is not thinking about separate rooms reserved for children and ruled over by bourgeois mothers and nannies, in this case, but instead about an expanded figure of the nursery-as-nation.

5 This book was conceived with a strategic deployment of the figurative versus real (historical or material) binary in mind, in part because I have differentiated a historical-realist approach to the nursery—found at the folk museum, for example, see the Prologue and Chapter 4—from my own interest in the nursery as a mostly empty and un-described space that can help us to think about our continued reproduction of normative ideas about children, gender, and the family. A major theoretical problem and point of debate in child studies is the question of the limits of the figurative: What, if anything, would constitute a non- or prefigurative child? My discussions of class and women's labor are informed by critiques of Lee Edelman's abstract, figurative Child, but scholars including Karín Lesnik-Oberstein and Neil Cocks have drawn attention to the ways in which analyses of the child within queer theory (including Edelman's) return to or continually locate a real child in a place safely external to (and therefore determining of) their analyses. In "Childhood, Queer Theory, and Feminism," Lesnik-Oberstein argues that "the child has a tendency to recur as a foundational or essential real, even in some queer and feminist theoretical writings which express an explicit commitment to questioning essentialist notions of identity" (39). In the final chapters of *The Peripheral Child*, Cocks differentiates Edelman's symbolic child from Kincaid's symbolic child, while critiquing their shared "ironic commitment to a certain 'substantialization'" and asking, "How secure is the anti-essentialism on offer?" (122). Even though I make use of the figurative/real binary in order to differentiate what I argue is the wide-ranging thematic significance of nurseries from their restricted naturalist presence in the dramas, I have also tried to avoid phrasing that would too neatly oppose figures and "real persons" or figures and "actual rooms."

6 For a historical consideration of the development of interiority and/as the figure of the child, see Carolyn Steedman's *Strange Dislocations*. Steedman writes, "From the end of the eighteenth century onward, there came into being complex ways of understanding childhood as a component of the adult self, and of envisaging the depths of the self to which childhood—the adult's personal history—was relegated" (96). While I take a greater interest in reading the absences in the dramas in order to engage our own, postmodern habits of thinking the child, Steedman's study of the afterlives of the figure of Mignon suggests that Ibsen's empty nurseries, as symbols for adult characters' hopes and fears, were also very much "of his time" (164).

7 For considerations of the racialization of innocence, see, for example, Robin Bernstein's *Racial Innocence: Performing American Childhood from Slavery to Civil Rights* and Kathryn Bond Stockton's *The Queer Child*.

8 For a consideration of romantic readings of Hedvig in *The Wild Duck*, see my article "A Scandalous Similarity?: The Wild Duck and the Romantic Child."

9 Edelman capitalizes the word "Child" in order to distinguish this political figure of "coercive universalization" from "the lived experiences of any historical children" (11). Whether this is ethical or possible has been subject to much debate within queer and child studies. Some critics have argued that Edelman's project (as polemic and as thought-experiment) is enabled

by his own white, male, academic privilege, that he dwells in this figure at the expense of real queer kids, and that he should have spent more time acknowledging the fact that the image that attends and constitutes the fetish and figure of the Child is also middle class and white. I discuss some of these criticisms briefly below and in Chapter 4. Unless I am referring directly to *No Future*, I do not capitalize the word child, partially in order to problematize or refuse a radical distinction between figurative Child and real children.

10 In "Det provoserende svangerskapet i Henrik Ibsens *Hedda Gabler*" (The Provocative Pregnancy in Henrik Ibsen's *Hedda Gabler*), Ane Hoel argues that Hedda's pregnancy is not certain, and that it results from wishful interpretation and takes place in Aunt Julie and the reader's mind rather than in Hedda's body. It is true that Hedda's pregnancy is never named *as such* in *Hedda Gabler*. Ultimately, however, whether or not Hedda is pregnant does not matter to my reading of the play, given that Hedda carries the Tesmans' "expectations." She takes either a fetus or these expectations out when she commits suicide. The fact that characters and most readers believe Hedda to be pregnant is enough for "us" (the normative collective) to lament the (potential of) infanticide-suicide.

11 See Franco Moretti's "Ibsen and the Spirit of Capitalism" in *The Bourgeois* for another reading of the future-focus of the late plays, in relationship to the tension between "bourgeois prose" and "capitalist poetry" (179): "in 'late Ibsen' characters speculate, looking far into the time to come" (185).

12 See, for example, Rose's *The Case of Peter Pan* (1984), Kincaid's *Erotic Innocence* (1998), Lesnik-Oberstein's "Childhood, Queer Theory, and Feminism" (2010), Bernstein's *Racial Innocence* (2011), Cock's *The Peripheral Child* (2014), and the articles in *GLQ: A Journal of Lesbian and Gay Studies'* special issue, *The Child Now* (22: 4, 2016). In *The Queer Child, or Growing Sideways in the Twentieth Century* (2009), Stockton argues that innocence itself queers the child, making it "strange (and appealing)" (296). In her contribution to GLQ's *The Child Now*, "The Child Now and Its Paradoxical Global Effects" (2016), she argues, "children are not just growing astray inside delay, as once they were. Delay itself is withering. Grandly telescoping. Children are (again) growing up too soon, in someone's estimation" (507).

13 Despite the cynical sound of his title—his acknowledgment that Rita and Alfred have conceived of their dead son as a pest—Aarseth argues that *Little Eyolf* provides insufficient evidence for pessimistic readings of its conclusion. I address this argument briefly in Chapter 3, where I present my own, rather pessimistic (or at least highly critical) reading of *Little Eyolf*'s conclusion.

14 The total number of conceived offspring in the empty nursery plays is four. Ibsen and Susannah Thoresen Ibsen themselves had only one child, Sigurd Ibsen, which has led to speculation regarding Ibsen's potentially prudish attitudes toward sex. In *I gode og vonde dagar* (*In Good and Hard Times*), Sogner et al. explain that the birthrate in Norway began to fall in the 1860s. It dropped first among the upper classes, although before this period they had more children than farmers and smallholders, due to lower marriage age and the use of wet nurses (52). Abstinence and withdrawal were probably the most common methods for preventing pregnancy, but information about other prevention methods (from homemade spermicides to fish bladder glue condoms) was also more widely available in the second half of the nineteenth century (Sogner et al. 52). According to Sogner et al., one of the reasons for large families being less desirable was that it became harder to hire maids and nannies after industrialization (53). None of this means that the small

number of children in Ibsen's plays or in his own family is typical of the family in Norway at the end of the nineteenth century, but it should serve to caution against assuming that family size can always be explained by either barrenness or prudishness.

15 See Frode Helland's *Melankoliens spill* (*The Play of Melancholy*) (2000) for a thorough discussion of the concept of melancholy in the context of Ibsen's late plays.

16 Ibsen's ideas about (dangerous) idealism on the heights are explicitly developed in the dramas *Brand* and *Når vi døde vågner* (*When We Dead Awaken*) and in the poem *På vidderne* (*On the Heights*).

17 As I discuss and challenge in Chapter 3, a possible exception is *Little Eyolf*, in which Rita imagines a charitable future of potential healing.

18 There is no scholarly consensus on what constitutes "late Ibsen." In this book, I define Ibsen's late plays as beginning with *Hedda Gabler*, and I am not alone in this. Toril Moi, for example, argues that a new phase of Ibsen's production begins with *Hedda Gabler* because Ibsen's greater interest in the "'bad' everyday" begins here: "*Hedda Gabler* thus inaugurates a new phase in Ibsen's modernism, one in which idealism comes across as a baffling anachronism" (318).

19 In "Reproduction and Queer Theory," for example, Anca Parvulescu insists that *No Future* is no longer a "theoretical model to be cultivated and reproduced" (87). I briefly discuss her claim and its significance for this book, in Chapter 4.

20 In "An Impossible Embrace," Dean offers a critique of Edelman's use of the psychoanalytical concept of the death drive and of his style ("and the irrational passion that style conveys") (126). Similarly to Muñoz, Dean welcomes Edelman's "thorough-going challenge to the social and political investment in 'family values'" (129). However, he challenges Edelman's interest in an ahistorical image of the Child because it entails a simplification of the (queer) child of psychoanalysis: "When [the capital-C Child] thus becomes unhinged from its living concepts and reduced to its often rebarbative vocabulary, psychoanalysis degenerates into a dogma whose principle function lies in producing the rhetorical effect of its authority" (129). My use of Edelman here is not intended as a wholesale endorsement of his theories. Dean insists, "Freud's theory of infantile sexuality, with its account of a universal predisposition to polymorphous perversion, long ago shattered the illusion of childhood innocence" (128). Unfortunately (and as Dean undoubtedly knows), Freud's shattering of childhood innocence does not seem to have shattered the concept sufficiently in many discourses and belief systems. Thus, Edelman's "melodramatic," "irrational," and "campy" ideas remain a good fit for pointing out related features in Ibsen studies (Dean 125–126).

21 Playing with Edelman's chapter title from *No Future*, "The Future is Kid Stuff," Muñoz reminds us that the future is "only the stuff of some kids. Racialized kids, queer kids, are not the sovereign princes of futurity" (Muñoz 95). We might add, as Muñoz does elsewhere, disabled kids to this list, both because scholars such as Kafer have theorized disability from within queer theory and because Eyolf is made to figure a form of futurelessness and preemptive mourning.

1 Endless Aunts, Endless Books

The Future According to *Hedda Gabler*

In the empty nursery plays, babies are dead or doomed, projects remain undone, and children's rooms are not occupied by offspring. Nevertheless, *Hedda Gabler* (1890) remains invested in reproduction, and not only in the sense that Ibsen uses reproductive figures and ersatz parentage to align mothers and fathers with creators, and offspring with projects. This chapter considers the significance of the forms that reproduction takes in this deeply pessimistic drama, asking, What future does *Hedda Gabler* ask us to imagine?

Each of the empty nursery plays also involves a proposal to refill empty children's space with improper occupants, objects, or creatures that are not the offspring of the family. In *Hedda Gabler*, these occupants consist of an endless collection of texts that will form a boring archive, to be compiled by Hedda's husband, Jørgen Tesman. Tesman is a "specialist," a collector and organizer of other peoples' papers—a talent that runs in the Tesman family (*HG* 12). Uninterested in the mode of archival preservation that animates her husband, Hedda burns an allegedly visionary manuscript about the "future history of civilization" written by Tesman's rival and Hedda's former comrade, Ejlert Løvborg (Durbach 52).[1] In Act Two, when Løvborg believes he has lost his manuscript, he tells his new comrade, Thea Elvsted, that he destroyed it.[2] Thea, the manuscript's transcriber and potential muse, insists that it is as if Løvborg had "killed a little child," and Løvborg agrees, seeming to confirm his role as both father and killer (*HG* 85). Hedda takes on their reproductive metaphor as the play comes to its climax in Act Three: "Now I'm burning,—now I'm burning the child" (*HG* 88). This drama of "child" burning represents the height of an apparent opposition in *Hedda Gabler* between vital creativity and secondhand collecting and copying.

The double meaning of apparent is crucial here: the difference between Løvborg's creativity and Tesman's specialization is evident, but it could also be misleading. My first argument in this chapter is that there are no examples of reproduction in *Hedda Gabler* that have a clear and uncertain relationship to vision and originality, or that are Fathered with a capital F. Løvborg's manuscript about the future is more creative than

Tesman's projects, but it is not for that reason undomesticated, irreplaceable, or uncopiable. During the course of the play, Hedda learns that she cannot put a stop to her husband's domesticated and domesticating archival collection, even by burning the supposedly inspired manuscript about the future, because Tesman and Thea will make an attempt to rewrite Løvborg's book, and perhaps this copy will be housed in the empty nurseries of *Hedda Gabler*.

Hedda Gabler is in many ways a drama obsessed with the Father and the past. It has sometimes been read as a story of decline, wherein the end of the family line is confirmed and settled by the hand of an improperly gendered (masculinized) baby-killer, who kills the future when she kills herself. Toward the end of Act Four, Hedda commits suicide while pregnant, which appears to invite a reading along the very familiar lines of reproductive futurism: no baby = no future. As Lee Edelman spells it out, "If [...] there is *no baby* and, in consequence, *no future*, then the blame must fall on the fatal lure of sterile, narcissistic enjoyments understood as inherently destructive of meaning" (*No Future* 13). One way to understand Hedda and her fate is to assume that she is condemned for failing to acquiesce to her reproductive role, for refusing to allow rooms and wombs to serve their proper function, and for refusing to become a carrier for the Tesman line. In an early essay, "The Irony of Decadence" (1953), Herbert Blau argues that Hedda embodies a dead end in the patriarchal line because she refuses to serve and assist procreativity or creativity.[3] She will not serve the family like Tesman's aunt, Miss Juliane Tesman. She will not assist in creative projects like transcriber Thea. She will not become a mother to her husband's children. Fixated on her father and his supposedly heroic world, she already "antedates" the material bourgeois world in which we find her, and thus cannot speak to the longings and needs of the present moment (in Blau's essay, the beginning of the second half of the twentieth century) (116). Because Hedda does not change and remains General Gabler's daughter, Blau defines "one of her most affective characteristics" as "a disturbing sterility that approaches the masculine" (113). Hedda's "essential sterility" emerges from her female masculinity, normatively defined, and from her difference from women characters who represent feminine service to the future through "sacrifice, charity, or love" (Blau 113).[4] Blau insists that Ibsen's drama contains no clear, internal principle from which to judge Hedda's character, making it profoundly anti-redemptive, a work of nihilism and decadent irony with nothing to say to the future.[5]

My aim is to pay attention to gendered patterns of association that exceed the story of the Father and the question of the freedom of the individual, which is arguably the leading question in approaches to gender and sex in Ibsen studies.[6] Rather than focusing on the contested relationship between universal personhood, femininity, and sex, I choose to dwell in aspects of Ibsen's drama that constitute a pessimistic and anti-redemptive critique of the patriarchal family. While Blau diagnoses a female-masculine sterility in Hedda's character, I emphasize the fact that Ibsen depicts a whole world in which *reproductivity approaches the feminine*. *Hedda Gabler*'s horizons of possibility consist of domestic-patriarchal endlessness, a world full of specialists, a family unit whose members will never lose their taste for engaging in secondhand projects, collecting new copies (whether babies or books), and transcribing and organizing the work of others. My second and primary argument is that the future is coming in *Hedda Gabler*, and that this future will be fully Tesmanized. The fulcrum of this argument is the maiden aunt, a non-procreative figure that nonetheless supports the family, guaranteeing its survival through secondhand mothering. To be Tesmanized, it turns out, is also to be *tantified*, or made aunted.

When Aunt Julie begins to expect Hedda's pregnancy in earnest in Act One, she announces that she will be visiting her nephew and his new wife every day. The aunt's visits, caresses, and expressions of concern exasperate Hedda, who loses patience in Act Two, uttering under her breath, "Oh, these eternal aunts!" (*HG* 44). Hedda's utterance combines a specific and ostensibly harmless figure with an adjective—*evig* (eternal or endless) in Norwegian—denoting ceaseless number and duration. It is an idiomatic, exaggerative expression of frustration, the way one talks about things that drive one to distraction. But it is also more than this, given that subtle ties between reproduction and auntliness can be found throughout Ibsen's drama. Taken together, these ties tell us, first, that the Tesmans are a family of domesticated, secondhand (re)producers, and, second, that the whole world of *Hedda Gabler* consists of *tantified* specialists. Hedda refuses to live in the Tesman family and in this world of aunts, which means that she is, after all, an anti-futural figure—just not in the simplistic baby-killing way that reproductive futurists might imagine. Hedda cannot kill the future because a future is coming, and it is this future that kills, its horizons of possibility driving her to commit suicide.

Forgetting the Father

Three main theoretical moves inspire my claim that *Hedda Gabler* is invested in feminizing forms of reproductivity: Edelman's polemical assessment of reproductive futurism, introduced above, Jacques Derrida's insistence that the archive marks both longing for, and impossibility of access to, the Father, to which I will return in the conclusion of this chapter, and Eve Kosofsky Sedgwick's advice in "Tales of the Avunculate": "Forget the Name of the Father. Think about your uncles and your aunts" (59).[7] Although Sedgwick's interests are aunts and uncles, she opens "Tales of the Avunculate" with a sociable command: "Let's begin—but only because everyone else does—with the

Name of the Father" (52). Before naming the difference that thinking about aunts might make in the case of *Hedda Gabler*, I will also begin—"just like everyone else"—by thinking about the name Gabler.

But before I can do this, I must admit that thinking about aunts in the case of *Hedda Gabler* does not enable me to make claims for forms of desire and creativity that take place between women, as others have done before me.[8] Sedgwick focuses on some of the ways in which aunts and uncles can offer queerer forms of kinship. In Ibsen's drama, the aunt is a figure that reinforces heteronormative-reproductive futures. As Joan Templeton writes, Aunt Julie is both "a paragon, approaching parody, of a familiar nineteenth-century type of self-sacrificing womanhood, the good spinster who devotes her life to a male relation" and the "*mater familias*" of *Hedda Gabler* (211, 213). The tangled webs of gender under patriarchy indicate that Ibsen's play is both feminist, that is, a drama that takes an interest in critiquing sexed forms of entrapment (marriage, sexual extortion, etc.), and sexist, that is, founded on a familiar understanding of the feminine as a secondary and corrupting force.[9] While Hedda is masculine-female—figuratively sterile, "[misidentified and maladjusted]," composed of "the rejected scraps of dominant masculinity" (Halberstam 9 and 1)—and the patriarchy is feminized (via Tesman), the feminine (Aunt Julie) becomes the passive-aggressive guarantor of the patriarchal family. *Hedda Gabler* remains caught up in an ambiguous mix of condemnation and commendation of its heroine, not only because Hedda Gabler must become Hedda Tesman or die but also because its commendation relies, in part, on effeminophobia, defined here as an aversion to emasculation and/as devitalization. Non-procreative aunts and the reproductive family go together because Pandora's lateness—the notion that that which is feminine is also dangerously secondary and corrupting (figured in the jar that figures a womb and brings ruin)—lingers in *Hedda Gabler*'s prescient suggestions.[10] The Gabler line is of the past, but it persists as an idealized and impossible fantasy. Any creature or product that might carry the Father into the future or lead to an alternative future remains latent, is subject to uncertainty, or is destroyed. Thus, thinking about aunts in the case of *Hedda Gabler* leads me back to Tesman, the name of the (lower case) father, a husband who represents the domesticated patriarchy, which is at once emasculated and persistent.

Many prominent aspects of *Hedda Gabler* suggest that Ibsen was more focused on the end of the Gabler line than on the future, more interested in the (ghost of the) Father than in the future of his daughter. Ibsen begins (titles his play) with the name of the father's daughter. In a letter to his French translator, Russian diplomat Count Moritz Prozor, he wrote, "My intention in giving [the play the name *Hedda Gabler*] was to indicate that Hedda as a personality is to be regarded rather as her father's daughter than as her husband's wife" (Ibsen, *Speeches and Letters* 297, trans. Sprinchorn). This description of titular intention suggests that Hedda is to be understood through association with the General, a man of higher social rank than Tesman (and, in the past, of greater wealth). It also suggests that she is future-less, tied to the past and caught in an impasse between two forms of patriarchal possession.

There are, as noted, two family names in *Hedda Gabler*: Gabler and Tesman. Addressing the equal significance of the Tesman name, Elin Diamond writes,

> In the play's fiction, Hedda Gabler is erased by Hedda Tesman [...] With her overdetermined connection to the father, Hedda Gabler troubles the representation of the wife. But Hedda Gabler cannot be viewed as 'freer' than Hedda Tesman; in effect it is the patriarchal 'Gabler' of her identity that causes her to become the 'Tesman' [...] Hedda is caught between her swelling (mother's) womb and her father's pistols and identifies with neither. (27)

Characters, critics, and audiences continue to obsess over the motivations and desires (or lack thereof) of the personality known by the name Hedda Gabler. No such person exists in the play, however, either legally or in the present moment of action. Both Gabler and Tesman, it turns out, represent the family and its temporality: the seemingly eternal patriarchy, whether in idealized or degraded form, with no foreseeable alternative future for its daughters in either case. Although critics and characters (especially Løvborg) refuse to stop saying Hedda Gabler, Ibsen has already set the record straight before the action even begins. The first name on the character list is "GEORGE TESMAN, research fellow in cultural history," followed by "HEDDA TESMAN, *his wife*" (*HG* 4, my emphasis).[11] Ibsen knows that his drama is about a personality that cannot carry its own name, technically speaking, and so he leaves us to shuttle back and forth between Gabler and Tesman. I am arguing that focusing on the Tesmanized future allowed by Ibsen's drama, rather on the disallowed future of Hedda alone, will enable us to understand the full story that *Hedda Gabler* tells about gender and reproduction.

Like Ibsen, Aunt Julie knows what it means for Hedda Gabler to become Hedda Tesman: she must become a carrier for the Tesman name (*HG* 47).[12] Several characters in the play use the title Mrs. Tesman to refer to Hedda, but there are only two instances of the full name Hedda Tesman, both spoken by Aunt Julie. This name and the way in which Aunt Julie uses it—always with pregnancy in mind—make it apparent that her interest in Hedda is part and parcel of her interest in the expansion of the family. In Act One, after Hedda has insulted Aunt Julie's new hat, Tesman distracts his aunt by drawing her attention to Hedda's altered appearance. Hedda insists that she looks the same as she did before the honeymoon, but Tesman asks his aunt to notice how "plump and buxom" she has become, how "much weight she has put on during the trip" (*HG* 15). Aunt Julie gazes at Hedda with folded hands and then uses those hands to grasp her head and kiss her hair: "God bless and keep Hedda Tesman," she pronounces, "For Jørgen's sake" (*HG* 16). Hedda Tesman is the name not only of the woman married to Jørgen Tesman but also, and even more properly, of the woman who appears to be pregnant and must be protected *for his sake*. Hedda extracts herself "gently," begging to be released, and although Aunt Julie releases her, she also closes in (*HG* 16). In Templeton's words, Hedda "hears her fate sealed" (214), as Aunt Julie now promises to visit Hedda "hver evige dag" (each and every day) (*HG* 16). Aunt Julie utters the name that spells out the facts of the trap. As Diamond observes, Hedda Tesman (imperfectly) covers over Hedda Gabler, and Hedda's meaning and value for others is increasingly limited to her procreative function, for the sake of the family.

In the opening pages of Act Four, Aunt Julie performs solemnity and uses the name Hedda Tesman for the second time, after arriving at the townhouse dressed in mourning to announce her sister, Aunt Rina's, death. Hedda has already heard the news from Tesman, but Aunt Julie states, "here in the house of life,—here I should bring the news of death myself" (*HG* 89). Although it is true that a dead body lies at Aunt Julie's and new life is expected at the Tesman's, the phrase "house of life" is an ironic description of the Falk townhouse, a place that Hedda does not want to live in, never leaves, and that will soon be the scene of her suicide.[13] Before Aunt Julie departs to prepare the body, Hedda asks whether she might help in some way and is politely refused:

> MISS TESMAN Oh, don't ever think of that! Hedda Tesman mustn't put her hands to such a thing. Or let her thoughts dwell on it, either. Not at a time like this, no.
>
> HEDDA Oh, thoughts,—they're not so easy to master—
>
> MISS TESMAN (*persisting*) Yes, my goodness, that's how the world goes. At my house we'll now be sewing a shroud for Rina. And soon there'll be sewing here too, I imagine. But of a far different kind, praise the Lord! (*HG* 90)

According to Aunt Julie, "a time like this" requires Hedda to think happy thoughts and sew (or at least direct the sewing of) clothes for an impending arrival. According to Errol Durbach, this conversation about shrouds and baby clothes indicates that Aunt Julie accepts time and the organic realities of birth and death, while Hedda longs to escape time and nature, and so destroys the future of "history in its most organic, most palpable form"—that is, in the form of her child (35, 52).

A non-procreative life, however, or at least a master-able relationship to biological reproduction, can make life as well as death more bearable for those who do not or cannot accept their status as vessels for non-chosen families. After referring to Brack's misreading of Hedda, his insistence that the claim of motherhood will give her life meaning, Diamond defines "the horror of the 'here' in realism: the room/womb which is in *Hedda Gabler* the source of the body's hysteria and of the play's action" (75). A third term, implied by the rhyme scheme, is tomb, which is not only an internal feature (a womb/tomb inside of Hedda) but also a name for the future that promises to entomb Hedda in an experience of living-death. Hedda does not accept her pregnancy because it is the embodiment of Aunt Julie's expectations, but the drama makes room for a "ludicrously aborted," revivified, and Tesmanized inhabitant: the to-be-recomposed manuscript about the future (Diamond 74–75).

Sedgwick concludes "Tales of the Avunculate" by asking (following Leo Bersani), "How can we stop redeeming the family?" Although she admits that forgetting the Father "can only partially work," she also insists that it "can work 'enough,' in the sense of making an unforeseen difference in the effect to which X presides over your obsessional process" (59). My strategic and good enough answer to Sedgwick's question is: Stop obsessing over Hedda's masculine sterility and start thinking about *Hedda Gabler*'s feminizing reproductivity. The world of *Hedda Gabler* is delimited and determined by Tesmanism, a mode of living in service to the family, of copying, organizing, and archiving the work of others. Thus, the future according to *Hedda Gabler* will involve more secondhand projects, overseen by "them all," the endless aunts for whom Hedda promises to be silent shortly before she kills herself (*HG* 107). In his drafting notes for *Hedda Gabler*, Ibsen addressed Tesman and Thea's plan to rewrite Løvborg's manuscript: "then those two sit there with the manuscript they cannot decipher. *And the aunt sits with them.* What an ironical comment on human striving towards development and progress" (Ibsen qtd. in Durbach 38, emphasis added). Although the aunt does not sit at the table with Tesman and Thea in the final draft of the play, a certain embodiment of the feminine, a certain feminizing presence, can be perceived as a threat to "human progress and development"—in this case in the form of an ironic tableau.

The claim that Hedda's refusal of motherhood and her decision to die constitute threats to the "future history of civilization" can distract us from the threat to alternative futures that the patriarchal family itself represents, making Hedda's perception of "endless aunts" a mere symptom of her own failure to acquiesce to reproductive heteronormativity—posing, as it often does, as what is and must be (Durbach 52). Addressing the limits of political think-ability and the "citizen as ideal," Edelman writes, "the social order exists to preserve" for the "fantasmatic" Child as "universalized subject [...] a notional freedom more highly valued than the actuality of freedom itself, which might, after all, put at risk the Child to whom such freedom falls due" (*No Future* 11). In other words, a common understanding of childhood and child-centric practices, policies, and habits of thought can distract us from threats to freedom by emphasizing possible threats to innocence in a politics of permanent deferral. Setting aside our fantasmatic attachments to the figure of the child as future, there is no reason to believe that a future is not coming in *Hedda Gabler*. Ibsen uses reproductive figures to reimagine the patriarchy as a emasculated but nonetheless persistent lineage of aunthood. Rather than barren apocalypse, he asks us to imagine the future as a boring and ridiculous continuance of the family that will domesticate or eradicate dreams of some alternative to Aunt Julie, Tesman, and Judge Brack's visions of "what is and what must be."

Aunts, Books, Endlessness

Aunt Julie is the first character to enter the stage in *Hedda Gabler*, followed by the Tesmans' longtime maid, Berte: "*Miss Tesman is a good and kindly looking lady around 65 years old. Neatly but simply dressed. Berte is a maid getting on in years, with a steady and somewhat provincial look*" (*HG* 5). In a letter to a Norwegian actress, Ibsen wrote,

> Jørgen Tesman, his old aunts, and the faithful servant Berte together form a picture of complete unity. They think alike, they share the same memories and have the same outlook on life. To Hedda they appear like a strange and hostile power, aimed at her very being. In a performance of the play the harmony that exists between them must be conveyed. (*Speeches and Letters* 299, trans. Sprinchorn)[14]

In the same letter, Ibsen described Berte—and so each member of the Tesman unit—as a "good-natured, simple, oldish person" (299). How can good-natured and simple old ladies threaten Hedda, the "most formidable humanized troll in Ibsen" (Bloom 354)? While Hedda is often offensive, manipulative, petty, and sometimes malicious, the Tesman unit is offensively inoffensive. Its members are curious about Hedda but cannot comprehend her worldview and motivations. The harmony of the Tesman unit contributes to Hedda's feelings of being bored and trapped and useless. While their unsophisticated qualities are not to her taste, it is certainly their "complete unity" and unquestioning faithfulness that strikes Hedda as "strange and hostile."[15]

All of the figures of reproduction in *Hedda Gabler*, from ersatz mothers to doomed fetuses (Hedda's unborn child and Løvborg's unpublished manuscript-child), constellate around Aunt Julie's "expectations" (*HG* 10).[16] When she and Tesman discuss the two empty rooms "between the back parlor and Hedda's bedroom" in the Falk townhouse in

Act One, she clearly understands them to be spaces for children (*HG* 11). Tesman and the play as a whole, however, suggest that they might house reproduction in another, academic and archival, but nonetheless fruitful (numerous) form. When Aunt Julie asks Tesman what he thinks of his new home, he describes it as "Excellent!" before admitting that he cannot divine the purpose of the extra rooms (*HG* 10). Amused by his apparent lack of understanding of the proper order of things—first love, then marriage, then baby in the nursery—Aunt Julie assures him that they will be in use "as time goes on" (*HG* 10). Tesman is struck with inspiration:

> Yes, you're quite right about that, Aunt Julie! In time, as I build up my library—huh?
>
> MISS TESMAN Of course, my dear boy. It was your library I meant. (*HG* 10)

Aunt Julie humors Tesman, playing as if she too imagined these nurseries as housing a "bogsamling" (book collection or library). She assumes that Tesman's realization of their true purpose will arrive when the "facts of life" become apparent and undeniable. The dream of space for a vast and growing library will then have to give way to the socio-architectural "needs" of little Tesmans.

When *Hedda Gabler* ends, however, the rooms remain in their current state, occupied only by expectations, or open to occupations of both proper (procreative) and improper (archival) varieties. The brief description of the empty nurseries of *Hedda Gabler* and their proposed future occupants make them one of the earliest links in the chain of text–offspring associations in Ibsen's drama. Tesman's proposed conversion of nurseries to libraries reiterates common and sometimes disconcerting associations, not only between babies and books but also between writing and the copy (as opposed to the original thing), derivativeness and survival (the threat to fantasies of originality posed by reproduction and living on).

Tesman and Aunt Julie's conversations in Act One make it appear as if aunt and nephew are quite different. After all, she focuses on the procreative future, while he thinks only of collecting books. In the end, however, the difference between the procreative and the archival makes no difference to the future according to *Hedda Gabler*. Ibsen is less interested in shoring up oppositions—including babies versus books, procreativity versus creativity, creatively envisioning versus archiving—than in making dramatic use of their proximity and inappropriate association, whether to comedic or disheartening (near tragic) effect. Accordingly, I do not strive to treat things like aunts and archives separately, but rather endeavor to show how they are dramatically entangled in *Hedda Gabler*.

In Act One, Tesman's penchant for academic collection is comedically juxtaposed with activities proper to a long honeymoon, in part by means of a prop: the small empty suitcase that Tesman carries with him into the main parlor in Act One. He tells Aunt Julie,

> Just think, Aunt—I had that whole suitcase stuffed full of transcripts alone. It's completely unbelievable what I managed to collect from the archives. Remarkable old documents that nobody knew about.
>
> MISS TESMAN   Yes, yes, you've really not wasted time on your wedding trip, Jørgen. (*HG* 8)

Tesman has gone where no man has gone before, or at least found what no one else bothered to care about, making copies of old documents for his research. The audience might snicker at the aunt and nephew's shared notion of what it means not to waste time on a honeymoon: engaging in studies and archival work, hunting for remarkable or peculiar old items, and making copies to take home. Tesman twice emphasizes the double purpose of his honeymoon, downplaying its extravagance: "Well, remember," he tells Aunt Julie, "I used it for research, too. All those archives I had to explore. And the number of books I had to read through!" (*HG* 9). All the books and all the old documents in all the old archives will continue to institute Tesman's future of academic collecting. His temporality is one of continual commencement and continual deferral by means of the texts of the past. His empty suitcase tells us, at least, that the honeymoon resulted in a successfully delivered "book pregnancy" (Templeton 212). Will these transcripts be stored in the empty nurseries, together with Tesman's book collection?

Tesman's passing proposal for turning empty rooms into libraries is one of several ways in which the drama designates him a domesticated man and an organizer and collector of the past. Consistent references to various forms of text, their creation and collection in undefined numbers, contribute to the primary temporal mode of the drama, which is expressed in terms of expectations, deferral, waiting, and the promise of endless accumulation.[17] Tesman's collection in Act One grows to include "*fagskrifter*" (disciplinary writings or specialist publications), bound and unbound books in Act Two. In Act Three, he gets ahold of the sections of Løvborg's new book manuscript about the future (*HG* 84). Finally, he inherits Løvborg's notes for dictation in Act Four, after Hedda has burnt the manuscript and after Løvborg has shot himself. Although the aunt does not sit with Tesman and Thea as they commence their attempt to rewrite Løvborg's manuscript in the final version of *Hedda Gabler*, she sits with Tesman when the conflict between Tesman (as collector) and Løvborg (as visionary creator) is introduced. Just as Ibsen couches the story of archival collection in a conversation about a honeymoon, he couches the potential for a battle of the books in a domestic scene that reveals Aunt Julie's status as "*mater familias*" (Templeton 213).

We learn about Tesman's predilections and the constitution of the Tesman family at the same time that we learn about Løvborg's already published book and Tesman's plans to continue to accumulate and review endless texts. When Tesman helps Aunt Julie by undoing the bow on her hat, we learn that she has been Tesman's primary caretaker, undoubtedly assisted by Berte and Rina (*HG* 8). Tesman's gesture inspires Aunt Julie to exclaim, "Oh my goodness,—it's just as if you were still home with us" (*HG* 8). He pats her cheek before they sit down to chat:

> What a blessing it is having you in the flesh, right before my eyes again, Jørgen! You—blessed Jochum's own boy![18]
>
> TESMAN And for me too! To have the chance to see you again, Aunt Julie! You, who have been both mother and father to me. (*HG* 8)

Despite international travel and his new residence in an "overly mortgaged, accidentally occupied villa," it is as if the orphaned and motherless Tesman never really left his own proper home with his mother-father-aunt (Sandberg 2). When he discovers that Aunt Julie has mortgaged her and Rina's pension to guarantee the new furnishings for the town house, he exclaims that she never tires of sacrificing herself for him.

Insisting that she lives to ease his existence, Aunt Julie reemphasizes Tesman's status as motherless and fatherless:

> Do I have a joy in this world other than smoothing the way for you, my dear boy? You, who have neither father nor mother to turn to? And now we've reached the goal, Jørgen! Things may have looked bleak now and then; but now, thank heaven, you've made it. (*HG* 11)

They might be near their goal—note that Aunt Julie says "we"—but this goal will soon be feared lost. Tesman is surprised and troubled to hear about the publication of Løvborg's first book. Aunt Julie quickly dismisses the possibility that it could be any good: "But lord knows, do you think it can amount to much? No, when *your* new book comes out— that'll be a different story, Jørgen! What will it be about?" (*HG* 12). Tesman's answer, "the domestic handicrafts of Brabant in the Middle Ages," startles and impresses Aunt Julie, while providing further evidence for his domestication and status as an academic "specialist" (*HG* 12). "No, just imagine," Aunt Julie exclaims, "that one can write about such a thing!"

(*HG* 12). Aunt Julie insists that Tesman has triumphed, thanks in part to her willing and joyous sacrifice, and in part to the fact that the threat Løvborg once posed has been removed: "The one who was the most dangerous for you—he's fallen the farthest now.—And he's lying there now, in the bed he made—poor, misguided creature" (*HG* 12). This little fable of triumph appears loaded with an entire unspoken backstory of competition, potential scandal, and tarnished reputation. Of course, Aunt Julie is not completely mistaken, just a bit premature. Løvborg *will* fall again, and farther, before his threat to Tesman is fully neutralized.

The potential for a battle of the books creates some of the early suspense in *Hedda Gabler*, although this suspense is muffled by the less romantic and more persistent threat of Tesman's mounting debt. The scope of Løvborg's threat to Tesman's professional expectations and the rapid neutralization of this threat (because Løvborg claims that he is uninterested in competition, loses control, loses his manuscript, and then dies) are revealed to characters and to the audience alike in the course of dramatic action.[19] In response to his aunt's enthusiasm regarding his own book project, Tesman now cautions that it will be some time before it is complete. He is confronted with a long list of sources, which are both essential for the project and will necessarily cause a delay in its completion: "I have these formidable collections, which have to be organized first, you understand" (*HG* 12). Luckily, the skill for dealing with "formidable collections" is a family trait, inherited from Aunt Julie's brother: "Yes, organize and collect,—you really are good at that. You aren't blessed Jochum's son for nothing" (*HG* 12).[20] Despite this delay, *Hedda Gabler* eventually gives us reason to believe that Tesman might triumph. Not only have his skills and industriousness brought him this far in life; but he might also triumph by means of adoption, or as a result of the secondhand project that he takes on as the play ends. In any case, slow and steady can win the race—especially when one's rival and his unpublished manuscript are taken out of the competition. Regardless of Tesman's naïveté when it comes to Aunt Julie's area of expertise (familial reproduction), she remains convinced of his talent as an academic. It is true that she evaluates Tesman's talents without having the capacity to do so, believing him to be a "shining light" when he is only a specialist (*Vi* 137).[21] Perhaps more important than whether or not Tesman can triumph as an individual, however, is simply the idea that it is possible to thrive as a specialist, collector, and organizer: some folks inherit and are nurtured in their capacity to foster the project of endlessly multiplying documents, facing accumulation and reproduction with glee.

In Act One, Tesman pursues Hedda with a pair of old slippers. This moment, which Templeton deems the "most successful of Ibsen's touches in characterizing" Tesman, unites the comedy of Act One with the "strange and hostile power" that the Tesman unit represents for Hedda— the threat of the friendly and familial, the "harmless" aunts and their "harmless" nephew (213). Tesman is thrilled to receive his "old morning slippers," embroidered by bedridden Aunt Rina, and he wants Hedda to share in his joy and memories (*HG* 14). When he describes the fact that Aunt Julie kept them for him as "really touching," Hedda responds, "I remember, you often spoke of them during the trip" (*HG* 14). Thus, longing for and discussing one's old slippers can be added to the named activities of the fashionable honeymoon that doubled as a research trip. Hedda tries to get away from Tesman, first moving to the stove and then to the table, where she explicitly states that his slippers hold no memories for her. In this case, Aunt Julie sympathizes with Hedda, and Tesman demurs without demurring: "but I thought, now that she's part of the family—" (*HG* 14). Hedda evades Tesman by interrupting him. She announces that the maid will never do, pretending to mistake the hat lying on the chair for Berte's, although she knows that it belongs to Aunt Julie. Hedda either does not realize or chooses to exploit the fact that Berte is not just *the maid* but also a former nanny and a member of the Tesman unit. By now, spectators will know what kind of man Tesman is: a bustling and foolish "*tantegutt*" (auntie's boy) (Templeton 213). His financial cluelessness, taken together with his childish naiveté and other forms of potential failure—ironically evoked in Aunt Julie's references to his success in marriage, education, and career prospects—might mislead one to believe that he is the kind of man who will be easily conquered or who will fail to persist.

While the domesticated, feminized, and childish aspects of Tesman's character have been recognized in the scholarship—in Templeton, for example, he is not only a *tantegutt* but also "an infantile adult" and "a boy/man entranced by his old slippers" (208, 214)—I wish to draw attention to the ways in which Tesman's comical-pejorative gendering is more thoroughly related to the schemes of gender and reproduction in *Hedda Gabler*, to its aversion to emasculation, and to its pessimistic attitudes toward the family and the future. If our admiration or sympathy for Hedda involves distaste for Tesman's feminine qualities, what implications might this have for feminist readings of Hedda as a character that "gives women access to the universal, as women"? (Moi 438). If Aunt Julie does not give women access to the universal, does Ibsen's "[relentless separation] of female biology from psychology" continue to assert a connection between masculinity and universal personhood, between the feminine and the sphere of domestication as a limited, emasculating sphere? (Templeton 230). And what does it mean if Tesman's persistence, survival, and success (within the bounds of the drama) result precisely from his relationship to secondhand mothers?

Hedda, who is always attempting to assert her status as *pas de la famille*—a person thus far un-Tesmanized (and un-Tesmanizable?)— differentiates herself in Act Two by criticizing her husband's pleasure in archival discovery. While Tesman is away, she tells Judge Brack that she longed to return home every day while on her honeymoon. Brack is surprised because Tesman repeatedly claimed in letters that they were having an excellent time. Hedda counters,

> Yes, *him*! Because he thinks the most wonderful thing he knows is to go and rummage around in the archives. To get to sit and copy out old parchment papers,—or whatever they are. (*HG* 39)

Hedda's dismissive final phrase indicates that she is unsure of, and does not care to know, the correct vocabulary for the tools of Tesman's trade. When Tesman returns home, interrupting Hedda's conversation with Brack, the unbound books under his arms and in his pockets confirm that collecting texts is not just an activity reserved for study trips in foreign lands. He announces that he is sweating from the labor of carrying them all, and Hedda asks what kind of books they are. Tesman replies, "They're some new *fagskrifter* [specialist publications], which I absolutely had to have" (*HG* 43).

Echoing the accumulation of texts, the Norwegian word for specialist publications or academic journals, *fagskrifter*, now accumulates through repetition, having first been uttered by the "fagmenneske" (specialist) himself (*HG* 40). Hedda repeats it as a question—"Fagskrifter?"—followed by Brack's mocking confirmation: "Of course. *Fagskrifter*, Mrs. Tesman," and they *"exchange a knowing smile"* (*HG* 43). Hedda uses the word again in disbelief at her husband's unending need to collect such uninteresting objects—"You need still more *fagskrifter*?"—and then Tesman assures her that his collection will never be complete: "Yes, dear Hedda, it's impossible ever to have too many. You have to keep up with what's written and published" (*HG* 43). Tesman now pulls out Løvborg's published book and offers to show it to Hedda, who refuses to look, for now. Still mocking and referring to specialization by means of the prefix *fag* (field or discipline), Brack asks, "Well, what do you think of it—as a *fagmand*?" (specialist) (*HG* 43). Tesman is impressed by the book and notes a change in tone from Løvborg's earlier way of writing, which was apparently less calm and steady (Thea's influence?) (*HG* 43). Hedda and Brack may mock Tesman all they like, but while the accumulating and collecting weigh Hedda down, Tesman looks enthusiastically forward to cutting the pages of new items for his collection.

The conversation between Brack and Hedda that Tesman interrupts upon returning home, all sweaty and laden with specialist publications, concerns the boring temporality of marriage. Like the word *fagskrifter*, the adjective *evig* (endless or eternal) and related words and phrases accumulate. Both Tesman and Aunt Julie are convinced that the long honeymoon abroad was essential, in large part because it is fashionable, and Hedda is a fashionable woman from a fashionable (but decaying) civil class background. Hedda suggests to Brack, however, that no expenditure could make up for the boredom of sitting with Tesman "as a couple in a railway compartment" (*HG* 42). Not only does it feel as if an "*evighed*" (eternity) has passed since she and Brack talked alone together, but the worst thing of all was always being cooped up with the same man, "evig og altid" (always and forever) (*HG* 39–40). Brack confirms by nodding and rephrasing: "både sent og tidlig" (literally both late and early, implying something like all the time or day and night) (*HG* 40). Hedda then adds emphasis by repeating her original word choice: "I said, *evig og alltid*" (always and forever) (*HG* 40). Although they agree that Tesman is a specialist, and that such people are not fun to travel with in general, Brack tests Hedda by suggesting that love might make a journey with a specialist bearable. She immediately rejects "that sticky word," which startles Brack:

HEDDA   Well, just try it yourself! Listening to the history of civilization day and night—

BRACK   Always [*evig*] and forever.

HEDDA   Yes! Yes! Yes! And then all this business about domestic handicrafts in the Middle Ages—! That is the most revolting thing of all! (*HG* 40)

At this point, Brack and Hedda appear in sympathetic relation: he is a person to whom she can confess her feelings; they repeat and trade each other's phrases and are in agreement when it comes to their assessment of Tesman as perfectly "correct and solid," with nothing "especially ridiculous about him" (*HG* 41). Brack now proposes that Hedda step down from the "train" a bit. With no taste for public scandal, however, she states that she would prefer a "trusted friend," who is not a specialist, to come aboard (*HG* 42). When they hear the front door open, Brack states that the "triangle is complete," but Hedda insists, "*lowering her voice*," that the "train goes on" (42–43; 252). Hedda's line suggests that Brack's proposal offers momentary diversion, but no real relief, from the everlasting boredom of marriage and the prospect of a future that promises more—an *evighed* (eternity)—of the same.

The temporality of the *evige* provokes Hedda's frustration with familial figures and institutions (aunts, nursery rooms, marriage), archival acts (collecting, copying, organizing), and textual objects. When Tesman returns home with his books, the *evige* takes place as a dramatic interruption of Hedda's hopes for more diverting experiences. *Evig* can mean eternal, as in timeless, interminable, or always in existence. However, and although "these eternal aunts" is a good translation for Hedda's colloquial utterance of frustration, in the context of *Hedda Gabler*, *evig* does not really suggest unending existence as much as persistence and continuation. It is associated with the promise of daily visits, with industriousness (not wasting time, even on one's honeymoon), with the temporality of marriage and academic life, with keeping up appearances (spending money one does not have), and with keeping up with what is published. The *evige* does not refer to immortality or to the absence and emptiness of death in this case—except in the sense that it contributes to Hedda's deadly boredom and is a factor in her decision to commit suicide. Instead, it refers to unwanted presences and relationships, to the processes, objects, and values of domesticated or domesticating specialization. Ultimately, the clash between this temporality and Hedda's desires—her longing to know "that some freely willed act of bravery can really still happen in the world" (*HG* 100)—constitutes a good deal of the play's prescience or futurism, because Hedda's longing cannot accept or withstand Tesmanization. In Act Four, when she learns that Løvborg died by an accidental shot to the groin, she exclaims, "Oh, this curse—that everything I simply touch turns ridiculous and vile" (*HG* 102). Ibsen uses Hedda Tesman to depict the desire for ideal and present-to-itself (undivided, singular, masterful) experience subjected to circumstances determined by vulgarity, domestication, and the limitations of sex roles. Hedda strains against her role as an academic's wife; she longs for power and freedom but is faced with mishap, scandal, and the unbearable expectations of her new family.

Sedgwick is interested in aunts and uncles because they are a bad fit, or because they can enable us to defy "the sleek 'same'/'different' scientism of modern gender and sexual preference" (60). Juliane Tesman and her sister Rina might interrupt a certain kind of "sleekness," exceeding as they do the primary reproductive unit of the bourgeois family; but the maiden aunts of *Hedda Gabler* are also a good fit. While aunts can figure a kind of resistance to the reproductive family, they can also figure, as they do for Hedda, its keeper. In *Hedda Gabler*, aunts are nonprocreative but nonetheless species-serving, enabling the persistence of the successful family and its domesticating, emasculating, and unimaginative aspects. "Naturally," the maiden aunt has a less direct influence on reproduction (or baby-writing, fetus-archiving, and re-delivering) than other characters. Nevertheless, it is the *reproductivity that approaches the feminine*—the adopting, collecting, copying, and organizing of the secondhand mother and her progeny—that promises a future in Ibsen's drama.

Burning the Future

Given that Løvborg's manuscript and Hedda's child appear to belong to the same promising category—undeveloped potential, nipped in the bud—we might associate their destruction with loss of hope or insist that the death of a child (whether literary or quick) truly figures the death of the future. Yet we cannot be certain of their value. Hedda's baby is unborn, and Ibsen provides few details about the manuscript, which means that it gains its status as a work of genius primarily through its visionary subject matter, its presumed potential, and its difference from Tesman's archival projects. Løvborg and the General's daughter also remain latent (as parents at least), and they too can appear superior compared with the Tesmans. Nonetheless, forms of depravity and degeneration already taint them. Løvborg is incapable of self-control, and Hedda's allure and intelligence are paired with her advanced age (she is 29), her boredom and fatigue, the "dull pallor" of her hair, and her status as the last child of the Gabler line (*HG* 13). Regardless of their uncertain value, all these doomed creatures do represent a category apart from the Tesmans in the sense that that they are futureless. Survival is for those who belong to, or can be adapted to, the auntly world of *Hedda Gabler*. I now take a closer look at the future that gets burned in *Hedda Gabler*, exploring the qualities of Løvborg's manuscript and asking whether it really exists in a realm apart, un-subject to the negative influence of domestication and secondhand mothering.

Only Thea and Tesman attest the value of Løvborg's manuscript—Tesman by expressing envy and calling it "precious" and "irreplaceable" (although he has not read it in its entirety) (*HG* 73–74), and Thea by means of her reproductive analogy: book as child. Of course, according to character testimony and other forms of evidence, these characters are feminized/feminine idiots. Although its identity and worth (as opposed to its general subject matter and comparative value) are unspecified and unverified, we do know that Løvborg's doomed manuscript has been dictated from notes and then transcribed, loved, perhaps even inspired, by a woman whom Løvborg eventually describes as pure yet stifling. Thea might be another corrupting maternal force, a de-virilizing stepmother, providing further evidence that secondhand or auntly mothering saturates the entire boring world of *Hedda Gabler*.

While Tesman's documents might promise to fill the empty nursery rooms (and his study, and his bedroom, and more?) Thea, Tesman, and Løvborg himself describe his manuscript as a singular work, an irreplaceable "child" (*HG* 50). When Thea comes looking for Løvborg at the Tesmans' new home in Act One, she explains that he came to town after the short period of restlessness (fourteen days) that followed the publication of his first book. The macro-considerations of this book, which covers "the course of civilization—in all its stages," have aroused great interest, and it has sold well (*HG* 21). Thea is afraid that Løvborg will be unable to sustain the abstemious lifestyle that she helped him cultivate when he was working as a tutor for her stepchildren. In Act Two, we learn that Løvborg himself does not regard this first book as significant. He advises Tesman to skip it, telling him that he wrote it simply to build up a favorable audience. He wanted, in other words, to ensure that his masterwork—"The one that I put myself into"—would not be rejected outright, despite its more radical subject matter (*HG* 50). Tesman is startled to hear Løvborg say that this manuscript is a sequel or continuation, given that his published book "goes right up to our time!" (*HG* 51). Løvborg explains that he has written about the future, which further startles Tesman: "About the future! But good lord, we don't know anything about that" (*HG* 51). Løvborg explains that his second work considers "the cultural forces of the future" and "the cultural development of the future" (*HG* 51). Tesman is as impressed by the subject of Løvborg's second book as Aunt Julie was about his own. "How extraordinary," he says, "It would never occur to me to write about such a thing" (*HG* 51). Hedda is not surprised to hear Tesman confess his lack of creativity. Standing by the glass door, she "*drums her fingers on the pane*" and says, "Hm—. No, no." (*HG* 51).

Ultimately, the most certain features of Løvborg's manuscript are its differences from Tesman's project.[22] In Act Three, Tesman remarks on the great value of Løvborg's manuscript, telling Hedda that the highlight of the evening was when Løvborg read aloud: "I do believe it's one of the most remarkable things ever written" (*HG* 72). Both Aunt Julie and Tesman approach historical research with naïveté, astonishment, and persistence (words that also happen to describe Tesman's attitude toward procreativity). Unsurprisingly, given his methods, Tesman's book will be more recognizably disciplinary than Løvborg's, more specialized and less theoretical. It will tell a story of the past reconstructed through documentary evidence rather than a story about the future dependent on inspiration. Moreover, while Tesman's project is methodical and archival, Løvborg has worked at a tremendous pace, writing both the published book and the manuscript in a single year.

These differences might encourage admiration for Løvborg at Tesman's expense, but they remain insufficiently convincing for two scholars, Max Nordau and Errol Durbach, writing nearly a century apart. In *Degeneration* (1892), Nordau—an admirer of Ibsen's talents and a decrier of his egomania—found the idea that either Tesman's or Løvborg's projects would merit a professorship "fit to raise a laugh in all academic circles" (348). For Nordau, the fact that Løvborg's manuscript cannot be reproduced means that it relies on "prophecy" and "inspiration," making it unscientific rather than special or visionary (1968, 348). He associates Løvborg's work with the past rather than the future, or with "the strange questions with which the causists of the Middle Ages used to occupy themselves" (348). In *Ibsen the Romantic* (1982), Durbach admits that it is "impossible to derive [Løvborg's] philosophy of history from Ibsen's text" (38). Given this lack of evidence, he turns to Ibsen's drafting notes: "The manuscript that H. L. [Løvborg] leaves behind is concerned to show that the task of humanity is: Upwards, towards the bringer of light. Life on the present social basis is not worth living.

Therefore imagine yourself away from it. Through drink, etc.—" (Ibsen qtd. in Durbach 38–39). According to Durbach's interpretation of these notes, an earlier version of Løvborg's character was interested in a spiritual rather than merely progressive (and so impotent) course of action for humanity; yet he could not imagine how such a course would be achieved, and so proposed alcohol-induced distraction and denial. The notes lead Durbach to propose that Løvborg might be "a Spenglerian before Spengler—a prophet of decline, dissolution and collapse, for whom the destiny of the future is a death of spirit, failure of conviction, and loss of nerve" (Durbach 38). In other words, they provide counter-evidence to those qualities of comparison (with Tesman's project) that tempt us to see the manuscript as a creative expression that would somehow enable a clearer view of the future's wondrous unfolding.

In putting forward his interpretation, Durbach disagrees with Muriel Bradbrook, who asserts in "Ibsen and the Past Imperfect" that Løvborg's project was "conceived through direct experience of life and by natural energy" (23). Bradbrook's interpretation might be very tempting indeed, given Løvborg's interest in the future. It implies that some projects are immediate and natural, not merely of the past (determined by the archive) but relevant and alive to what is to come, distinct both from Tesman's history as record of domestic practice and from the manuscript that will eventually result from the "[reconstruction]" process, re-created in the image of Tesman as "stepfather" (Bradbrook 23). Bradbrook's interpretation also reinforces the idea that Løvborg's manuscript is precious and tragically nipped in the bud. This is, indeed, where a familiar hope for the good future might be held out in *Hedda Gabler*: in the possibility represented by the unborn and the unpublished, and in "a fantasy of completion" in "a future continuously deferred" (Edelman, *No Future* 114). Such a fantasy can only be sustained because the unborn and the unpublished are destroyed and therefore persist in a mode of permanent potential. Hedda herself believes for a time that Løvborg "has more courage in the face of life than the others"—although she does not link this courage to his writing project (*HG* 73). Her disillusionment on this front coincides with the unfolding action of *Hedda Gabler*, with its revelations concerning both the origins and the fate of Løvborg's manuscript.

The scenes surrounding the burning of this manuscript comprise the obvious buildup and dramatic climax of *Hedda Gabler*, with its obvious cliché: reproductive metaphor, or the baby-book, a figure of bio-literary confusion that will soon have no future, just as Løvborg, Hedda, and Hedda's fetus will have no future.[23] Løvborg's moment of triumph—his ability to produce a work that impresses and astounds a Tesman—is itself quickly nipped in the bud. In Act Three, the story that Tesman tells of the night's festivities, which turned into a "bacchanal," crushes Hedda's hope that Løvborg would show more courage and control than others (*HG* 73). After reading from the manuscript and arousing Tesman's envy that anyone could write "such a book," Løvborg gave a confused speech about his "muse"—an unnamed woman, but Tesman is sure it must be Thea (*HG* 73). Then, when the party was splitting up in the morning, a "curious" and "tragic" thing happened: Tesman is almost ashamed to say it, but Løvborg simply dropped the manuscript on a street corner (*HG* 73). He shows Hedda the "precious, irreplaceable manuscript," making her promise not to tell anyone "for Ejlert's sake" (*HG* 74). Once he has rested, Tesman plans to return the manuscript to Løvborg, but Hedda claims that she wants to read it first. Tesman refuses, knowing that Løvborg will be "completely desperate" when he wakes up and realizes that it is missing (*HG* 75). Hedda *"looks searchingly at him"* and asks, "Can't such a work be rewritten?" (*HG* 75). Although Hedda does not care about specific issues of form or content (she never reads the manuscript), she appears to be particularly interested in singularity or irreplaceability. In an ironic comment, given that he will begin just such a project as the play ends, Tesman responds, "Oh, I don't see how it could. Because the inspiration, you know" (*HG* 75). Luckily, a letter has arrived, to which Hedda *"casually"* draws Tesman's attention (*HG* 75). Aunt Rina is finally dying in earnest, and for the moment, this news trumps all other concerns. The death of an unseen, invalid aunt leaves Hedda in convenient possession of a supposedly irreplaceable work of genius.

Believing that the manuscript is lost forever, Løvborg is broken and hopeless by the time he arrives at the Falk town house in Act Three. After Thea arrives, Løvborg confesses falsely that he tore the manuscript up and threw it in the fjord. She accuses him of figurative *Kindermord* and exits, declaring "Everything before me is dark now" (*HG* 86). Løvborg now makes the second, true confession to Hedda: he committed a crime worse than *Kindermord* by simply losing the manuscript, and he is convinced that the act of misplacing and its consequences matter more than the simple fact of loss: "The devil knows whose hands it has fallen into. Who's had their fingers in it" (*HG* 87).[24] The doubled notion of manipulation expressed here—hands and fingers—suggests altering influence and potential abuse of the work. It prefigures Tesman and Thea's plan to rewrite (while altering and abusing?) the manuscript-child. Hedda makes a fleeting attempt to neutralize the conversation by getting literal: "Well,—but when all is said and done then—then it was only a book" (*HG* 87). Løvborg, however, counters Hedda's realist reminder by insisting "Thea's pure soul was in that book" (*HG* 87). For Løvborg, Hedda's verbal acceptance of this truth—"Yes, I understand"—means that she should also understand that his relationship with Thea has "no future any more" (*HG* 87). In fact, Løvborg has no desire to create a future at all, and he tells Hedda that he will kill himself as soon as possible. Although Hedda's reasoning no longer includes her desire to see "vine leaves" of triumph in Løvborg's hair (because she has lost faith in such things), she now gives him one of her father's pistols as a "souvenir" and asks him to promise her to do it beautifully (*HG* 88).

Perhaps Hedda fails to tell Løvborg that she has the manuscript because she wants to commit a supremely powerful act that will somehow rupture the world of collecting and copying and reproduction in which she finds herself. Tesman has assured Hedda that Løvborg's manuscript is inspired and remarkable and cannot be rewritten. She has witnessed both Løvborg and Thea express despair at its loss. After Løvborg leaves, she listens at the door to be sure that she is alone before burning it. The burning scene pairs Hedda's controlled indifference with the drama and suspense of irreversible and passionate destruction. Her gestures are slow and calculated. She takes the package out from the drawer in the writing desk, pulls a few pages out halfway, and glances at them. She then sits with the manuscript in her lap before opening first the stove and then the package. She throws a few sheets in, then a few more, and then the rest. Hedda's words during the scene are extraordinary and emphatic: "Now I'm burning your child, Thea!—You with the curly hair! [...] Your child and Ejlert Løvborg's [...] Now I'm burning,—now I'm burning the child" (*HG* 88). Løvborg appears to be the secondary target, here, although he is more profoundly affected, given that Thea is able to move on and imagine a future when the play ends. It appears that the manuscript, its materiality, and content (paper and ink, text and ideas) do not matter to Hedda, but its supposed irreplaceability does matter, because power and radical acts of destruction matter to her.

When all is said and done, I am less interested in the identity and value of the manuscript itself—which will remain forever uncertain—than in thinking about the *family dynamics* that produce and host both Tesman and Løvborg's book projects. How seriously are we supposed to take Ibsen's characters when they use reproductive figures of speech, or when they entangle life and life's work, creativity and procreativity, writing and parenting by means of reproductive metaphor? Is Ibsen's understanding of vocation, art, and creativity in some sense mirrored in his characters' reproductive figures and claims, or does he want us to question the father–child/artist–"child" bond?[25] In *Hedda Gabler*, at least, the father–book bond remains sufficiently intact to be threatened by a third element: Thea, the mother or stepmother, who has "had her fingers in" Løborg's destiny (*HG* 86). After Thea leaves Hedda's home, uncertain of what she will do now that she believes the manuscript has been destroyed, Løvborg explains to Hedda that he is trapped between two modes of living, neither of which hold interest for him, and he blames Thea: "It's the courage and daring for life that she has broken in me" (*HG* 86). Previously, Løvborg assured Hedda that he never told Thea about their "audacious" and "illicit" comradeship, when Hedda solicited from him stories from a world "that [a young girl] is forbidden to know anything about" and then threatened to shoot him when he took it too far (*HG* 57–59). Løvborg's reason for keeping the nature of his relationship with Hedda to himself is that Thea is "too stupid to understand that sort of thing" (*HG* 59). Too stupid to understand a comradeship based on "lust for life," Thea can nonetheless serve as a transcriber for an inspired book about the future (*HG* 58).

Perhaps Thea's stupidity (according to Løvborg) is insignificant, because she only played a secondary role in its creation, or perhaps it tells us something fundamental about the project. After all, she claims that it was her child too, and that she has a "right" to know what happened to it (a right unfulfilled within the confines of the drama) (*HG* 85). Significantly, when Løvborg gave his confused and drunken speech the night before, he did not name the woman who inspired him. One could work through all the evidence that suggests that Thea is, indeed, Løvborg's muse—or argue that the muse is really Hedda (the most likely candidate, in my opinion), or that it is Miss Diana, the singer-huntress in whose bedroom Løvborg eventually dies—but the fact is that this woman remains unnamed. The pertinent question in this context, then, is not which woman inspired Løvborg, but rather what it would mean if the book manuscript was mothered by a woman too stupid to understand the fascination with intoxication and taboo (admittedly tempered by cowardice, weakness, and fear of scandal) that supposedly characterized Hedda's interest in Løvborg and their comradeship. Could Løvborg's book about the future only be written after Løvborg's courage and defiance were brought to heel by purity and idiocy, or after the fruit of his musal inspiration found a stepmother in Thea?

Even if Thea's mothering is not the same as Aunt Julie's, these characters share in common the ability to make masculine creativity (re)productive through domestication. As Durbach insists, Bradbrook's positive interpretation of Løvborg's manuscript is born out neither by his character nor by his assertion, made after the loss of the manuscript, that the person who gave her "soul" to the project has functioned as a devitalizing force in his life (*HG* 87). Against Løvborg, Tesman, and Thea's assertions of the manuscript's originality and precious potential, and against Hedda's possible belief that destroying the manuscript will somehow impact the auntly-archival world in which she lives, *Hedda Gabler* suggests that the book about the future is mainly a *mise en abyme*: a book about the future inside a play that promises a bad future, a murdered "child" inside a play about a pregnant woman who decides to kill herself, and a figure for Tesmanization of the future in a *tantified* world. Even if Løvborg's manuscript is beyond Tesman's imaginative-intellectual capabilities, better-than-*tantified* is good enough neither for Hedda nor for *Hedda Gabler*. Ibsen's drama does not let readers and spectators in on the details of Løvborg's vision of the future, because both Hedda and Ibsen are more interested in letting that future burn.

Both of *Hedda Gabler*'s unborn children are destroyed, but *Hedda Gabler* also stages survival, a future that persists and can outlast the fire. The literary child is recoverable—at least to the extent that its remains can be revised and incorporated into Tesman's specialization process and book collection. Because this project is just getting under way when the play ends, we do not know if the rewriting will take place, or if the recomposed manuscript will be archived in an empty nursery-cum-library. If Tesman and Thea truly succeed in reanimating the book about the future, it will have a kind of afterlife, either as a pale copy or parody of its original self or as a copy of a copy.

Them All

As characters discuss the circumstances of Løvborg's death, Thea and Tesman express longing that his torn up (in reality, burnt up) manuscript—the one "that would have cemented his name permanently" (*HG* 99)—could be put back together. Prompted by Tesman's longing ("what I wouldn't give"), Thea suggests that it might in fact be possible, because she brought the notes for transcription with her to town (*HG* 99). They have been lying quietly in her pockets the entire time. When she hands the notes to Tesman, he comments on their confusion and messiness. Nonetheless, he and Thea feel compelled by even the slightest potential for resurrection and decide to enter into a partnership, Tesman exclaiming, "It *will* work! It *must* work! I'll dedicate my life to this!" (*HG* 100). This re-visionary venture, a memorial project for the author of the futureless book about the future, will likely cause further delay in the completion of Tesman's own manuscript. When Hedda questions his vehemence, Tesman explains to her, "My own collections, they'll have to wait. Hedda,—do you understand me? Huh? It's something I owe to Ejlert's memory" (*HG* 100). Significantly, this delay represents the perfecting of Tesman's mode of reproductivity rather than a change or flaw. Echoing his aunt's sentiments from Act One, Tesman insists, "setting other people's papers in order, it's exactly what I do best" (*HG* 103). Tesman's capacity for copying, collecting, and organizing can also be applied to objects and creatures beyond those directly relevant to his research interests. When *Hedda Gabler* begins, the Tesmans are startled and thrilled that their son has managed to collect Hedda, but she is dislodged from her place as the crowning jewel of Tesman's collection when the transcription notes become available. New or newly (re)discovered items will always be coming, to be perused, put in order, and added to the Tesman archive.

Whether or not I am correct in my contention that Løvborg's manuscript might already be authorized by what Løvborg describes as Thea's domesticating and devitalizing influence, we know for certain that the archival process represented in *Hedda Gabler* does not need to preserve originality to proceed. As Leonardo F. Lisi reminds us in his reading of what he calls Ibsen's "darkest play": "Wherever we look, the play resists the idea that we are dealing with original or unique occurrences and characters" (42). Thea's relationship to Løvborg, for example, promises to repeat itself, as she and Tesman sit down to start the long project of decoding the transcription notes. At first, they try to work in the back parlor, but the light is too poor, and so they move back into the main parlor. These movements allow Brack to speak to Hedda alone, and then for Hedda to retire to the back parlor, where she pulls the curtain shut, leaving the "visible space for the first time since arriving on the stage" (Diamond 76). Before performing this first but not quite final leave-taking, Hedda comments on the repetition: "Isn't it strange for you, Thea? Now you sit here with Tesman,—just like you sat with Ejlert Løvborg before" (*HG* 106). In response, Thea expresses a strong desire to "inspire your husband as well," and Hedda assures her, "Oh, that will certainly happen—in time" (*HG* 106). This is Hedda's last prediction concerning the future, a future that she has already decided will not include her. A closer look at the events leading up to Hedda's suicide will support my claims that the world of this drama is determined by endless aunts, and that it is not Hedda, but rather Tesmanized horizons of possibility, that kills.

In the opening dialogues of Act Four, Hedda lets us know that she will soon die, and that the cause of death will be submission to the absurd exigencies of her new family, exacerbated by increasing uselessness and increasing restrictions on her freedom and ability to control others successfully. Hedda uses Tesman's earlier confession of envy to justify her destruction of Løvborg's manuscript, distracting Tesman from the fact that she has committed a crime by destroying lost property. This move, which is perhaps necessary to protect herself from scandal (silencing Tesman), requires that she acquiesce, precisely, to familiarity. She implies that she is willing to make sacrifices to protect Tesman, making him feel as if she is finally joining the Tesman unit. This is also the moment in which she tells Tesman that she is pregnant—or allows him to believe as much without quite saying it. Tesman finally catches on and is thrilled. His enthusiasm embarrasses Hedda, who expresses concern (not for the first time) that "the maid" might hear (*HG* 93). For Tesman, Berte is not "the maid" but his former nanny, so he wants to tell her about the pregnancy right away. Hedda "*[clasps] her hands together in desperation*," exclaiming "Oh, I'll die,—I'll die of all this," before regaining control and naming, "*coldly*," what it is that will kill her: "all this—absurdity" (*HG* 93). Such absurdities—as well as the ways in which Hedda's resistance to them makes her increasingly vulnerable to Brack—are finally deadly for Hedda. It is not just the fact that Berte will have access to the private details of her life, but also the fact that she must submit to an entire simulation of dedication to the Tesman unit and its continuation.

Tesman acquiesces to Hedda's desire not to tell Berte for the moment, but he insists that he tell Aunt Julie both about the pregnancy and about the fact that Hedda has begun using his first name. Tesman's association of burning love and old aunts echoes the comic association of honeymoons and archives (or sex and rummaging through libraries for the purpose of copying old documents) from Act One: Aunt Julie cannot know about Hedda's burning of the manuscript, but she can "share" in Hedda's burning passion for Tesman (*HG* 94). Of course, Hedda does not regard these associations as comical, even if she can recognize that they are absurd. Tesman now wonders whether such behavior is "common among young wives," apparently understanding Hedda's behavior to be the result of her pregnancy rather than an expression of its rejection (*HG* 94). Hedda can only direct Tesman's question to Aunt Julie, the absurd font of wisdom on all things reproductive.

This is the penultimate low point for Hedda, because she must perform loyalty and tolerate familiarity in order to secure her secret. This low point is short-lived, however, and followed by a similarly short-lived triumph. Just after Hedda and Tesman discuss Hedda's "burning love," Thea returns. She is concerned that Løvborg has "met with an accident" (*HG* 94). Judge Brack enters shortly thereafter, confirming Thea's worst fears (without revealing the whole truth): Løvborg is dying at the hospital (most likely already dead) from a shot to the chest (groin). In her moment of triumph, and although Løvborg did not manage to shoot himself in the temple—the chest is "good too"—Hedda dares to call this death courageous: "Ejlert Løvborg has settled accounts with himself" (*HG* 98). She can momentarily tolerate the knife's edge of scandal—Tesman "(*whispers slowly*) Oh, Hedda, we'll never come clear of all this" (*HG* 99)—and her husband's plan to rewrite the book that she tried to eradicate, because she feels personally liberated by Løvborg's suicide. She is, however, quickly disillusioned by Brack, who is also a "specialist," it turns out, that is, a man of the law (*HG* 100). At first, Hedda resists Brack's condescension and correction: "Oh, I know well enough what you want to say. Because you are also a kind of specialist, you too, just like—well! [...] Ejlert Løvborg had the strength and will to break away from the splendor of life—so early" (*HG* 101). Brack now crushes Hedda's faith in Løvborg by informing her of the scandalous facts of his death by accidental shot to the groin.

Hedda cannot maintain her feeling of liberation and is more vulnerable to Brack than ever. He knows too much, especially concerning the source of the pistol involved. Tesman's plans for rewriting the manuscript, which did not interrupt Hedda's feelings of liberation before, become intolerable post-disillusionment, as his skill for sorting other people's papers is reconfirmed in light of Løvborg's failure. Tesman has already returned to his usual, cheerful, and industrious mode of being, declaring that they must "pull [themselves] together": "Good lord, there's no use brooding over what's taken place. Huh?" (*HG* 100). Months and months will be given to the reconstruction, and Hedda will be pushed into Brack's company. Brack explains to Hedda why Løvborg must be accused of stealing the pistol and assures her, "Now, luckily there is no danger, so long as I keep quiet" (*HG* 106). Hedda realizes that she is now fully in his control. When she exclaims that she cannot bear the thought of being "unfree," Brack responds, "People generally learn the accept the inevitable" (*HG* 106).

Although Brack's character and his threats of blackmail are often read as intensely masculine, the endless aunts of Hedda's original utterance echo in his promise to visit Hedda every evening. Endless aunts are equally present in Hedda's last lines and in both Tesman and Brack's responses to Hedda's "beautiful" death (*HG* 107). Because she cannot be of help to Tesman and Thea and is informed that she can expect to spend a good deal of time with her blackmailer/seducer "from now on," Hedda claims fatigue and says that she will lie down on the sofa in the back room. After a short pause, she begins to play "a wild dance melody" (*HG* 106). Tesman asks her not to play, out of respect for the dead:

> TESMAN (*runs to the doorway*)
>> But, dearest Hedda,—don't play for dancing tonight! Think of Aunt Rina! And about Ejlert, too!
>
> HEDDA (*sticks her head out between the curtains*)
>> And about Aunt Julie. And about them all. From now on I'll be silent. (*She closes the curtains again*) (*HG* 107)

Whom Hedda means by "them all" is not made explicit. The most likely candidate, I argue, is endless aunts—members of the Tesman unit and other specialists who are not dead but can be included, according to Hedda, in the list of those for whom she should be silent.

Tesman decides that his work with Thea might make Hedda unhappy, and so he decrees that Thea will move into the empty room at Aunt Julie's, so that they can work together in the evenings there. Hedda's disembodied voice emerges from the back room, breaking her promise to stay silent. She lets Tesman know that she can hear every word they say, and then asks yet another version of the same question she has been asking herself and others since the beginning of the drama: what is she supposed to do with herself? Tesman announces that the solution is Brack, who is relaxing in the armchair. Brack shouts out in a cheerful tone:

>> Certainly, each and every evening, Mrs. Tesman! We will definitely have a pretty good time together here, the two of us!

HEDDA (*loud and clear*)

Yes, don't you wish judge? You, the
only rooster in the coop—

(*A shot is heard from within. Tesman, Mrs. Elvsted and Brack
jump*). (*HG* 107)

Brack's cheerful declaration of "hver evige aften" (each and every evening) reinvokes the boring and ultimately deadly temporality of the
evige (*HG* 107). Hearing the shot, Tesman runs into the room, followed
by Thea; they expose Hedda's body, and screams emanate from the
back room as a confused Berte enters. Tesman announces that Hedda
has managed to do what Løvborg could not: she has shot herself in
the temple. Brack remains "*slumped down [halvt afmægtig*, or halfway
powerless] *in the armchair*," uttering one of the drama's most famous
lines: "But good god,—people don't do such things!" (*HG* 107). For Diamond, the lines that spoil Hedda's beautiful death are also a sign of the
survivors' inability to understand and diagnose the hysteric, who is both
acting and dead serious (75). For Brack, Hedda is not people: she has
not done what people do (accept the inevitable), and she has done what
people do not do (shot herself to avoid acceptance). This is a *tantifying*
moment for Brack, providing further evidence that he, too, is a specialist, a person who cannot understand will and beauty. Even Brack is one
of "them all," the endless aunts of *Hedda Gabler*. The resurrection of
Løvborg's manuscript is not the only guarantee of the bad future's arrival in this drama. Revision or no, those who remain do what they can
to make Hedda's "better" (beautifully corrective) death fall flat.

Hedda Fever

In a certain sense, my focus on one implied future—the persistence of
the auntly or *tantified* patriarchal line—violates both the formal closure
of the dramatic text (nothing happens after the play ends) and the open
possibilities of its realism (who knows what might happen to Brack,
Thea, and the remaining Tesmans after Hedda commits suicide). My
aim in this chapter, however, has not been to offer predictions or readings of the future itself, but rather to explore an implied futurism that
emerges from plans and expectations, from the gendered implications of
Hedda Gabler's reproductive figures and iterative structure, and from
broader habits of thought and reproductive rhetoric found in criticism.
I have taken cues from Tesman's plan to house his book collection in the
space of empty nurseries, from Løvborg's subject matter (the future),
and from the fate of his manuscript (burning and proposed resurrection
in secondhand form). Finally, I have treated the gap between Hedda's
death and the ending of the play as a future. Aunts and their derivative,
domesticated progeny both enclose and outlive the father's daughter, if

only for a few moments. Despite the burning of the manuscript-child and Hedda's suicide-coterminous-abortion, *Hedda Gabler* suggests that *the reproductivity that approaches the feminine* will go on.

Ibsen's pessimistic re-imagination of the patriarchy as a lineage of aunt-hood takes place within the conflicting temporalities of archival desire, or within a commencement that is also a deferral, a repeated re-launching of a past. In *Archive Fever*, Derrida acknowledges and deconstructs the desire for immediacy that represents the strange heart of the archive: the desire to uncover origins, so that they might speak in their own name—thus undoing (impossibly) the need for archives. The impossibility of such uncovering is what makes the archive necessary as a collection of signs, a system of classification, an order, a name, a law, and a place (or home). But archival desire remains the desire for an access that would undo the archive's necessity. Significantly, Derrida argues that the decline from the original (figured in the Father) exists only as a fantasy, a "homesickness" without a home (91). In her desire for the beautiful and freely willed act, in her disregard for what is written, copied out, and preserved, and in her distaste for the patriarchal family as endless, absurd trap, Hedda appears to be *en mal d'archive*, or to suffer from archive fever, "a homesickness, a nostalgia for the return to the most archaic place of absolute commencement" (Derrida 91). What *Hedda Gabler* knows, however, is that there is only originary repetition. The patriarchy is a series of nominal usurpations (like Tesman for Gabler), a system of brothers rather than a relationship with the Father.

In *Hedda Gabler*, Ibsen creates drama by dividing the archive into two and simplifying or making literal its functions. Tesman provides the space (the nurseries) and the name, under which the children—whether literary or quick—will one day be organized. He is the archivist and persistent (surviving) patriarch, but it is Hedda who represents that which is "*en mal de*": the trouble, the illness, the passion or need for archives (Derrida 91). In a sense, Ibsen uses Hedda to separate out the very heart of the process, or that aspect of archive fever that abhors the necessity of gathering signs together, of remembering so as to forget whatever might be heterogeneous, and thereby instituting the future in the name of the past (Derrida 3). Despite her "coldness," Hedda is the embodiment of that strange heart, and she remains surrounded by the bloodless (yet cheerful and warm) Tesman unit and their secondhand consignation, or "*gathering together [of] signs*" into "a single corpus" that creates and ensures a bad (unoriginal and secondary) future (Derrida 3). Tesman represents the archival temporality that just keeps chugging along, adding up, and copying, like Hedda's train metaphor for marriage: the form of *tantified* endlessness that surrounds, smothers, and, in the end, survives Hedda. Hedda is under a kind of "house arrest," and thus, the heart remains within the body of the drama until death. This dramatic body, I have argued, is almost fully *tantified* and becomes even more so when it expels (or absorbs?) Hedda as a foreign body, leaving behind the survivors, or all the endless aunts of *Hedda Gabler*. Unlike Tesman, Hedda longs for immediacy, when the origin can "present itself in person [...] without mediation and without delay" (Derrida 93). This latter time or temporality is, of course, a fantasy more than a practice. Derrida concludes the theses section of *Archive Fever* by noting the tension between Freud's deconstruction and reproduction of patriarchal logic. Freud "illuminated" the fact that the "archontic," or the principle of "paternal and patriarchic" rule, "is at best the takeover of the archive by the brothers" (Derrida 95). At the same time, Freud is still making "his inheritors" ("so many brothers") wonder whether they might "yet speak in their own name" (Derrida 95). And if the brothers are uncertain whether they might speak, Derrida asks whether the daughter can have lived as "anything other than a phantasm or specter" (95).

We have been asking who is to blame for the failure to keep the Father with a capital F and his "good" future in *Hedda Gabler*, while alternately placing blame on the sons who cannot live up to heroic ideals and the daughter who refuses to serve the new patriarchy by adding her offspring to her husband's archive. In "Against Survival," Edelman argues that Shakespeare's *Hamlet* "survives as a foundational text of Modern Western culture in part because it anticipates modernity's ideology of cultural survival" (148): the son who keeps the word of the Father, his brain an "educational supplement that makes [the child's] survival equivalent to a book [...] a supplement that renders the biological organism a mere substrate for the imperative of the Ghost" (153). General Gabler certainly haunts the scene in *Hedda Gabler*, but Ibsen also makes the father's (brother's) book-of-the-future literal, and then mocks it for its inability to survive as anything other than a poor copy, another domesticated brother's takeover. As part of its critique of the patriarchal family, *Hedda Gabler* disallows alternative futures in favor of insisting that the future, which is coming, will offer more of the same. Although Hedda, the father's daughter, does not manage to embody an alternative future, she dies in order to show us the deadness at the heart of the patriarchy, its future-creating modes that amount to copying, accumulation, and more of the same.

When Hedda destroys Løvborg's manuscript, it seems that she is laboring under the idea that she can put a stop to Tesman's reproductivity by burning a hole in his archive. Her faith in the manuscript's originality and irreplaceability, however, emerges not from a reading of the text but instead from her faith in Løvborg's superiority and her husband's assurances. Ibsen shows us that alternative futures do not emerge from this kind of faith. In fact, it is Hedda's destructive act that enables the final project of *Hedda Gabler*, making the future available to Tesman and his organizing talents. Sedgwick warns us that the project of forgetting the Father "can only partially work" (59). As I have already confessed, thinking about aunts in the case of *Hedda Gabler* leads me back to the Tesman unit. At a certain point, Ibsen imagined that Aunt Julie would sit with Thea and Tesman as they began rewriting the book about the future. I have argued that endless aunts are everywhere in *Hedda Gabler*, even if Aunt Julie is not present in the final version of the drama. If something better came before the secondary mother of the future and her auntly offspring—like man before Pandora, like a rooster before the chicken and the egg—it dies with Hedda. Without expressing faith in the problematic and persistent (ancient as well as contemporary) idea that a certain embodiment of the feminine can threaten progress and true human development, one can sit with *Hedda Gabler*'s effeminophobic tendencies in order to advocate for Hedda as a radical critic of the family and an "advocate of abortion" (Edelman, *No Future* 31)—while simultaneously rolling one's eyes at the idea that abortion kills the future.

In Chapter 2, I consider *The Master Builder*, whose nurseries—rather than remaining relatively static, empty spaces to be filled with occupants of uncertain number—are themselves in a state of uncertainty and multiplication. Halvard Solness, the titular master builder, has continued to build nurseries, despite the fact that he and his wife, Aline, have no children. *The Master Builder* also depicts a dramatic culmination, an event of occupation that takes place in the course of action rather than in some possible future: a guest, Hilde Wangel, spends one night in the middle nursery of the current Solness residence. Hilde, it turns out, is an uncertain child, a useful and troubling figure for thinking through the strange calculations of erotic innocence.

Notes

1 See the Introduction for further discussion of Durbach's reading of Hedda's suicide in relation to Edelman's concept of reproductive futurism.

2 In *Hedda Gabler*, "Kammerat" (comrade) refers to relationships between men and women—first Hedda and Ejlert, and then Thea and Ejlert—that involve unusual or inappropriate closeness (intellectual and potentially erotic) (see *HG* 28–29).

3 I focus on Blau's essay because it contains a phrase that is particularly useful to me: "a disturbing sterility that approaches the masculine" (113). I would argue, however, that reproductive-futurist understandings of Hedda can be found throughout the entire history of the reception of *Hedda Gabler*, from Herman Bang's 1891 lecture on the play, published in *Tilskueren* in 1892, to the recent volume, *Ibsen's* Hedda Gabler: *Philosophical Perspectives*. Some contributors to the latter volume struggle, precisely, with the meaninglessness of Hedda's "narcissistic enjoyments" (Edelman, *No Future* 13).

4 According to Jack Halberstam, "female masculinity is generally received by hetero and homo-normative cultures as a pathological sign of misidentification and maladjustment, as a longing to be and to have power that is always just out of reach" (9). See Jenny Björklund's "Playing with Pistols: Female Masculinity in Henrik Ibsen's Hedda Gabler" for an attempt to re-read Hedda in light of female masculinity.

5 For a more recent analysis of *Hedda Gabler* through the lens of nihilism (as a philosophical concept rather than an accusation), see Leonardo F. Lisi's "Nihilism and Boredom in *Hedda Gabler*" in *Ibsen's* Hedda Gabler: *Philosophical Perspectives.*

6 I do not regard the question of the freedom of the sexed and gendered individual as unimportant or closed, but it has already been admirably addressed by Joan Templeton, especially in "The *Doll House* Backlash" in *Ibsen's Women,* and by many others. The fact that some Ibsen scholars continue to suggest that questions of sex and gender are separate from the "broader" questions of freedom and humanity—even after Templeton, and even after Toril Moi reanimated some of Templeton's claims in different ways in *Ibsen and the Birth of Modernism*—results from the fact that unmarked personhood is stealth-masculinized, as well as from ideological resistance to thinking through both sexual difference and the matter of gendering.

7 Sedgwick probably has the Lacanian concept of *le nom/non du père* in mind when she uses the phrase Name of the Father. The primary work of her essay, however, is to critique and resist the "vertiginous oscillation of 'same' and 'different'" in deconstructivist approaches to the life and work of Oscar Wilde (56). Sedgwick performs this resistance in order to seek out "some alternative approaches" to thinking desire and kinship, as well as possibilities for less neatly "complementary" models for relationships in and beyond the family, which she argues are already suggested in Wilde's writing and by the historical terminology of queer social relations (56–57).

8 See, for example, Virginia Blain's "Thinking Back through Our Aunts: Harriet Martineau and Tradition in Women's Writing" and Yopie Prins's "Greek Maenads, Victorian Spinsters." Blain's biographical project is to consider "a non-traditional order of literary inheritance": "legacies from literary aunts to nieces" that enable us to look away from "metonymic concepts of Mother- and Daughterhood" (224). Hedda is a niece by marriage, and part of what happens "between women" in this play involves not escape from the patriarchal family (except by death), but instead a seemingly petty and antagonistic power struggle between an aunt who serves the Tesman family and a wife who is, but does not wish to be, in service of the same family line. See also Ellen Mortensen's "Feminine floker i Ibsens *Hedda Gabler*" for an analysis of the play's rather explicit, but critically overlooked, representation of desire between women.

9 I am not, of course, the first person to insist that *Hedda Gabler* is both feminist and sexist. Diamond, for example, writes, "Realism's putative object, the truthful representation of social experience within a recognizable, usually contemporary, moment, remains a problematic issue for feminism, not least because theatrical realism, rooted in part in domestic melodrama, retains the oedipal family focus even as it tries to undermine the scenarios that Victorian culture has mythified—the angel in the house, the lost child, the poor but faithful husband, among others" (4).

10 In *The Mother in the Age of Mechanical Production,* Elissa Marder explains how Pandora's "box" is really a jar that resembles a womb. She also describes Pandora's arrival as follows: "[...] early men were born of the (Mother) Earth rather than from any woman. In those happy days before woman was made, there was no illness, no misery, no toil, no death, hence no birth, and no children. The invention of the first artificial woman puts an end to that prehistorical era and inaugurates the dawn of human time and history. Human history, therefore, begins with Pandora's arrival into the world of men; she brings 'death,' 'birth,' and sexual difference with her in addition to all the other 'ills' associated with mortal life" (10).

11 Two reasons internal to the world of the play for forgetting Hedda's married name are (1) attachment to her former (available and "maiden") status and (2) the relative newness of her marriage. Tesman has a hard time remembering Thea's new name as well. He refers to her by her maiden name, Rysing, four times in *Hedda Gabler*. Hedda takes note of this habit and corrects him on one occasion. In this subtle way, Ibsen's interest in the transition from father's daughter to husband's wife (and in desires that linger beyond the bounds of marriage) exceeds Hedda's character. For a different, post-character reading of Hedda's disappearance in relationship to the name, see Julia Jarcho's "Cold Theory, Cruel Theater" (2017). Jarcho discusses the ways in which *Hedda Gabler* dramatizes self-erasure, in part through the future-less-ness of Hedda's name. She reads Hedda (split between or taking place across character and role) as a willing participant in "a theatrical attrition of the self" (11).

12 Although he does not utter the name "Hedda Tesman," Judge Brack, who refers to motherhood as a "capacity" that makes its "serious" claim on "most women," also understands the implications of Hedda's becoming Tesman, and he is interested in taking full advantage of Hedda's entrapment (*HG* 47).

13 Although Fjelde translates the Norwegian phrase "statsrådinde Falks villa" (*HG* 11) as "Secretary Falk's town house" (*The Complete Major Prose Plays* 226), "statsrådinde" refers rather to the secretary's wife. The association of the townhouse with an older woman is reemphasized in Act Two, when Hedda claims that it smells of "lavender and salted roses" (*HG* 46). She thinks that Aunt Julie might have brought the smell with her, but Brack says that he believes it to be the lingering scent of the widow. This scent is further proof that the world of Hedda Gabler is saturated with a post- or secondarily reproductive, yet persistent, femininity.

14 The letter is addressed to Kristina Steen, actress at the Christiania Theater, who had communicated in a letter to Ibsen's wife, Susannah, that another actress, Mrs. Wolf, did not wish to play the part of Berte. It was composed in Munich on January 14, 1891.

15 Some scholars regard Aunt Julie as good, giving, and existing in proper relationship to the organic realities of life. See Durbach and Blau, for example. Other scholars take a critical stance toward Aunt Julie and other members of the Tesman family because they care only about that family's survival, operating in a mode of private or domesticated "goodness" that threatens the good (falling short of more universal social-moral principles) and threatening Hedda's desire for something better (Adorno 94). See, for example, Lisi and Adorno's *Minima Moralia*. For a discussion of Adorno and *Hedda Gabler*, see Frode's Helland's "The Scars of Modern Life" in *Ibsen's* Hedda Gabler: *Philosophical Perspectives*.

16 Aunt Julie expresses her hopes for Hedda's pregnancy by means of euphemistic phrases: "But now listen, Jørgen—don't you have something—something special to tell me?" (*HG* 9). Tesman cannot think of anything special, beyond the news that he has received his doctorate, which he already announced the night before when he met his aunt at the pier. Aunt Julie persists, "Yes, of course, yes. But I mean—whether you have any kind of—expectations—?" (*HG* 9). Tesman appears not to understand her euphemisms, and he states that he expects the professorship. Aunt Julie interprets his lack of understanding as a refusal to discuss procreant matters, a form of modesty or embarrassment: "My goodness, Jørgen—I'm your old aunt after all!" (*HG* 10). Perhaps incapable of being more explicit, she now changes the subject twice, first to the expense of the honeymoon and then to their new place of residence.

17 For a discussion of the temporality of waiting in *Hedda Gabler*, see Lisi.

18 The adjective "salig" (blessed) indicates that Tesman's father is deceased (*HG* 89). Aunt Julie also uses this adjective to describe Aunt Rina, after she dies toward the beginning of Act Four.

19 Shortly after his arrival at the townhouse in Act Two, Løvborg assures Tesman that he will not stand in the way of his professorship. He intends to give lectures, but he tells Tesman, "I'm going to wait until you have your appointment," because he only longs to triumph over Tesman "in peoples' opinion" (*HG* 53).

20 Like her nephew, Aunt Julie is a collector and organizer rather than a firsthand creator, taking on the care of her brother's child and her invalid sister, Rina. After Rina dies, she makes plans to continue the practice of adoption: "I won't let blessed Rina's little room stand empty [...] there's always some poor invalid in need of care and attention, unfortunately" (*HG* 90). In *Hedda Gabler*, the sacrifice and devotion of maiden aunts is subject to a great deal of (elitist) irony and granted a good deal of power—power that does not serve the individual but the private unit of the family. The word "unfortunately" is especially significant, because the invalid's misfortune comprises Aunt Julie's purpose in life. She informs Hedda in Act Four that it is no "cross" or burden (*HG* 91). Along with caring for future Tesman babies, it is something "that an old aunt can put her hands to" (*HG* 90–91).

21 The phrase "shining light" comes from *The Wild Duck*, in which Dr. Relling and Gregers Werle openly discuss the supposed consequences of auntly mothering, or the fact that Hjalmar Ekdal was reared by "two warped, hysterical maiden aunts" (137). What Gregers believes to be a loving upbringing is in Relling's opinion a disservice. Relling believes that the Ekdal family's exaggerated understanding of Hjalmar's talents and value to the world has had an unfortunate influence on him. The problematic qualities of auntly upbringing, according to Relling's diagnosis, are hysterical femininity and childishness, unstructured by the proper guidance and normal bounds of adult masculinity. Such improvised and alternative families are breeding grounds for a shallow and derivative existence, especially when one adds the disease of idealism to the mix. Relling's claims evoke fear of the queer (or improperly gendered) family and its potentially far-reaching influence. Although this character's opinion on the matter should not be assumed to be Ibsen's, it is clear that the aunts of *The Wild Duck* have something in common with the aunts of *Hedda Gabler*, and thus, that aversion to the fruits of auntly mothering exceeds one character's opinion.

22 Resisting Helland's ironic dismissal of Løvborg's talents, Asbjørn Aarseth points to Løvborg's positive public reception (230). I am not sure that collective, public admiration for Løvborg's first book (written to manipulate that very public) is a reliable indicator of talent in the world of *Hedda Gabler*. In any case, and as stated below, my point is not to disparage Løvborg so much as to pay attention to the implied *family dynamics* of his manuscript's production.

23 I call the book-as-child conception of the manuscript a cliché because reproductive metaphors are so common and familiar. In *Against Reproduction*, Stephen Guy-Bray calls the reproductive metaphor a "dead or at least a zombie metaphor": "the idea that the author is the parent of his or her work" has become "so much a part of what everyone apparently knows" (4).

24 Fjelde translates Løvborg's statement of dismay as follows: "God only know what hands it's come into. Or whose got a hold of it" (287). Not only is this

translation unnecessarily distinct from the original, but it also avoids the more specific implication of manipulation contained in the phrase "havt sine fingre i" (had their fingers in) (*HG* 87). Løvborg is reusing Hedda's phrasing here. She has just referred to Thea's power as a form of manipulation: "That sweet little idiot has had her fingers in a human destiny" (*HG* 86).

25 As I address briefly in the Epilogue, I would argue that Ibsen asks us to question the parent–child/artist–"child" bond most explicitly in *John Gabriel Borkman* and *When We Dead Awaken*.

2 Age Is Just a Number
Strange Calculations in
The Master Builder

Bygmester Solness (*The Master Builder*) (1892) is the middle work of the three empty nursery plays. It represents a peak or reproductive high point for the pattern of children's rooms in these plays for two main reasons: first, because its nurseries, rather than their proposed occupants, are of uncertain number and as if proliferating; and second, because one of these nurseries is actually occupied during the action. Whereas characters in *Hedda Gabler* and *Little Eyolf* propose improper occupations that will take place beyond the bounds of each drama, Ibsen chooses to stage a fulfillment in *The Master Builder*. Between Acts One and Two, Hilde Wangel spends the night in the middle nursery. The peak position of this drama creates a fitting shape that resonates with Ibsen's constant thematic and dramatic treatment of the juxtaposition of valleys and heights, as well as with one of its most explicit messages: what goes up must come down. Who, or what, brings master builder Halvard Solness down?

Retrospective dialogue in *The Master Builder* reveals information about Solness's professional climb, his family, and his fateful first meeting with Hilde. Audiences learn of Solness's usurpation of his former boss Knut Brovik's position (although Brovik is a trained architect and Solness is not), of his church building days, of the fire that provided him with the means to succeed (land to subdivide and on which to build) but left his wife in a permanent melancholy for all that burned, of the death of their twin babies shortly after the fire, of Solness's decision to give up church building after he parted ways with God while hanging a wreath on "a new tower on an old church" (Sandberg, *Ibsen's Houses* 159),[1] of his forgotten meeting with Hilde, a "devil child" dressed in white, on whom his tower climbing made a fierce impression (*BS* 32), and of his period of building homes for happy families, which he is currently renouncing. The present action of *The Master Builder* shows Solness in a state of uncertainty and fear of usurpation, which is interrupted by Hilde's arrival, ten years to the day after their first meeting. While Solness and his wife are estranged and cannot manage to talk to one another without accusation, misunderstanding, and frustration, Solness and Hilde find much to discuss, including dreams, robust consciences, devils and magical servants, castles in the air—and, of course, that fateful meeting, when Hilde claims Solness kissed her "[m]any times" (*BS* 34). Egged on by Hilde and full of plans for new (and impossible) building schemes, Solness attempts to re-create his earlier climb in the third and final act of the drama. Having reached the top, he plunges to his death, dashing his brains on the rock quarry below. Aline faints; the ladies gathered to witness the dedication scream; Hilde thrills; and the crowd from the street storms into the garden.

Paul Gorceix, scholar of Belgian symbolism, compares Aeschylus, Maurice Maeterlinck, and Ibsen on the subject of death, asserting that while fatality is divine in the first case and associated with mysterious higher powers in the second, "for Ibsen, conversely, death is in us" (15). Despite Solness's defensive stance with regard to usurpation, he appears to be engaged in self-sabotage. By clinging desperately to ideals of potency and mastery, he invites his own death. Ibsen chooses Hilde, a seductive young woman who appears to be stuck in a childish fantasy, as the external manifestation of vitality and fatality alike, as the imperiling helpmate who urges Solness to climb the final tower. In *Ibsens Samtidsskuespill* (*Ibsen's Contemporary Plays*) (1999), Asbjørn Aarseth claims that

> a central problem in the interpretation of [*The Master Builder*] is how we best can position ourselves in relationship to the mysterious Hilde Wangel, the girl who makes her entrance with a reckless, captivating charm [...] and who seems to carry a message for the aging master builder about both the past and the future, but most of all about an uncompromising joy in life. (270)

This chapter re-approaches this central problem by centering Hilde's status as a queer occupant of an empty nursery. Before Hilde arrives, Solness has built six nurseries for no babies; she shows up and is told she can "be the child here for a while" (*BS* 28). Solness's ambition, his fear of the future, and his death are strangely united in his invitation to Hilde, an uncertain child who has always been on the verge of something other than innocence.

Although all of the empty nursery plays deploy themes of accumulation, supplementarity, and replacement, *The Master Builder* offers the most explicit association of the emptiness of nurseries with the empty, malleable, desire-inducing figure of the child. In this chapter, I consider the strange calculations of *The Master Builder*, its play with misleading numbers and ages, and critical responses to Hilde's first encounter with Solness. I argue that Hilde's characterization, her power, as well as her disempowerment, rely on what James R. Kincaid calls child loving: an eroticization of the child as a figure of uncertainty and emptiness, a "Romantic heritage" which is also legible as "a dangerous nineteenth century inheritance" in late twentieth- and early twenty-first-century interpretations of *The Master Builder* (*Erotic Innocence* 7). Some scholars, including Elinor Fuchs, are quick to label Solness's encounter with Hilde pedophilic in a manner that makes it sound as if child loving is primarily a matter of the perverse individual's "willed desire" (Kincaid, *Child Loving* 9). In "Estragement," Fuchs closes her list of reasons why Solness is a "startlingly unsympathetic protagonist" with the claim that he "on at least one occasion may have sexually molested a 12-year-old girl" (73). While Hilde rounds up in *The Master Builder*, insisting that she was "twelve or thirteen" when she met Solness, Fuchs emphasizes Solness's lack of likeability by rounding down and combining the qualifying word "may" with the phrase "on at least one occasion"—perhaps doubting that pedophilic encounters can happen just once (*BS* 26). I would not call Fuchs's description inaccurate, although it might be anachronistic, given that its accuracy depends on what we currently understand to be essential features of human development, power, and the limits of consent: "It is because big and older people are more powerful than small and younger people that sexual contact between them is wrong" (Kincaid, *Child Loving* 24). My goal, however, is not to insist on what does or does not constitute molestation, but to draw attention to the ways in which *The Master Builder* makes use of, and is used to contribute to, a version of child loving that is part of our "general cultural geography of and for desire" (Kincaid, *Child Loving* 9). In both *Child Loving* (1992) and *Erotic Innocence* (1998), Kincaid's daunting (and reviled) task is to put pedophiles, parents, pedagogues, and "us" into the same category, not because we all engage in the same activities, but because we are all formed by a culture that reproduces the "heavily eroticized" division between adult and child, desiring youth and investing the child with powers of seduction (Kincaid, *Child Loving* 6–7). Motivating my analysis is the question of how we should read Solness's relationship with Hilde responsibly today, while engaging some historical awareness and acknowledging our embeddedness in—or refusing to exempt ourselves (irresponsibly) from—that "geography."

The person who knocks on the door of Solness's workroom in Act One appears to carry an uncanny or deconstructive threat, in the sense that her youth is perceived as the promise *and* primary threat to his middle age, her femininity to his masculinity, her potency to his impotency (or is it the other way around?). Hilde is both seduced and seducer, hostage and host. Was the eroticism that she embodied in the past neutralized by her childishness? Or do the regressive pleasures that she appears to promise, and her status as a frozen adolescent (not quite a child, then as now), constitute a primary threat in *The Master Builder*? Ibsen uses Hilde to depict uncertainty when it comes to the difference between childhood and *something else*. Because of her extended adolescence and because she occupies an empty nursery, she represents the desire to collapse differentiation into a singular figure of fulfillment: the lover-child, who is both compliant and resistant, a vanquished-vanquisher, an all-in-one nursery dweller, nymphette, and "bird of prey" (*BS* 69). My broad aims in this chapter are to explore the ways in which Hilde's power over Solness emerges in relationship to figures and spaces of innocence and irrational desires to add things up, while resisting the conception of childhood as faulty (or traumatized) foundation, a doomed architecture of adult life permanently destabilized by violations of innocence.

Making the Uncertain Child

In Act Three, Solness embarks on a new scheme, acquiescing to Hilde's insistence that he do "the *impossible* again!" (*BS* 99). Although he suffers from acrophobia and has only hung the dedicatory wreath on one previous occasion, he will now climb the tower of his new house and have another conversation with God, daring him to judge him by revealing both his new building plans and his intention to climb back down and kiss Hilde again, "many, many times" (*BS* 99). As he reveals his plans to Hilde, she cheers him on, punctuating his descriptions with phrases such as "Yes—yes—yes!" and "Yes, tell him that! Say that to him" (*BS* 99). She stretches out her arms and mentions the music that she heard the first time he climbed, prompting Solness to "*look at her with his head lowered*," asking,

> How have you become the way you are, Hilde?
> HILDE   How have you made me the way I am?
> SOLNESS (*short and fast*)
> The princess shall *have* her castle. (*BS* 99–100)

Hilde places responsibility for her becoming with Solness, either believing that he has, in fact, *made her*, or knowing that no utterance could be more appealing to the master builder, more likely to lead to her "castle." Aarseth lists a variety of ways in which one might interpret Solness's fall: as "an expression of madness resulting from a meeting between a sick older man and an overeager young woman"; as "an example of hubris that leads with frightening necessity to nemesis in agreement with the ethos of ancient tragedy"; or as "an example of modern dramatic rhetoric formulated as erotically tinged exertion of the will in the decade of vitalist romanticism" (270–271). He then wonders whether Ibsen might simply be pushing the boundaries of plausibility when it comes to depicting "the strange power a person can be imagined to have over another" (271). Aarseth locates Hilde's "strange power" in her capacity to conquer Solness, to bring him down by goading him to climb; but if the master builder has "made" Hilde, we might question whether she can be powerful as something other than a fulfillment of his own desire.

A range of understandings of Hilde's power and disempowerment are legible in criticism, from Hilde-as-embodiment-of-Nietzschean-will to Hilde-as-permanently-ruined girl, suspended in a pedophilic embrace.[2] I am arguing that what appears to be a spectrum with opposed understandings at its ends is really a knot or bind, because Hilde's power over Solness emerges in relationship to those aspects of her character, including sex, age, and memories of an erotic intergenerational encounter, that are more commonly associated with weakness and disempowerment. I am not the first person to insist that Hilde's role in *The Master Builder* must be understood "against the background of those unseen, empty nurseries" (Young 153) and in relationship to a persistent "girlish eroticism" (Templeton 268). In the conclusion to this chapter, I will explore some scholarly interpretations of Hilde's first encounter with Solness from our own turn of the century (1980–2019), articulating a critique of what might be called pedophilic (dis)empowerment. In this section, I define the pedophilic in relationship to Kincaid's concept of child loving—a nineteenth-century inheritance and broad cultural phenomenon—and begin to consider why this concept corresponds with the construction of Hilde as an uncertain child in *The Master Builder*.

The decade between Solness's first encounter with Hilde and her return to claim the promised kingdom, as well as her occupation of the nursery and her turnabout seduction of Solness, have pedophilic characteristics that emerge precisely from the fact that the "definitional base" of the "division between adult and child" has been "at least for the past two hundred years heavily eroticized":

> the child is that species which is free of sexual feeling or response; the adult is that species which has crossed over into sexuality [...] Of course, other binaries are involved too, those involving innocence and experience, incapacity and competence, empty and full, low and high, weak and powerful. (Kincaid, *Child Loving* 6–7)

The Master Builder at once destabilizes and preserves the division of innocence and experience by capturing Hilde in the division between child and adult. Hilde herself insists that she was already something other than a child when she first met Solness, and yet their relationship consists of fantasy-driven interactions that Kincaid defines as the very stuff of erotic innocence. Hilde invites Solness to play her game. When he fails to understand what his next building project should be— or what the "loveliest, absolutely the loveliest thing in all the world" is (castles in the air)—she momentarily reverses their roles, "*shakes her head a bit, pouts and talks as if to a child*": "Master Builders—they are very, very silly people" (*BS* 88). According to Kincaid's definition, pedophilic desire removes the "child/adult" barrier; it consists of a world of "play" that is "unconstrained and never-ending," often without the "'fulfillment' (or closure)" of sexuality centered on the "genital or copulative" (Kincaid, *Child Loving* 15). *The Master Builder* does not so much remove the barrier between child and adult as play in it, almost closing the gap in the past (by means of the successful climb followed by a longed for or willed or executed kiss) and then reopening it by making space for Hilde's queer occupation (a different kind of fulfillment) and ensuring that she will never receive visits from *The Master Builder* in a tower room fit for a princess.

Whatever happened ten years ago in Lysanger, the period of time between Solness's first encounter with Hilde and her entrance in Act One can be described as a pedophilic decade because it is a period of "play" that has suspended Hilde in an adolescent "fairy tale" (Templeton 269). Although the decade technically ends on the day that Hilde shows up, it is also "unconstrained and never-ending," because *The Master Builder* also reopens the past, and because it loves to play with numbers and ages and fulfillment, making these categories nonsensical.

It is very likely too early to look for a strong form of intentional ethical condemnation of pedophilic desire in *The Master Builder*. In *Child Loving*, Kincaid uses sources from the Victorian era to highlight the difference of late twentieth-century attitudes toward children. His goal is to disallow later definitions of the child and ideologies of child-centrism from covering up an era in which the child was still in the making—or at least when the difference between child and adult, as well as obsessions over the innocent and/or non-sexual nature of the child, were "created but not occupied": "we vastly overstate the dominance of this view of the child in the Victorian period, expressing and exposing a need of our own" (78, 72). Kincaid argues, for example, that the Victorians were much less worried about intergenerational sexual encounters than we are today. Although Carolyn Steedman is critical of Kincaid's sometimes sweeping rhetoric concerning the child as a "field of desire," and of his "irresponsible" and "illogical" conclusions concerning what we should do about it, she confirms his caution against assuming that perceptions of the child in the nineteenth century resemble our own (8, 166). She insists, for example, that we err by failing to recognize the "nineteenth century's lack of interest in the actual chronological ages of its 'child,'" particularly "as we watch what is *for us* the irreducibly paedophilic gaze turned upon the girl-child" (Steedman 7–8, emphasis added). In Kincaid's analysis, significantly, it is precisely the twentieth-century assumption of pedophilic desire that is irreducible, not pedophilia itself. Although *The Master Builder* is clearly interested in ages and a form of (dangerous) "innocent" eroticism, it does not follow that it defines the relationship between childhood or adolescence and sexuality in the ways that we do.[3]

Even when erotic encounters between girls and men were viewed in a negative light in the turn of the century Western context, the adult male could be conceived as the victim of seduction rather than as the inevitably more empowered person who is supposed to be mature (without desire for inappropriate persons and objects). In "The Tale of Enchanted Hunters," Olga Voronina considers the "commonplace" figure of the nymphette or "underage seductress" in Victorian literature.[4] She writes,

> for Victorian writers a girl-child was not as much an icon of virginity as a variation and marginalization of the myth of the powerful female. Angelic in appearance, unaware of her sensuality or repressing it, she was associated with the Fall either in the social (Carroll's odalisque images) or spiritual (Lilith) sense. What is most striking, though [...] is that the Victorian admirer of a demonic child finds himself deep in sin and on the brink of death and despair not because he believes that he has done anything wrong, such as stepping beyond what was morally permissible or giving in to uncontrolled desires, but because he is convinced that the object of his affection is able to cast an evil spell on any male she captivates. (153–154)

Although we do not meet Hilde in the form of the "girl-child" in *The Master Builder*, and it would seem a bad fit to call her "angelic" or repressed (or Victorian), Ibsen's drama certainly combines innocence and wickedness in its memorial description or retelling of Hilde's childish figure. She was one of several school girls, all referred to as "dævelungerne" (the devil-children), dressed in white and holding flags; but she was the only one who screamed up and waved her flag, making Solness dizzy at the height of his climb (*BS* 31). Many scholars have commented on the sexual innuendoes in this scene. It has been read as "a narrative of lovemaking in which Solness functions as a masterful, experienced male who brings an aroused, inexperienced young woman to orgasm" (Templeton 267); and when the climb is re-created in Act Three, Hilde's cheering for Solness literalizes the notion of a fall built into conceptions of improper seduction. Hilde herself calls Solness's behavior toward her on that day ten years ago "uskikkelig," a term that might be translated as naughty or ill-mannered and certainly suggests that there was a degree of inappropriateness in his behavior (*BS* 39). But the arch of their story, from climb to (real or imagined) kiss to return to climb to fall, marks Solness as the final victim. It might be tempting to claim that wickedness outweighs innocence in Ibsen's descriptions of Hilde, although she has also been interpreted as a figure of positive vitality (by Georg Brandes, for example) as well as a death-dealing "instrument of retributive justice" (Young 153). In any case, it is likely less anachronistic to describe Hilde as a conqueror who "gets her way"—in the simultaneous form of "young girl" and "*femme fatale*"—than as an obvious victim of molestation (Aarseth 261, 271).[5]

Some readers might have noticed that I do not differentiate between pedophilia and hebephilia. This is because I do not seek to specify or diagnose or to insist on puberty as the boundary between child and adult, although puberty can clearly serve as a strategic or definitional boundary in other contexts. Hilde's adolescence is not determined by puberty in *The Master Builder*, but rather by means of her simultaneous attachment to and estrangement from childhood. The difference between the child and something else—a person who is not quite a child—sometimes matters quite a bit to Hilde. This difference also fails to matter when it suits her to play the child for Solness—or with Solness, given that he too plays, or longs to play, childish games. The precision of the category of hebephilia, and its assumption that childhood ends when another period of life begins, would be beside the point here, given that the point of Hilde's occupation of a nursery is imprecision, a bad fit in turns melancholic and playful. It is this kind of child—the child that is "not, in itself, anything" (Kincaid, *Child Loving* 5)—that matters in *The Master Builder*, because this child is "the embodiment of desire and also its negation" (Kincaid, *Child Loving* 5, 7). As with Alice and Peter, two exceptional figures from English literature in critical child studies, Hilde's characterization does not "set up a static binary with the adult," but engages in a "shifting dynamic," "blocking fulfillment, keeping the chase and desire alive" (Kincaid, *Child Loving* 276). As will be seen, Kincaid's description of the child suits how *The Master Builder*'s nurseries are built to house both melancholic loss and Hilde, how Solness simultaneously fears and longs for youth, and how quantities and ages matter precisely as instabilities in this play.

Numbers

Frode Helland evaluates the domestic dynamic of the Solness household, concluding, "This, then, is homey coziness at Solness': a situation characterized by isolation, death, stiffening, silence and estrangement" (*Melankoliens spill* 98). It is this dynamic that Hilde both interrupts and confirms by playing the lively yet death-dealing (uncertain) child, the one and only occupant of empty nurseries in the empty nursery plays. Ibsen intersperses references to these nurseries in the dialogue of the first two acts of *The Master Builder*. We know for certain that there are three nurseries in the current house in which Solness and Aline have been living since the fire; and three more have been built in the soon-to-be-dedicated new house. It is tempting to assume that there were three nurseries in Aline's family home. This temptation arises, in part, because subsequent nurseries appear to be copies of original spaces. As Helland indicates, Solness's habit of rebuilding nurseries suggests melancholic compulsion, a dwelling in estrangement, a refusal or inability to mourn and move on from the losses of the past. It also gives the "impression of an empty mimetic pattern" (Sandberg, *Ibsen's Houses* 162). Mark Sandberg writes, "The nurseries seem to have a logic of their own, as if no matter where Solness might move, there will always be three unused children's rooms" (*Ibsen's Houses* 163). When Hilde questions Solness about his building projects, he is ready with causal explanations ranging from the apparently practical (we have nurseries because we once had children) to the mystical (I have been successful because I can call on "helpers and servants," and they answer my call) (*BS* 65). Solness and Aline's explanations for feelings of guilt and grief adjoin recognizable and normative rationalizations, while also evoking more abstract, and perhaps more fundamentally melancholic, fantasies about permanent potency and other modes of uncanny impossibility. In this section, I consider *The Master Builder*'s strange calculations by means of the nursery, its interest in quantities, proliferation, and fulfillment, its irrational fantasies that are nonetheless anchored to the desire to add things up.

When we first hear about the nurseries in the current home, Solness emphasizes that they are complete, which implies that they are ready for an overnight guest and creates a subtle correspondence between completion and emptiness. Solness tells his wife that Hilde will spend the night, and Aline plays the good host, inviting Hilde to rest while she makes "a room [...] a little cozy" for her (*BS* 28). In the original Norwegian, Aline uses *værelse* (room) rather than *barnekammers*, the word for the nurseries in *The Master Builder*. Solness asks her,

SOLNESS   Can't we use one of the nurseries? Because *they* are completely finished, they are.
FRU SOLNESS Oh yes. We have more than enough room there. (*to Hilde*) Sit yourself down now and rest a little (*She exits to the right*) (*BS* 28)

Solness's description includes three forms of emphasis: the repetition of the subject "they," or "de" in Norwegian, which is further emphasized by italics in the first instance, and the qualifying adverb "completely," or "fuldt." It is not entirely clear why he speaks so emphatically. Are parts of the interim house still under construction or unfinished in some sense, despite the fact that Solness and Aline have been living there for more than ten years? Was this house always intended as a mere holding place between the old home and the new house?[6]

After Aline leaves, Hilde wanders about the room, looking at various objects, while Solness stands in front of his desk, looking at her. Following this scene of bodily mirroring—hands on their backs, eyes surveying—Hilde "*stops and looks at him*," asking,

          Do you have several nurseries?
SOLNESS   There are three nurseries in the house.
HILDE   That's a lot. So you have an awful lot of children, then? (28)

Hilde's assumption that Solness has "an awful lot" of children is an early example of her often exaggerative and impertinent manner of speaking, which also suggests that many children could be housed in three such rooms.[7] Although Aline's comment concerning "more than enough room" is suggestive, there is no dramatic irony in these first references to nurseries. The audience and Hilde now learn together that there are no children in the current Solness residence: "No, We don't have any children" (*BS* 28). The explanation for this incongruous situation is not given until Act Two.

In addition to figuring a curious form of excess—several nurseries for no children—the nurseries of *The Master Builder* evoke Solness's desire for fulfillment. When Aline re-enters toward the end of Act One, she announces that "the room" is ready for "Miss Wangel"—again using *værelse* rather than *barnekammers* (*BS* 41). Solness must verify that Aline has readied one of the nurseries, as previously proposed:

> SOLNESS (*to his wife*)
> The nursery room?
> FRU SOLNESS   Yes. The middle one. But first we'll go to the table and eat.
> SOLNESS (*nods to Hilde*)
> Hilde will sleep in the nursery then. (*BS* 41)

Between Solness's doubled use of the word "nursery," Aline confirms that she has readied the requested room by specifying the "middle one." Solness's repetition, his double-checking, and his nod to Hilde comprise a strange overemphasis on something that might not quite make sense to the audience. Why is he so intent on Hilde's occupation of a nursery room? In "*Ibsen the Romantic*," Errol Durbach understands Hilde's occupation of a nursery as the activation of the "incest-taboo," which will prevent Solness from beginning a riskier, more adult relationship with Hilde (133). Hilde will play the child, and this will prevent Solness's relationship with her from being "fulfilled," or from becoming a "sexually threatening liaison" (Durbach 133).

When Act Two opens, a fulfillment of a different sort has taken place: Hilde has spent the night in a nursery, interrupting the emptiness of these rooms. Solness asks Aline about their guest and hears that she has been up for hours. "*[A]fter a short pause*," he tells her,

> Then we found a use for a nursery after all, Aline.
> MRS. SOLNESS   Yes, we certainly did.
> SOLNESS   And I think that's better than that they all remain empty.
> FRU SOLNESS   The emptiness is so completely horrible. You are right about that. (*BS* 44)

Solness insists that use is better than emptiness, but this dialogue evokes further questions concerning the use of empty rooms and the kind of hospitality being offered to Hilde. It is not only Solness but also family friend and physician Doctor Herdal and Aline who have made Hilde's acquaintance prior to the opening of the drama. It was Aline who invited Hilde, when they met at a sanatorium, to stay with them if she ever came to town. Why would Aline agree, or at least not object to, the idea that the nursery is the best place for their guest, if guestrooms are also present in the interim house? (*BS* 28) Although Aline and Solness are otherwise estranged from one another, each doubting the other's intentions, they appear to be a team of sorts when it comes to hosting Hilde in a nursery for the night.

Unused but furnished rooms have a tendency to collect dust, to smell musty and stale, and to look dated. In literature (and in the real world), they are sometimes reserved for ghosts or the memorialization of the dead. While attempting to work out the fictional reasons for, and architectural chronology of, the nurseries in *The Master Builder*, both Helland and Sandberg mention Solness's insistence that the nurseries in the interim house are complete. Helland suggests that these particular nurseries could have been built before the fire, with the twins in mind. Although Solness, Aline, and their boys were still living in Aline's childhood home when it caught fire, when and why the interim house was built is not actually stated. Sandberg insists that these nurseries most likely never served "a practical function," given that the twins did not live long after the fire: "Halvard and Aline came to the house only as a result of the accident. In the eleven years that have passed since the twins' death, though, it seems that the rooms have remained fully furnished, as if still waiting for future occupancy" (*Ibsen's Houses* 163). More than a decade has passed, and no one has converted the nurseries. Helland imagines that Solness's descriptive phrase, "fuldt færdige" (fully prepared or completely finished), means that these rooms have been and remain furnished and decorated for the dead children, "with the colors, carpets and objects (for example, toys) that normally belong in such rooms" (*Melankoliens spill* 106). However, the dialogue and stage directions do not specify décor. Clearly, this lack of specificity encourages readers who take an interest in nurseries to begin asking questions about the undescribed space, as we attempt to understand why they have been built and preserved and re-built, and why—when everything gets added up—such rooms can be used as evidence for evaluating Solness's "mental health" (Helland 106).

When we learn about the next set of rooms—three more nurseries "without children" in the new and as-of-yet-undedicated house—we might begin to suspect, together with Hilde, that Solness is mentally unstable, or that he "lingers repetitively with emptiness" (Helland, *Melankoliens spill* 107). Suspicion of madness arises in *The Master Builder* because Solness's behavior and mindset are incomprehensible to others, and also because he continues to build nurseries for no children in sets of three. Significantly, it is Solness himself who evokes the topic of madness, in part because he believes himself to be special and uniquely gifted, and suspects that his wife and Herdal are misdiagnosing him, not being special themselves. Before Hilde enters the "finely decorated, smaller parlor" in which Act Two takes place, husband and wife discuss Aline's inability to stop thinking about the past and its losses. Although Solness has just asserted that things will get better when they move to the new house—because "there will be so incredibly much *there* that will remind you of your own home" (*BS* 45)—he now confirms what Aline herself contends: the new house will never constitute a true home: "Just as empty. Just as vacant. There as here" (*BS* 47). Each spouse attempts to take on the full burden of guilt for the grief and pain of their current situation, and they accuse one another of having ulterior motives and hidden, reproachful feelings.

Solness openly accuses Aline of believing him to be ill or crazy, a claim that he already tested on the doctor in Act One:

SOLNESS (*takes up a position in front of her*)
                                        Don't you find a sly, hidden meaning in
                                        the most innocent words I say?
FRU SOLNESS   *I*, you say! *I* do that!
SOLNESS (*laughs*)

                                        Hahaha! It makes sense, of course,
                                        Aline! When you are dealing with a
                                        sick man in the house, then—.
FRU SOLNESS (*anxiously*)
                                        Sick! Are you sick, Halvard!
SOLNESS (*bursts out*)

                                        A half-crazy man then! A ruined man!
                                        Call me what you will! (*BS* 47)

Startled and confused by her husband's outburst, Aline has to sit down, and Solness confuses her further by insisting that he is perfectly well, to which she rejoins, "No, of course! But what is the matter with you then?" (*BS* 48). Solness now insists that the burden of guilt is his rather than hers. His debt to Aline is what causes the profound disturbance in his feelings, and yet he assures her that he has no definite reason to feel guilty (while she suspects him of being unfaithful). Solness's claim on unwarranted yet "bottomless guilt and debt" to his wife is evidence (or irritation) enough for Aline to acquiesce to his perversely stated self-diagnosis: "Then you are—sick after all, Halvard" (*BS* 48). Solness does not share with Aline what he has already shared with Herdal and will soon tell Hilde: he suspects that he has a kind of telepathic power, a means of making things happen, of controlling people and events by magically aided will and inner troll-ness.

In the dialogue that follows, Solness and Hilde are united by the label "crazy" and by their insistence that it does not fully apply to them. Hilde's entrance in Act Two interrupts the spousal dispute described above. The topic of conversation appears to shift radically, from guilt and blame, unspoken truths and diagnoses, to Hilde's night in the nursery and a shared yet distinct experience of the dream of falling. For Hilde the dream is thrilling; for Solness it is "chilling," but they both try to tuck their legs up under them while it happens (*BS* 49). Apparently tired of being the third wheel, Aline announces that she must go into town and will return with some items of clothing for Hilde, whom she believes will be subject to stares if she walks in the streets dressed in her "tourist's costume" with a sailor's collar and cap (*BS* 24). Solness confirms that people might think that Hilde *"also"* is "crazy" (*BS* 49). He uses the word *"also"* to continue confessing—again, ironically or perversely—that he himself is mentally unstable, and now asks Hilde whether she has noticed his madness. At first, she insists that she has yet to notice any such thing, but then, "(*reconsiders and laughs a bit*) Well yes, maybe in just one way anyway" (*BS* 50). Solness urges Hilde to confess what she means, but she simply responds, "No thanks,—I'm not as crazy as that" (*BS* 50). Before leaving, Aline insists that Hilde will tell Solness what that "just one thing" is when she is gone, given that he has known her "ever since she was a child" (*BS* 50).[8] This is, indeed, what happens. After a short discussion of Aline's coldness—Hilde would like her to be warmer and to stop using the word duty—and of Solness's building plans—Hilde insists that only Solness should be allowed to build—she finally tells Solness that the nurseries in the current house appear to her as the sign of his mental instability.

The disclosure of this "one thing," however, is delayed again until after Solness confirms that the house under construction also contains three nurseries. When Hilde corroborates Solness's conviction that no one else should take the position of master builder, he assumes that this must be the "one thing" that makes him appear insane. Hilde, however, denies that this is so and again refuses to tell him why. Solness brings her over to the bay window and directs her attention to the new house, visible just beyond the stone quarry, with a tall tower still surrounded by scaffolding. She *"looks at him"* and asks,

> Are there nurseries in that house too?
> SOLNESS   Three, just like here.
> HILDE   And no children.
> SOLNESS   None will come either.
> HILDE (*with a half-smile*)
>   Yes, then isn't it like I said—?

SOLNESS   That—?
HILDE   That you are—well—a little crazy after all.
SOLNESS   Was that what you were thinking about?
HILDE   Yes, about all the empty nurseries that I lay and slept in.
          (54–55)

Finally, Hilde has confessed what she considers to be evidence of Solness's mental instability: the "one thing" is the second (or third) set of nurseries. Solness attempts to explain the nurseries, dispelling Hilde's suspicions by telling her "We *did* have children,—Aline and I" (*BS* 55). Of course, having had children in the past is not a credible reason for continuing to build nurseries in the present.

In addition to being legible as a feature of irrational fixation brought on by unresolved, melancholic grief, the dialogue concerning empty nurseries in *The Master Builder* can encourage a wild goose chase, an attempt to work through the strange logic of the drama's numbers and quantities. Hilde's occupation of the middle nursery suggests a fulfillment that itself consists of tension between the limited (*only* one) and the singular (to be *the one*, or at least to be indefinitely copious enough to represent a near-realization). Is Hilde's occupation of the middle nursery a restricted drop in an ocean of emptiness that leaves the Solness home and marriage just "as vacant" as ever? Or is it somehow boundless? Helland notes that Solness understands Hilde's occupation to be an improvement on absolute emptiness: He "appreciates that they have filled at least one 'nursery,' so that one can no longer say that the totality, '*everything*,' is characterized by emptiness" (*Melankoliens spill* 89). Solness expresses a passing hope that Hilde's occupation means something "better," that it can counter the all-encompassing lack in his private life. Its impact is nevertheless restricted, given that Aline cannot share, and soon convinces Solness to abandon, his optimism concerning a more fulfilling future in the new house. From this perspective, Hilde cannot really replace the babies that did not grow up in the nurseries and that manage to represent, by means of their absence, the future of futureless-ness that Solness insists on recreating.

When Hilde confesses her reason for doubting Solness's mental stability, however, she uses a vague colloquial expression, both exaggerating for effect and suggesting that her occupation was somehow numerous or filling. She thinks of "all the empty nurseries that I lay and slept in" (*BS* 55). Hilde has spent one night in one empty nursery, but somehow, it is as if it she slept in *many* empty nurseries, a series of uncertain number that can be described as "all." Although Hilde's description is inaccurate in one sense, what she emphasizes is how these empty rooms express a form of paradoxical proliferation, a reproduction of emptiness, as well as how one night in the middle nursery can represent a fulfillment, an experience of singularity as all. Just as multiple ages are as if united in

Hilde's figure—as I discuss below, she is a permanent adolescent who can play at being a not-quite child and woman—her phrasing suggests that multiple spaces, perhaps even temporalities (many rooms and an unspecified number of nights), are as if collapsed into a single room and a single night's occupation.

After Solness tells Hilde the story of the fire and the death of the twins, she asks him whether things cannot be made good again. He denies this possibility, and then she confronts him for the last time with his seemingly pointless building project: "(*looks at him with an indefinable expression*) And yet you still build all these nurseries" (*BS* 59). Hilde describes what Solness has done in the past (built more than one set of nurseries) in present tense, as if he continues and will continue to build— implicitly uniting the nurseries with the castle that she has already demanded. This comment encourages Solness to ask whether Hilde has noticed how "the impossible—it sort of lures and calls to you?" (*BS* 59). She thinks about his question and quickly recognizes the call of the impossible as the voice of the troll, a creature that also lives inside her. This shift from nursery-building to the impossible is not really a change of topic, because the impossible is associated with Solness's desire to freeze time, suspending himself in the status quo of mastery, and with Hilde's desire to turn back time in order to re-witness a singular act from the past. The impossible refers both to the first climb in Lysanger and to the second, fatal climb at the end of the drama. The impossible is also a suitable description for Hilde's boundless occupation of "all the empty nurseries," and for other spaces imagined as being fit for a troll-princess and suspended nymphette (*BS* 55).

The Master Builder tempts us to get carried away by its delusional rationality, its quantities and numbers, calculating various impossibilities and looking for a good fit, despite the fact that nursery-room-to-occupant ratios do not follow simple calculations. After noting the unique logic of Solness's nursery rooms, or the way in which they appear to promise continual repetition of the pattern of emptiness, Sandberg writes,

> Note that the sign of repetition is not the nurseries themselves, since all houses might logically contain *one*; instead it is the excess of the number three (one more than the number of Solness children), repeated three times, that makes the presence of the rooms unusual. (*Ibsen's Houses* 163)

It is both the multiplication of the rooms (times three) and their numerical bad fit for the twins that makes them "unusual," according to Sandberg. Of course, nursery rooms are, in fact, signs of repetition, intended to house reproduction in the form of offspring, or little copies of humans. As I show in my analyses of *Hedda Gabler* and *Little Eyolf*, nurseries "have a logic of their own" even when they are not unnecessarily re-created in additional houses and multiplying by threes. Although their realist presence is not "unusual" in the other two dramas, they nonetheless serve to house the sneaking feeling that all forms of reproduction are already supplementary, a matter of originary replacement and poor fit rather than an "ultimate beginning where everything is perfect or can at least be made good" (Rose 138). Moreover, the idea that each child should have a room of its own is conditioned by class rather than by addition and division. Note that Sandberg is tempted by the number nine, or three times three. Two small (dead) bodies cannot be made to fit perfectly into nine rooms; but if there are actually nine nurseries, then Hilde's occupation of the middle nursery constitutes an occupation of the perfect middle, with four nurseries on either side. This number—nine: a mystical prime number squared—is misleading and seductive. It is misleading because we do not know whether the original home actually contained three nurseries (there might only be two sets of three, or even some other unknown number, in which case no perfect middle would exist). It is seductive because it is also a perfect fit for Aline's "nine lovely dolls" (*BS* 81).

Although *The Master Builder* has left the word nursery behind by Act Three, these dolls carry over some of the logic of empty nurseries. When the act opens, Hilde has already occupied the middle of the nine (real or imagined) nurseries of *The Master Builder*. She has also been offered the tower room in the new house—a room fit for a "princess"—and she has succeeded in convincing Solness that whether he actually kissed her or not, he probably willed it and "should have" done it (*BS* 77). Throughout the act, Hilde continues to persuade Solness to release his fears, to be greater than all other builders, and to take on impossible projects, including a castle with a "terribly high tower," from which they might look down upon those who still bother with churches and "homes for mother and father and a flock of children" (*BS* 88). Aline and Solness have yet to give up dwelling in their losses, however. Solness believes that Aline is in perpetual mourning for their twin boys, and this appears to be the case in Act Two when she exclaims, "But the horror that happened in the wake of the fire—! *That's* what it is! That, that, that!" (*BS* 46).

In Act Three, however, when Aline and Hilde sit on the large veranda overlooking the garden and discussing Aline's many losses, Aline appears to have forgotten the nurseries' proper occupants. Hilde mentions both the burning of Aline's home and "that which was worse"—in fact, the "worst" of all (*BS* 80). Aline does not understand and twice asks for clarification. When Hilde reminds her that she "lost both little boys," Aline insists that these deaths are a matter unto themselves, the result of a higher will or plan: "And one must bow before such things. And be grateful for them" (*BS* 81). Although Aline does not always manage to be fully grateful, and despite the fact that she sometimes conceives of her loss as just punishment for lacking strength when tested, she insists that the twins are in a better place:

> Oh, no, no, Miss Wangel,—don't talk to me anymore about those babies. We should only be happy for them. Because they have it good,—so good now. No, it's the small losses in life that cut so deeply in one's heart. To lose everything that others deem meaningless.
>
> HILDE (*lays her arms on Aline's knees and looks warmly up at her*) Darling Mrs. Solness,—tell me what that is!
>
> MRS. SOLNESS   As I say, just little things. All the old portraits on the walls burned. And all the old silk dresses burned. The ones that had been in the family for such a long time. And all of mother's and grandmother's laces—they burned too. And think,—the jewelry also! (*heavily*) And then all the dolls. (*BS* 81)

When Hilde asks Aline to explain her relationship to these dolls, Aline tells her that she continued to live with them even when she was grown, even after her marriage—although she kept them hidden from Solness. She is particularly sad that no one tried to rescue the dolls during the fire. She asks Hilde not to laugh at her, making clear that she believes there was "life in them too, in a way": "I carried them under my heart. Like small, unborn children" (*BS* 82). Again, *if* there were already three nurseries in the original home, then there are just the right number of nurseries for Aline's dolls. This good fit, however, is suitable only to the extent that these nurseries multiplying by threes are ideal rooms for ghosts, burnt up dolls, and queer occupants like Hilde, who understands how one night in one such room can stand in for many nights in "all" such rooms.

Hilde also understands quite well that Aline's fixation is morbid, that her mourning for dolls is melancholic, not fully reconcilable with her grief for the twin boys, not a means of moving on but the occupation of a tomb. Although this tomb clearly makes an impression on Hilde, she quickly shakes it off, as her future plans involve the occupation of much higher places. In Act Three, when Solness joins Hilde on the veranda and Aline has left to talk to the doctor, Hilde tells him that she "just came up out of a grave," where she got "frost" in her body (*BS* 83). Solness assumes that he understands Hilde's comment. He confesses to her that it is both painful to him and a relief that his wife generally leaves when he arrives, and he agrees with Hilde's attempt to specify the nature of his feelings: "That [he doesn't] have to continually witness how hard [Aline] takes the situation with the little boys" (*BS* 83). After a pause, Solness begins to ask Hilde for more details about her conversation with Aline.

She remains silent, refusing to answer three queries in a row, neither mentioning the dolls nor other details. She allows Solness to assume that she and Aline mostly talked about the twins, but a *"nervous twitch"* runs through her body when he states as much (*BS* 84). Hilde *"nods quickly a few times"* and then announces that she plans to leave (*BS* 84). When Solness objects, Hilde insists that she cannot do bad things to a person she knows (only to a stranger). When he insists, however, that he needs Hilde to have something to live for beyond his lifeless duty to his wife, lamenting that he has lived all these years chained to a dead person, Hilde gives up her ethical qualm, deciding that it is "nuts" to give up seeking happiness just "because a person one knows stands in the way!" (*BS* 85–86).

Hilde now leads Solness into a conversation about future building schemes and the kingdom that he still owes her (*BS* 88). She restates her demand from Act One, now specifying that kingdoms usually involve castles and insisting that Solness begin building at once: "a castle on the table! It's *my* castle! I want it *right away*!" (*BS* 87). Although Hilde understands that Aline's obsession with dolls is a melancholic fixation, it is not clear that she understands her own motivations in terms of fixation: her insistence that her life—indeed, that which means more to her "than life"—is to see Solness climb a tower again (*BS* 71). In Act Three, Dr. Herdal remarks on Hilde's "mountain uniform," and she responds, "But I'm not going to the heights to break my neck today. The two of us will be good and stay down to watch, doctor" (*BS* 82). Is this just a manner of speaking, or is it evidence of more murderous desires?

Sandberg extrapolates from Helland's characterization of Solness's repetitive building projects as a personal "melancholic reaction to loss," suggesting that "nurseries might convey a central point about architecture's durative features more generally" (162). I wonder whether the broader conceptual term, encompassing melancholy and architecture alike, is not reproduction, given that it can cover the full range of repetitive production, from baby-making and child-rearing to house-building to dwelling in fantastic castles in the air. Sandberg writes,

> Using Helland's productive framework [...] one might extrapolate and claim that Ibsen's architectural imagination is itself essentially melancholic. We see that in the tendency of built structures to repeat and rigidly outlast their original functions, in the difficulties they have accommodating the changing needs of future inhabitants, and in their overwhelming inertia. (162)

Sandberg highlights Ibsen's reliance on architectural figures to convey the tension between structure and function, between inertia (or unmoving solidity) and the future. *The Master Builder* offers a particularly dizzying example of these tensions because it asks us to contemplate the proliferation of inertia, a seemingly radical denial of proper function in favor of empty structural re-creation. Because the main architectural spaces under consideration, in this case, are supposed to house offspring, a subtle version of reproductive futurism also arises here: a real future, a future that counts, would involve living babies and women capable of birthing and rearing them, rather than doll-mothers like Aline and impenetrable adolescent seductresses like Hilde.

The nurseries in *The Master Builder* make the relationship between reproduction, emptiness, and repetition explicit by depicting the reproduction of empty rooms rather than children, by housing Hilde the uncertain child, and by depicting Aline as a mother fit for burnt up dolls. In Act Two, Solness explains his wife's melancholy to Hilde by insisting that his success has deprived her of her own talent for building:

> Building up the souls of children so that they could rise in balanced and in noble, beautiful forms. So they could mature to be upright, adult human souls. This was what Aline had a talent for.—And all of it, it's lying there now. Unused—and unusable from here on out. (*BS* 60)

Solness's metaphor applies to mother-builders as well as children-buildings. According to the master builder, human life is architectural, and properly mothered children can serve as the foundation for adult life, which should rise up like the towers that fascinate Hilde and Solness (but in a more ethical, "upright" and "noble" sense). Of course, Aline is currently more fixated on dolls and duty than on the kind of motherhood that Solness describes. Robin Young suggest that this is because Aline "may always have been emotionally crippled by her own childhood," which would presumably make her unqualified for the building project that Solness describes (155). We cannot know whether Aline was "always" destined by be an unfit mother, but Solness's description of her calling certainly seems a bad fit for her current fixation. Aline's defunct architectural-maternal calling echoes in Solness's numerous empty rooms, but the child itself is also a figure for emptiness that is (imperfectly) fillable, a blankness that welcomes and resists inscription, a vacancy begging to be filled with anxiety and "depravity," a foundation on which to pile up anxious, normative stories about futures that will count (Kincaid, *Child Loving* 78). In the next section, I re-approach the problem of Hilde Wangel by exploring her embodiment of this child, her relationship to the variability and amorphousness of childhood, youth, and adolescence.

Ages

Another way in which *The Master Builder* tempts us to add things up is in terms of age. Hilde is sometimes very precise about dates and the passing of time, and then she allows precision to fall away when it is more useful to be vague and to round up. According to Hilde, her arrival at Solness's house marks the day on which his promise expires. Her time as his guest concludes ten years of waiting, a period of time that I have called a pedophilic decade inaugurated by the possible Lysanger kiss. Hilde refuses Solness's claims in Act One that he has forgotten the details of their first meeting and demands that he tell her the exact date: "Yes, on which day did you raise the wreath on the tower? Well? Say it right away!" (*BS* 36). Solness remembers that it took place ten years ago, sometime in the fall:

> HILDE (*nods her head slowly several times*)
> It was ten years ago. The nineteenth of September.
> SOLNESS   Oh yes, that seems right. Well, you remember that too, you do! (*stops*) But wait a moment—! Yes,—today is also the nineteenth of September.
> HILDE   Yes, it is. And the ten years are up. And you didn't come—as you had promised me. (36)

Hilde is right on time, not giving Solness the opportunity to be even a day late. According to Helland, this perfect timing provides evidence that Hilde is not serious, that she is play-acting rather than expressing a firmly held belief in Solness's promise: "Because, provided that she believed, fully and completely, that Solness was going to come and get her on the nineteenth of September, should she not have made sure to be home on that day?" (*Melankoliens spill* 68). Of course, when Solness asks Hilde in Act Three if she ever fancied anyone else, she insists that she did so only occasionally, out of frustration with his failure to arrive. This implies that she expected him earlier and was always waiting for his return. Whether or not Hilde tells the truth about her own memory and beliefs, the mix of precision and strategic uncertainty when it comes to her age is one aspect of her erotic innocence, at once attaching her to and estranging her from childhood.

The Master Builder puts a wide range of age categories in play, including not only childhood but also youth, old age, middle age, adolescence, and infancy. These various ages matter profoundly for Ibsen's broad interest in mastery and anxiety, reproduction and mortality, as well as for Hilde's characterization: who she appears to be, why she belongs in the nursery, and how she both invigorates and imperils Solness. Fuchs argues that *The Master Builder* is part of Ibsen's "three-play meditation on age, on what it means to cycle off the planet and be succeeded by new life" (73). The first drama in this end-of-life "meditation" (which includes *John Gabriel Borkman* and *When We Dead Awaken* but excludes *Little Eyolf*, a play that deploys age in other ways), *The Master Builder* offers an "almost parodic image of the decline and fall narrative" (Fuchs 74). The opening scenes emphasize fatigue and illness: members of Solness's staff and household suffer from old age and sickliness; Aline is

weak and melancholic; Solness himself appears powerful, but is paranoid and anxious. Joan Templeton observes that these scenes "establish
the unhappiness that makes Solness take Hilde for an immediate and
miraculous remedy for what ails him" (*Ibsen's Women* 264). Solness's
take, of course, is a mistake, which is why Templeton refers to Hilde's
entrance as a "*coup de théâtre*," writing, "Not since *Ghosts* has there
been such a sense of fatality in an Ibsen play. Hilde enters bringing Solness's death with her as though she were carrying it in her knapsack"
(266). In addition to its stark juxtaposition of youth and vitality (coming
up) and aging and morbidity (going down), *The Master Builder* indicates
that childhood can consist of many ages, can be put on or played as a
role, can last much longer than it "should," even unto death. Part of the
power of the child is located in its forms of persistence.

In Act One, Solness introduces the concept of "omslaget" (the turnabout), an inevitable usurpation or replacement process, whereby members of a younger generation, who are eager to leave childhood behind,
take the master's place. Somebody will make a claim, he tells Herdal,
demanding that Solness step back, "and then all the others will storm
in, threatening and screaming: make room,—make room,—make room!
Yes, you just wait and see, doctor. One day the young people will come
here and knock on the door" (*BS* 24). Herdal fails to see this as a threat
to Solness's position, but Solness insists that the arrival of youth will
entail his end. His pronouncement is followed by what Fuchs calls a
"corny but memorable moment": Ibsen's "famous knock knock joke: enter youth" (73). Although Hilde's knock causes Solness to jump or start,
he does not fear her or associate her with the eventual storming in of demanding youth. She certainly embodies youth, being only twenty-two or
twenty-three years old, but her particular relationship to the turnabout
is as of yet unclear. After Hilde asks to the spend the night and informs
Solness and the doctor that she has only the clothes on her back—plus
a very dirty pair of underclothes in her traveling pack—Herdal laughs
again and jokingly praises Solness's talent for prediction:

> Youth came and knocked on your door after
> all.
> SOLNESS (*enlivened*)
> Yes, but in a different way.
> DOCTOR HERDAL   You can be sure of that. Undeniably so! (*BS* 27)

This conversation splits the idea of youth into different types, with apparently different bearings on the situation at hand. Although Hilde
brings a version of turnabout with her, taking over the role of seducer,
both Herdal and Solness are convinced that her arrival as an embodiment of youth—the image of health and energy—are quite different
from the feared usurpation. The portent of youth is divided in this case

because of Hilde's sex, as it is perceived, welcomed, and enjoyed by the middle-aged men who greet her in Act One.

Youth proliferates across *The Master Builder* in the mode of opposition, or as Solness puts it after he confesses his fear of the turnabout to Hilde later in Act One: "youth against youth" (*BS* 41). Hilde is not just unlike the young men who pose a professional threat. She is also unlike Kaja, Solness's bookkeeper. Both Aarseth and Helland have commented on ways in which Hilde's entrance functions as an interruption of the "intrigue plot" of the opening scenes (Aarseth 248). Her arrival pulls the drama in new directions, yet also carries over major themes, including intergenerational, gendered power play—or the use of young women by older men to stave off the arrival of young and conquering men. Prior to Hilde's arrival, Herdal and Solness discuss Solness's manipulation of an old man (Brovik) and his son (Ragnar) through the employment and manipulation of a younger woman (Kaja, Ragnar's cousin and fiancée). The gender-age category of "young girl," as Kaja is described in the opening stage directions, is thus introduced as a controllable control mechanism (*BS* 5). Unlike Kaja, Hilde appears to promise revitalization while also posing a sexualized mortal threat. Hilde manages to turn the tables: "Solness had such a power [a Nietzschean *Wille zur Macht*] over Kaja and over Hilde as a child, but in the drama's present, spectators can observe that the roles are changed" (Aarseth 278). Thus, within the category of youth, *The Master Builder* makes use of the following oppositional binaries: male versus female, instrument versus threat, disempowered versus empowered, youth on the verge of growing up (taking on a profession or getting married) versus youth interested in recreating childish pleasures and perpetuating childish desires.

At the same time, youth is also constantly threatening to collapse back into itself, to reunite as a combined threat to the master builder. Toward the end of Act One, Hilde encourages Solness to let young people in, so that they can bring "the good" along with them (*BS* 41). Solness vehemently resists her suggestion, insisting that the youth who come "under a new banner," are a threat (*BS* 41). Hilde responds to Solness by asking him, her drawn mouth *"quivering"*: "Can you use *me* for something master builder?" (*BS* 41). Solness's vehement no becomes a yes, but he uses the same language to describe Hilde's arrival. This is the moment in which Solness announces the contest—youth against youth—but Hilde is also figuratively correlated with battle, coming "under a new banner" as well, although she gives Solness reason to believe she is fighting on his side (*BS* 41).

In Act Two, after Solness and Hilde discuss "vikingtrods" (the indomitability of Vikings) and Hilde's two-fold identity as bird-of-prey and captive—her desire to be the captured woman of a "man of violence," while remaining free from the cage of her family—Solness declares that he must have called to her "inwardly," precisely because she is youth: "You are youth, you are, Hilde" (*BS* 68–69):

HILDE (*smiling*)

The youth that you are so afraid of?

SOLNESS (*nods slowly*)

And that I am so sorely drawn to, at bottom (*BS* 69–70)

Like the child in Kincaid's formulation of child loving, youth in *The Master Builder* is very clearly "the embodiment of desire and also its negation," or, as Kincaid spells it out, "that which we are not but almost are, that which we yearn for so fiercely we almost resent it, that which we thought we saw in the mirror and almost wanted to possess yet feared we might" (Kincaid, *Child Loving* 5, 7). Solness's attraction to Hilde resembles "youth loving" in precisely this mode of simultaneous longing and fear, of (self)recognition and difference—across the adult/adolescent and male/female boundaries. Although it still takes some convincing, Solness finally acquiesces to Hilde's request that he acknowledge Ragnar's talent for building in writing. In his analysis of Hilde as a character who brings Nietzschean ideas into play, Helland writes, "For Solness to live up to Hilde's expectations, he should either neglect Ragnar as irrelevant, or welcome the struggle with him" (Helland, "Ibsen and Nietzsche" 55). Inspired by Hilde's insistence that she has never loved anyone but him and that she is still waiting for her kingdom, Solness calls Kaja into the parlor, hands her the inscribed plans, and fires both her and Ragnar.

In Act Three, it appears that Hilde has managed to clear the grounds for her castle, but she also functions as a conduit for a kind of youth that she is not, clearing the grounds for Ragnar to build. Hilde's description of Solness's second climb—"For now, now it is finished" (*BS* 103)—is given in the words of a "divine plan," yet indicates achievement of her "*private* fulfillment" (Helland, "Ibsen and Nietzsche" 70). Although Helland insists that Hilde does not "consciously" seek Solness's death, he argues that her "use of the Biblical expression," paired with her shawl-waving and loud hurrah, seems "to imply [...] that the risk that Solness will die is now worth chancing" (69). Hilde's insistence on her possession of Solness—that he "made it to the top" and is now "*My,—my* master builder!" (*BS* 24, 104)—is also paired with the less private fulfillment of Solness's original prediction regarding the storming in of youth. Both Ragnar and the "young people" with whom he has often discussed Solness's mythic first climb are on the scene, all believing that "no power in the world can get him to do it again" (*BS* 101, 92). These young people "storm into the garden" right after Solness falls, and Ragnar announces to Hilde that Solness "didn't actually make it" (*BS* 103). Thus, Hilde's seduction not only provides Ragnar with the acknowledgment that he needs to begin building on his own, but also removes Solness from the earthly scene of building altogether. When all is said and done, these two apparently distinct representatives of youth stand side-by-side. According to Helland, their opposed interpretations of Solness's climb represent "the two foundational interpretive paradigms of the drama itself," which are "registered in and ironically anticipated by the text" in the forms of Ragnar's and Hilde's spectatorship (*Melankoliens spill* 212). In addition to reading Hilde as the guarantor of the appearance of Solness's success (of his achieved, yet purposeless and terminal climb), one might read her as an unwitting facilitator of the turnabout, a role that would be proper to the woman-child, regardless of her perverse worldview. Hilde serves to make things "right" by removing a barrier for the next generation. Still, her particular version of youth is not defined by transition into adult life, but instead by ties to childhood and childish fixation on Solness's performance of mastery.

Hilde is referred to as a child five times in *The Master Builder*, not because she is currently a child, but because her relationship to childhood remains uncertain, then as now. The word *barn* (child) is also used in other contexts in the drama: as a diminutive applied to Ragnar and Kaja by old Brovik, in reference to the twin babies that died and the dolls that burnt up, to describe the consciences of Vikings, who returned from raids "happy as *barneunger*" (children) (*BS* 68), and as part of other compound words, *barnekammers* (nursery), *barnesjæl* (children's soul), and *barneflokken* (flock of children), the last of which symbolizes what makes a house a home. The diminutive "little" is also applied to both Kaja and Hilde. While Kaja accepts this term from Solness as an endearment, Hilde tells him that she did not like being called "little Hilde," even when she was twelve or thirteen (*BS* 6, 40). Twice, Solness states that Hilde was just a *barn* (child) when they met, a statement that she contradicts each time. In Act One, Hilde is in turn bemused and slightly offended when Solness appears not to remember her. When Herdal uses her last name, Solness realizes that she is the daughter of "the district physician up in Lysanger," whom he met "that summer" when he built the tower on the old church (*BS* 26).

> HILDE (*more seriously*)
>> It certainly was that time.
> SOLNESS   Well, that was a long time ago.
> HILDE (*looks at him unwaveringly*)
>> It is exactly ten years ago.
> SOLNESS   And at the time you were just a child, I imagine.
> HILDE (*casually*)
>> About twelve or thirteen anyway. (*BS* 26)

Hilde does not quite specify her age. She uses the word "ialfald" (anyway or at any rate) and the number thirteen to distance herself from Solness's assertion that she was a "just a child."

Whether or not Hilde was a child when she met Solness in Lysanger, she manages to re-inhabit the child in the present. After Solness suggests to his wife that Hilde should sleep in an empty nursery, he offers her the role of interim child in the home:

> We have no children. But now *you* can be the child for as long as you are here.
>
> HILDE
>
> For tonight, yes. I won't scream. I'll see if I can't sleep like a stone.
>
> SOLNESS
>
> Yes, you are undoubtedly very tired, I can imagine.
>
> HILDE
>
> No way! But just the same—. Because it's so intensely wonderful to just lie and dream. (*BS* 28)

It is significant that Solness offers Hilde the role of interim or replacement child before he remembers "what happened up there" in Lysanger, before he realizes that *she* was the little devil in white that made him dizzy, before she reminds him or convinces him that he (wanted to or should have) kissed her "many times" on that same day (*BS* 34). The Norwegian word "sålænge" (for as long as) suggests a vague period of time, or that Hilde can play the child for as long as she chooses to visit, but Hilde specifies that she will play the child for only one night. At the same time, she will not act like a baby or small child, because she will try to sleep soundly and not scream.

Before they return to the uncertainty of Hilde's childhood for the second time, Hilde manages to entice a confession from Solness. At first, he denies her claims that he bent her back and kissed her, but Hilde turns her back on him and remains silent and mostly still—with the exception of an impatient arm gesture—until he concedes to "everything [she] wants" (*BS* 35). "Now, you see," Hilde exclaims while turning back to face him, "I managed to coax it out of you in the end!" (*BS* 35). Hilde explains Solness's denial as an expression of shame, because "one doesn't forget that kind of thing" (*BS* 36). Solness tries to explain it by reframing it as a game meant to frighten a child rather than a seduction, but Hilde insists that she found nothing frightening in it. Solness responds:

> | | Well, or tease you a bit then! I don't remember it, god help me. But it must have been something like that, because you were just a child then. |
> |---|---|
> | HILDE | Oh, maybe I wasn't just a child after all. Not the little miss that *you* believe. (*BS* 37) |

Common sense tells Solness that his behavior toward Hilde must have been a joke, intended to frighten or tease her. What else could it have been, given that she was "just a child"? This time, Hilde resists the label more directly, although she qualifies her resistance with "maybe." She also indicates that her status as just a "little miss" ("tøsunge") is a matter of Solness's current belief rather than a fact related to her age at the time. Templeton describes Hilde's insistence on "her maturity at age twelve" as a sure sign of "arrested development": she "confuses sexuality with adulthood," and this confused form of sexuality—what Templeton calls Hilde's "abnormality"—involves not maturation, but rather profound naïveté and a desire to re-attach "herself to another older man" after leaving her father's home behind (Templeton 268).

Hilde's status as the improper occupant of an empty nursery and her future plans to occupy a castle in the air clearly locate her in closer proximity to childhood than to youth on the cusp of adulthood. The most precise age-label for Hilde—although the label is not, in and of itself, precise—is probably adolescent. When Solness asks her if she slept well in Act Two, Hilde responds,

> Marvelously well! Like in a cradle. Oh,—I lay
> there and stretched myself like—like a princess!
> SOLNESS (*smiles slightly*)
> Truly a good fit then.
> HILDE   I should think so. (*BS* 48)

Hilde remembers a comfortable night, in which she slept as if in a cradle. She remembers stretching, and she stretches herself from baby to princess, agreeing with Solness that the empty nursery was truly suited to her metamorphosis.

Ibsen does not call adolescence by a unique name in *The Master Builder*, although *ungdom* (youth) can suggest something similar in Norwegian.[9] Adolescence, the age that "'came of age' in the decades around 1900" according to John Neubauer, has been interchangeably conceived as a necessary period of delay between childhood (innocence) and adulthood (experience) and as a period of struggle with the perversions and wickedness of childhood, an age lacking in innocence in this latter conception. In *The Fin-de-siècle Culture of Adolescence* (1995), Neubauer defines adolescence broadly as an age that

> stretches from the onset of puberty until the time that the individual
> is sexually mature and reasonably integrated into adult society [...]
> It covers, roughly, the years from twelve or thirteen to eighteen or
> twenty [...] Whereas puberty depends on physiological changes [...] ad-
> olescence knows no physical determinants and depends on the way so-
> cieties structure their families, education, and institutions of labor. (6)

Hilde is probably too old to be defined as an adolescent by means of her proximity to puberty, although this was not the case ten years ago, when she first met the master builder. She is definitely not located in the later phase of adolescence, where individuals are "assuming or working towards professional and familial responsibilities" (Neubauer 6). In any case, adolescence is an age category defined by in-between-ness, being too childish to be adult (still a princess) and too adult to be childish (no longer a little girl).

In *Child Loving*, Kincaid discusses the discordant, shifting, and multiplying status of childhood during the Victorian era, when experts in the English context named categories such as adolescence, infancy, childhood, boyhood, and girlhood in dis-alignment with legal ages concerning crime and punishment (68–69). Disagreeing with those who insist that "the separateness of childhood was axiomatic in Victorian ideology," Kincaid tells us that these categories appear in many ways to have been even less robust and certain than they are today, puberty representing no "chasm" between two species (child and adult) (Spilka qtd. in Kincaid and Kincaid 63). Concerning adolescence, which has perhaps become the chasm itself in our times, Kincaid writes, "Virtually all writers [...] recognize [adolescence] as a social institution that has, once manufactured, given us more trouble than Hyde gave to Jekyll" (69).[10] Although he had been arguing for the amorphousness—indeed, the expansive nothingness—of "the child," Kincaid has to admit that it is actually "under somewhat better control" than adolescence (69). This is due not to childhood's greater definitional specificity, but rather to its possible/sometime association with innocence, passivity, and non-sexuality, whereas adolescence is "a 'stage' designed to encourage and thus contain a medley of rebellious, unproductively selfish, nominally revolutionary, and uncontrollably erotic feelings" (Kincaid, *Child Loving* 59). Hilde is certainly "rebellious," "selfish," "erotic," and "amorphous," and her adolescence is also "inconveniently lengthy"—lasting a decade and longer (Kincaid, *Child Loving* 59).

In Hilde's case, adolescence is not enabled by an official "moratorium," a period of time in a context that isolates and privileges the unique development of the pubescent and immediately post-pubescent person and her cohort (such as secondary school), but instead by Hilde's always uncertain and playful attachment to childhood (Neubauer 7, 76, 80). In all of the empty nursery plays, Ibsen manages to freeze the proper occupant (the child). In *Hedda Gabler* and *Little Eyolf*, he prevents the child from growing up and exceeding its age category by killing it—thereby leaving the remains of its significance under the surface or in the depths of interiority. He also mobilizes yet defers improper occupants, making their occupation a matter of future plans. Unlike the endless books and poor fosterlings of these dramas, the improper occupant of *The Master Builder* has grown up (in terms of years) and left behind the "cage" of her childhood home (*BS* 86). She also manages to bring about and survive the death of the master. In this way, Ibsen makes it clear that the empty nursery is a space for housing desire that cannot contain desire, or prevent it—and its desired object: childish youth, the supposed sign of futures to come—from spilling over into other spaces in the house. Hilde does not remain in the middle nursery. Having occupied it between Acts One and Two, she is already in the process of imagining new rooms and new spaces to occupy.

At the turn of the century, psychologists and authors who depicted adolescent characters described or worried over their access to a room of their own—not a nursery for all the little children, but a private space free of siblings and nannies, in which one could "daydream" and fantasize (Neubauer 67). Such a space was, "of course, a luxury of the affluent," and it contained dangers of its own: privacy + fantasy = masturbation, which is why some considered "adolescent solitude dangerous" (Neubauer 67–68). Adolescent rooms, like adolescence itself, were supposed to lack "utility and rationality" (Neubauer 69). If the nursery confirms Hilde's attachment to childhood, the dream of a tower room confirms her adolescence, as well as a fantasy of never-to-be-fulfilled sexual availability. Hilde's adolescence allows Ibsen to dwell in the irrationalism and anti-utilitarianism of the "aesthetic," in egoism rather than altruism, in endless play rather than maturation. Scholars have located Hilde in an "autoerotic" stage, in a mental room of her own, which does not open itself to proper sexual development (Weigand qtd. in Templeton 365)—although Hilde and Solness fantasize about his visits:

> SOLNESS (*softly*)
>> Will the master builder be allowed to come up to the princess?
> HILDE   If the master builder *wants*.
> SOLNESS (*more slowly*)
>> Then I think the master builder will come.
> HILDE (*nods*)
>> The master builder, he will come. (*BS* 88)

Ibsen also uses Hilde to draw out the adolescent characteristics in Solness, which are perverse and destructive, as well as imaginative and dismissive of boring and deadening ideas like duty, responsibility, and guilt. In the next and final section of this chapter, I turn from ages and rooms to a late twentieth-century rhetorical locating of power in the pedophilic itself, a move that appears to be motivated, in part, by implicit fear of the molested girl's impenetrability.

Pedophilic (Dis)empowerment

Hilde's location between the occupation of an empty nursery and the dream of taking up residence in the terribly high tower of a castle in the sky is an allegory for erotic innocence, the almost kingdom that precedes fulfillment. She is (or plays the role of) a once and future princess, once promised a kingdom, still promised a kingdom. As stated in the introduction to this book, I am interested in drawing attention to the ways in which we continue to use Ibsen to reproduce ideologies of childhood innocence, gender, and the family during the decades surrounding our own turn of the century. Thus, I conclude this chapter by engaging with two familiar ways of understanding erotic innocence in some scholarly interpretations of Hilde: first, the paradox of child loving, in which the child is understood to be asexual or latent—an erotically "safe" or neutralized figure—yet childhood still manages to represent the most dangerous, all-encompassing, and potentially damaging phase of life when it comes to exposure to sexual ideas and experiences; and second, the threat that intergenerational desire is understood to embody due to its departure from a normative chronology, in which sexual maturity means a penetrability that can lead to procreation, that is, to a meaningful future.

My aim is not to correct the interpretations that I analyze, but to highlight how the child in Ibsen studies is often "a product of ways of perceiving, not something that is *there*": "Adolescents are stuffed back into childhood when it serves our purposes, as it often does when we are talking about molestation or crime [...] The child is functional, a malleable part of our discourse rather than a fixed stage" (Kincaid, *Erotic Innocence* 19). The thinkers considered here wield the child deftly, in all its empty flexibility. They do not always bring the child under explicit critique, so it remains as if self-evident, even as it slips and slides into territories supposedly improper to it. By bringing the child under more explicit critique, I would like, in particular, to gain some critical distance from anti-pedophilic descriptions that preserve the exceptional status and power of the pedophilic, while offering no way out of the conceptualization of childhood as fragile foundation.

Durbach (1982) calls Hilde from ten years ago a "nubile adolescent" who is "thrilled" to have her "first sexual experience," but he also suggests that her encounter with Solness was pre-sexual, involving as it did a person who was not yet "sexually eligible" (128). Of course, this notion of pre-sexuality or latency is the first part of the paradox of erotic innocence. Sooner rather than later, latency slides into more dangerous territory, in this case by persisting when it should not. Although Durbach insists that "kissing a thirteen-year-old 'dævelunge'—a devil child—is sexually quite safe, in a way that kissing a sexually eligible adult devil is not," perversion arises anyway, because the avoidance of "commitment or fulfilment" is preserved in, and by means of, this safety (131–132). Hilde was a safely improper object, "protected by social mores from violation" (which seems to imply that Solness, and most people, are not social deviants who would have intercourse with a thirteen-year-old girl), but the character of her relationship to Solness in the present is yet another symptom of his failure to engage life properly (131). Durbach's interpretation of the possible Lysanger kiss suits an understanding of this relationship as pedophilic in the "playful" sense that Kincaid describes, as a game of impossibility that Solness chooses to play because he cannot fulfill the needs and purposes of an adult life, building a home for his wife or enabling her to fulfill what he believes to be her calling as a builder of "the souls of small children" (*BS* 60).

Durbach's concept of safety is clearly paradoxical, combining absurdity with danger in the end. In "the final analysis," Durbach writes, "ideal, prelapsarian sexuality [...] makes Romantic nonsense of human consummations": "To put it crudely: time, turned ten years back, has the effect of relocating Paradise in the nursery" (132–133). While the "asexual erotic" couple of *The Master Builder* talks idealizing childish nonsense, sensical "human consummations" would be imperfect and fallen, but also properly sexual as opposed to being childishly, and therefore perversely, erotic. Durbach does not consider Hilde's insistence on the uncertainty of her having been a child. There is no seductive, spell-casting girl, no explicit nymphette in his analysis (beyond the descriptor nubile). His definition of the sexual also appears to rely, implicitly, on the union of sex and intercourse, penetration and reproductive possibilities, adulthood and romantic risks worth taking for the payoff of familial fulfillment. Durbach's insistence on this payoff is aligned with Solness's own melancholic assessment of "what he had to give up" for professional success: "a home for a flock of children. And for a father and mother too" (*BS* 59).

In *Ibsen: the Dramaturgy of Fear* (1999), Michael Goldman categorizes the possible Lysanger kiss as an explicit example of molestation and makes a strange attempt to historicize—impossibly, he himself insists—Ibsen's depictions of child abuse. Like Young, Goldman applies the identity category of the "wounded child" not just to children but to any character or person who has ever been a child (Goldman 70). He finds this category to be central both to Ibsen's oeuvre and to the nineteenth century's self-awareness, generally speaking. Goldman expresses some hesitation concerning whether this awareness emerged as a diagnosis of social problems, as the result of industrialization, or simply as a core aspect of identity—did the nineteenth century "perhaps simply [discover abuse] in its heart"? (Goldman 71). Regardless of its origins, Goldman insists that the double bind of this awareness emerges from the "cruel undecidability inherent in the crime" (71). In real life as in *The Master Builder*, we cannot know for sure what/whether child abuse happened, which renders abuse a fantasy-riddled trap that ultimately makes the attempt to historicize impossible (presumably because the conclusion concerning "what really happened" has to be drawn by an adult who cannot, can no longer, or does not want to know what really happened).

Goldman claims that the undecidability of abuse means, in the end, that "the history of child abuse can never be written," which seems to suggest that thinkable subjects for history (indeed, written histories?) are not "inscribed in fantasy, in the intertwined fantasies of victim, abuser, and observer" (and reader?) (71). These claims appear to grant both child abuse and history exceptional and exceptionally opposed statuses founded on the fantasy/reality binary. While child abuse is impenetrably fantastic, history relies on observers and readers (not victims and perpetrators) who are sufficiently free from the grip of fantasy to decide "what really happened."

Despite the uncertainty that Goldman expresses concerning the origins of the nineteenth-century awareness of child abuse, he is very certain of its effects: "The radical damage of child molestation goes far beyond the physical damage, which may indeed be nonexistent. It takes place in the determining mental life of the child, in the imagination, or rather at the base of the imagination" (71). Trauma does not just happen to the child, doing damage to the very base of its imagination, it also constitutes our life of the mind in post-childhood: "it is on such foundational traumas to the imagination that the mental life of the adult is built" (Goldman 71). If the undecidability of the crime of child abuse is a trap, this formulation of its effects is also radically determining, suggesting that trauma is both inevitable and essential to the construction of adult "mental life" because it "is" the foundation. In his reading of the possible Lysanger kiss, Goldman implies that the crime of child abuse is such a dangerous thing to imagine and desire that *it does not matter whether it actually happened*:

> The question is unanswerable: Did Halvard Solness pause on his upwardly mobile track to commercial success to crush an impressionable thirteen year-old girl to his body and kiss her on her lips, or was there simply a moment when, simultaneously, she imagined it and he desired it? We never know, we *can* never know, but it destroys them both. (72)

Note the temporality of Goldman's description: the encounter is described as a "pause," a hiatus or deviation from Solness's rising to "commercial success." Whether committed or longed for, the imagined and possible-but-uncertain break in upward progress was so harmful that the "crushed" girl, who is thirteen in this account, and the "crushing" man (or the man who simply wanted to "crush" the girl) both become victims of their "simultaneous" imagining and desiring. They are not just damaged, they are "destroyed."

Goldman's fervor, which is clearly anti-pedophilic, makes the first encounter between Solness and Hilde appear more salacious in criticism than it does in the drama, or at least than it does in Hilde's description of what happened after the first climb:

> HILDE (*looks at him steadily*)
>   You took and kissed me, master builder Solness.
> SOLNESS (*with an open mouth, rises up from his chair*)
>   I did!
> HILDE   Uh huh, you did. You took me in both arms and bent me over backwards, and kissed me. Many times. (*BS* 34)

Although one might just as well imagine—if one dares to "pause" to imagine such a thing—Solness dipping Hilde gently backward and dangling her like a dance partner, Goldman imagines Solness crushing an "impressionable" Hilde "to his body" (72). Goldman's use of the verb "crush" suits his interest in emphasizing destruction, given that crushing is suggestive of compression and defeat. One might like to be able to stick with Hilde's less detailed and more matter-of-fact description of the event, but Goldman's understanding of the foundational force of child abuse, of its crushing end to development and permanent radical uncertainty, appears to depend on Hilde's status as having been a child in the sense of being disempowered or unable to consent; and if she was unable to consent, then we cannot take her at her word. We have to know better than the once-and-future wounded child, a person destroyed rather than sustained or conserved into adulthood. Of course, if Goldman's concept of childhood trauma as foundation is fully operational, then Solness is also a once-and-future wounded child, which means that the ultimate power in this encounter is found not in persons but in the endless cycle of child abuse—in a pedophilic kiss, whether it happened or was simply "imagined or desired" (Goldman 72). I am not sure that *The Master Builder* locates such radical power in the Lysanger kiss, or that it expresses awareness of this kiss as a clear instance of abuse, even if it is profoundly interested in Hilde's suspended state of and for desire.

I resist not only this insistence on the power of the pedophilic but also the subtext that locates another form of destructive power in impenetrability. This subtext implies that erotic innocence, due to its out-of-joint relationship with time, can never be cured by normative sexual maturity: the molested and arrested girl = a dangerously impenetrable girl. Goldman's insistence on Solness and Hilde's destruction, on their having been crushed, whether physically or mentally, suggests a permanent and mutual sealing off, which Young also emphasizes in *Time's Disinherited Children* (1989): "Psychologically, and in terms of the play's patterns of imagery, the moment at which Solness kisses her has sealed off an image of them both in Hilde's mind, as impenetrably as the forest of thorns seals off Thornrose from the world of men" (159). I have argued that Hilde's decade of waiting represents a form of child loving as suspension in the early, uncertain years of adolescence. Young's allusion to Sleeping Beauty suggests that the cure for this suspension would involve a breaking open of fantasy performed by a figure from "the world of men," that is, a man who could penetrate Hilde's mental "forest of thorns." (But aren't we still inside fantasy, even when this penetrating man arrives, given that the fairy tale allegorizes successful penetration?) As Aarseth notes, it is Hilde who masters the master in the end; but Young insists that her eventual possession of Solness, her insistence that he is *her* master builder, is not "triumphant erotic passion (she has never possessed him in that sense)" (160). Possession is presumably a euphemism for sexual penetration here, without which there is only "the satisfaction of a childish imagination" (150). Young's interpretation of Hilde is a prime example of the simultaneous horror and preservation of the paradox of erotic innocence, given that innocence is supposed to prevent the erotic from taking place, yet also sustains it as a negative future anterior or what will *not* have been.[11]

For Young, it is Hilde's particular formation, her having been made impenetrable, that ultimately serves to break open the "sealed ritualized world of the Solness marriage, for which time has stopped with the death of the children" (161). He reads Hilde's function in Solness's fate as "an ironic reversal of roles," by means of which the past secures the future by permanently decimating it, or by interrupting the status quo, which means "[restoring] the marriage to truth and time"—but "only by destroying it" (Young 161). Like Durbach, then—and although Young uses the term erotic to mean sexual, rather than opposing the erotic to the sexual—Young reserves the sexual for the adult world, while also locating danger in the persistence of innocent or non-adult sexuality (which is not *really* sexuality). Although all of the main characters in *The Master Builder* fail "to live in time and fulfil [their] potential" according to Young, Hilde manages to break "down the doors of time" precisely because she is "a child who refuses to grow up," an "adolescent" who equates "sexual fulfillment with death" (155). "As everyone knows," what makes time keep moving is children; and the only thing that can put a stop to childless persistence—a living on that denies "life, time, development" (Young 155)—is the childish adolescent, who is deployed as the simultaneous embodiment and mode of condemnation of "the fatal lure of sterile, narcissistic enjoyments" (Edelman, *No Future* 13). Hilde is both the seducer and the victim, a doubled example of the dangers of intergenerational desire.

As I have suggested, interpretations of Hilde as a youthful seductress—"youth's amoral and ruthless representative," who finally gets her way, a suspended nymphette who turns the tables on the master builder (Aarseth 269)—are probably less anachronistic than interpretations of her as nothing more than the deadly fruit of victimhood, taking revenge without obtaining a truly vital form of retribution. A third interpretation of Hilde's power involves her advocacy of Nietzschean will, or her message about "an uncompromising joy in life" (Aarseth 270). Hilde wants Solness "to be capable of acting freely in the radical sense," with a creative, vital conscience (Helland, "Ibsen and Nietzsche" 60). He should be like a child himself, embodying the "special form of innocence" that Zarathustra demands in the final spiritual transformation from "lion to lamb" (61). Hilde clearly wants Solness to be able "to say yes to himself," but I would stress that she herself has no "special capacity for active forgetfulness" (63). Although I do not pursue this third interpretation of Hilde at length here, I wonder whether it can account either for sexual difference or erotic innocence, for Hilde's desire "to be captured" by a "man of violence" as well as to take the "prey" that she desires (*BS* 68–69). I am not sure that any of these readings of Hilde's (dis)empowerment can satisfy desires for a more queerly feminist future. Hilde herself questions Solness's fixation on the loss of all chances for happiness: "But can't that maybe still be put to rights?" (*BS* 59). Perhaps this question could be posed to our own fixations on Hilde's devilry and/or ruination, but not if answers cannot tolerate her status as a nursery dweller and seductive adolescent, who conquers by being conquered, and who makes the way for youth by refusing to forget the past.

The next chapter focuses on *Little Eyolf*, the third and final empty nursery play, which includes a child in its character list. At the end of Act One, the one-and-only son, Eyolf, drowns. He remains absent and inaccessible in the acts that follow, but nonetheless serves as the pivot around which dreams of "making good" (Rose) will continue to turn, including the charitable project of refilling his rooms with the poor children who live by the shore. As the drama ends, Eyolf's parents propose a future of children's rooms filled to the brim with (almost) proper occupants. Many critics read this conclusion as redemptive, opening to a future of potential healing for the bereaved, who seek to go and look up, in search of more ethical modes of being. I explore the drama's suggestions of inversion (wherein going up can mean going down) and the alternative trajectories of lost boys through its landscape, opening a more varied understanding of Ibsen's dramatization of lost innocence.

Notes

1 In *Ibsen's Houses*, Mark Sandberg works through Halvard Solness's "complicated housing history," emphasizing the significance of "composite," "mixed," or "hybrid" styles or characteristics (158–159). He acknowledges that Ibsen's builders, perhaps the master builder most explicitly, are stuck

between a rock and a hard place: while the "combination of new and old never bodes well in Ibsen's architectural world," the dramas also acknowledge that "building one's own structure on someone else's leftover foundation" is "the actual position of every person born into the world" (158–159).

2 Aarseth refers to several critics invested in exploring Ibsen's engagement with and critique of Nietzschean ideals, including Harald Beyer, A. H. Winsnes, Michael W. Kaufman, and Theoharis C. Theoharis. See also Frode Helland's "Ibsen and Nietzsche," which I discuss briefly in this chapter.

3 See, for example, Lydia Kokkola's *Fictions of Adolescent Carnality: Sexy Sinners and Delinquent Deviants* (John Benjamins Pub. Co., 2013) for a discussion of contemporary representations of the relationship between adolescence and sexuality.

4 Voronina aims to intervene in the standard treatment of Nabokov's *Lolita* as a product of the American 1950s, reinterpreting it "as Nabokov's commentary on the Victorian ideas of beauty, artistic inspiration, and child sexuality" (148). She implies that *Lolita* represents an early attempt at ethical evaluation of pedophilia, asking whether

> Nabokov, aware of the existence of this archetype [pretty little girls … as victims of sexual preying or as underage seductresses] as well as of its peculiar Victorian features, created his nymphet in order to revive, relive, and bring to a close the Humbertian discourse that no one before him cared to judge ethically, rather than from an aesthetic point of view. (148)

Voronina claims that the intertextual implications of Humbert Humbert's persona as literary critic have been overlooked in scholarship reluctant to "[conduct research] from the point of view of the author and not of the narrator" (149).

5 Aarseth emphasizes the fact that Hilde's name is a "homonym for a verb that can mean to get one's power, to capture, lure, fool," which Ibsen uses in a variety of dramas (256).

6 See Sandberg's *Ibsen's Houses* for in-depth consideration of the tensions between house and home in Ibsen's contemporary dramas.

7 Hilde assumes that three rooms mean a lot of children, but it is possible that she is unaware of the practices of child-rearing and living arrangements for servant girls. Nannies often slept in the same room with the children, and turn of the century handbooks for mothers and nannies suggest that multiple rooms were ideal, if financially feasible, so that offspring could be moved into another room when cleaning, airing, and setting the fire took place, so that they would not be subject to too much cold, damp, or poor air quality. In *The Lady from the Sea*, Hilde's proper naïveté is expressed when a teenage version of her character suggests that her sensibilities are offended when Lyngstrand mentions that he is renting a room at the midwife's house.

8 Aline adds "so you say" to the end of this comment, expressing doubt concerning both Solness's claims and the significance of long-term acquaintance for Solness's current familiarity with Hilde (*BS* 50).

9 Ibsen was certainly aware of puberty and of adolescence as a phase of life distinct from, or taking place between, childhood and adulthood. In *The Wild Duck*, Dr. Relling warns Hjalmar Ekdal and Gina that Hedvig (who is fourteen years old) is in "a difficult age," that she is experiencing "stemmeskiftningen" (the change of voice) (86). In *The Lady from the Sea*, we also meet Hilde as a morbid teenager with what might be regarded as particularly adolescent fantasies about love and death.

10 Kincaid supports his claim that almost "all writers recognize [adolescence] as a social institution" by inserting the phrase "not just [Philippe] Ariès" (69). In a footnote, he cites Ariès's *Centuries of Childhood* and "Thoughts on the History of Homosexuality," as well as Deborah Gorham's *The Victorian Girl and the Feminine Ideal* and Stevi Jackson's *Childhood and Sexuality* (1982).

11 See Bruhm and Hurley's discussion of the future anterior temporality of queer childhood in "Curiouser: On the Queerness of Children" in *Curiouser*.

3 A Dead Child Cannot Look Back

Lost Boys in *Little Eyolf*[1]

Ibsen's antepenultimate play, *Lille Eyolf* (*Little Eyolf*) (1894), presents readers with at least two orders of lost boys: the lame and drowned son, lured to the depths by the Ratmaid, and "all the naughty boys who will take his place" (*LE* 76).[2] In Act One, Alfred Allmers tries to explain a recent change in plans to his wife, Rita, and younger half-sister, Asta. He will abandon his book project on "Human Responsibility" in favor of a boy project (*LE* 19). That is, he will be a better father to his son so that Eyolf can fulfill the expectations of the family line. The Ratmaid, a pied-piper/werewolf figure who travels the surrounding countryside offering exterminating services, arrives on the scene in Act One, momentarily interrupting Allmers's explanations. Her brief visit appears to constitute a fantastic interlude in the otherwise realistic play. Allmers and Rita insist that they are not plagued by anything that "gnaws and nibbles,— and creeps and crawls," and the Ratmaid soon exits (*LE* 16). Shortly thereafter, Eyolf too exits, unnoticed by the adults in the room. As the act comes to a close, we realize that he wandered down to the water's edge and drowned. Eyolf's death puts an end to Allmers's replacement project—boy for book—but it also serves to open the past. *Little Eyolf* is a "begivenhetsfattig drama" (drama lacking in events) (Aarseth 294). Its second and third acts consist almost entirely of retrospective, revelatory dialogue, enabled by "the subtle [and not to subtle] permissiveness of sorrow" (Goldman 96, my addition). Perhaps most significantly, we discover the primary source of blame, guilt, and heartache in the Allmers marriage: Eyolf was permanently disabled as an infant, when he was left alone and fell from a table while his parents were having sex.

Little Eyolf closes with Rita's own plans for a replacement project. She imagines a new identity for herself in an attempt to come to terms with her grief: philanthropic foster mother. Allmers has decided that they should part ways, and he asks Rita to tear down all the shacks by the waterfront, where the boys who failed to save Eyolf live—although they know how to swim. He conceives of this demolition project as a parting gift to his wife, a mission to fill Rita's life after both son and husband are gone. Rita, however, has another mission in mind. She tells Allmers, "(*slowly and decisively*) As soon as you have left me, I'm going down to the shore to bring all those poor, mistreated children back up with me into this house" (*LE* 76). The poor children will take up residence in Eyolf's empty "stuer" (rooms or parlors) (*LE* 77), and this occupation will, according to Rita, fill the empty space that Allmers has created inside her with something "that could resemble a kind of love," in a charitable future of potential healing (*LE* 77). Although Allmers questions Rita's capabilities and motives at first, he shortly decides to join her, hoping that they will receive "visitation of the spirits [...] above" (*LE* 79).

In *Ibsens Samtidsskuespill* (*Ibsen's Contemporary Plays*) (1999), Asbjørn Aarseth reviews examples from the long tradition of pessimistic readings of *Little Eyolf*'s conclusion. The driving question in this scholarship, according to Aarseth, is not whether or not Rita will complete the project in some future that exceeds the play, but whether or not the ending and character development is believable, whether or not she and Allmers are deemed capable of true compassion and dedication (281). He finds that pessimistic readings are based on "the effect of irony," often attributed to Ibsen's intentions, and on unfavorable judgment of the characters, rather than on textual evidence (Aarseth 290). I disagree with the claim that there is insufficient textual evidence for suspicious readings of *Little Eyolf*'s conclusion. After all, the drama establishes a clear pattern of incomplete projects and replacement. Nonetheless, this chapter neither faults *Little Eyolf* for its failure to sustain dramatic illusion, nor doubts Rita and Allmers's compassion, nor reproves them for inauthentic grief. Rather than dwelling in "the impression of self-deception and bad faith" alone, it adds to the pessimistic tradition by reconsidering the significance of class and fantasy in the drama, and by following the distinct trajectories of lost boys through its landscape (Young 179).

As well as constituting a fantastic break with the realistic world, the entrance of the Ratmaid is a link to the landscapes and people that surround the upper-class estate. While the heights of this estate continue to offer a place where endeavors to restart life's projects, fantasies of unending love, and dreams of charitable replacement and redemption are possible, the territories navigated by the Ratmaid suggest different lived modes of existences, as well as offering routes of escape. I argue that the plan to refill Eyolf's rooms breaks neither with the upper-class privilege and isolation that characterizes the Allmers marriage and estate, nor with habits of looking away from a child in favor of idealizing the innocent potential of the child.

The concept of innocence has been thoroughly critiqued in children's literature and queer and critical child studies. In her analysis of *Peter Pan*'s afterlives, for example, Jacqueline Rose calls innocence a fantasy of "origins" that expresses faith in an "ultimate beginning where everything is perfect or can at least be made good" (Rose 138). Despite such critiques, innocence remains (as if) intact in many places, including late twentieth- and early twenty-first-century readings of *Little Eyolf*. As my use of the phrase "lost boys" suggests, *Peter Pan* (1928) and *Peter and Wendy* (1911) are principal inspirations for this chapter's approach to Ibsen's drama, its child, its replacement projects, and its treatment in criticism, not only because J. M. Barrie's play and novel provide an exceptional figure for child studies (a boy who neither dies nor grows up, a boy who is innocent in a non-sentimental way) but also because Ibsen, like Barrie, "empties the nursery" (Gilead 286).[3] Although Ibsen does not return a child once taken away, his characters make plans to fill the nursery up, offering that child's rooms to other occupants. The fantasy island on which Peter lives is sometimes called Neverland, sometimes the Never Land, and other times Never Never Land. The doubling of never represents both death as an absolute limit to life and the refusal of this limit that Peter embodies as a boy who is not dead but does not really live. Rita's replacement project is also a refusal of this limit, in the more normative sense of understanding children as interchangeable representatives of the future. *Little Eyolf* makes explicit use of the recuperative motif of emptying and refilling a child's rooms, thereby associating reproduction and the future with substitution and replacement. Its retrospective structure and distinct orders of lost boys—the dead son, the sister who once played at being a brother (Asta), and the "naughty boys"—undermine the notion of ultimate beginnings, showing that innocence is propped up by loss and always involves repetition.

Verticality and Inversion, or Going Nowhere

Several claims in this chapter emerge from a reading of the landscape of *Little Eyolf,* and of characters' actual or imagined movements through it.[4] The explicit arrangement of the drama is vertical: the landscape rises from the fjord to the mountain heights, and the characters go down to the shore and climb back up under the course of action. They also aim to choose higher duties as the weight of responsibility sinks deeper. Allmers and Rita might associate ethical and existential forms of progress with an upward trajectory, but I will show that up and down, development and retreat, surfacing and drowning, are unstable categories in *Little Eyolf.* Its landscape is not only constructed along a vertical configuration of familial attachment (below) and aesthetic or pleasurable detachment (above) but also by means of class differences and by the movement patterns of minor characters. I acknowledge these alternatives in an attempt to open up a varied understanding of the structure and movement of the play—not just vertical but also inverted, horizontal, and orbital-recuperative (round and round and/or back and forth)—which is essential for defining the difference between Allmers and Rita and the lost boys.

The central landscape feature of *Little Eyolf* is the Allmers estate, a large house surrounded by gardens and grounds stretching from the edge of the fjord up to "forest-covered hills in the distance" (*LE* 5). In Act

One, the staged or visible-to-the-audience space of the house is a "richly decorated garden room" with glass doors leading out to a veranda (5). The waterfront includes a wharf, mentioned several times throughout the play, that is visible to the characters from the doorway of the garden room. The waterfront also includes a private location near the shore, described in the stage directions for Act Two: "A small, narrow valley" surrounded by trees, with a stream, path, and boathouse (*LE* 34). Act Three takes place in an "overgrown highpoint in the garden," from which the fjord is distantly visible, with a plunging, fenced-off cliff and stairs leading down to the left (*LE* 60). Finally, the broader world of *Little Eyolf* includes the mountain heights to the east where Allmers went walking; the waterways and roads that lead south; the mountain heights in the north that will soon be conquered by Asta's suitor, road engineer Borghejm; the until-recently-rat-infested islands in the fjord; a general idea of surrounding country, around which the Ratmaid travels; and the horizontal stretches of the North Sea, down and out to the west.

The landscape of *Little Eyolf*, in its physical and psychological manifestations, suggests a seaside-to-heights setting and a vertical (counter) idealism common to several of Ibsen's works, in which characters search for ever-higher ground and an ever-higher calling, but are frequently brought down to the ground by chance/fate, temperament/habit, or avalanche. In "National Language and International Drama," Inga-Stina Ewbank argues that the "geography of the mind" found in Ibsen's breakthrough verse play, *Brand* (1865), serves as the model for all of the plays that follow (63):

> The sense of an actual vertical landscape—of peaks to which the characters aspire and depths which they wish, or dread, to penetrate—forms the deep structure of the prose plays. It spills over, not only into metaphors, explicit or submerged, but also into the verbs and adverbs of the dialogue, as characters act, think and feel in terms of 'up' and 'down.' (64)[5]

At the end of *Little Eyolf*, Rita imagines that she will go down in order to take the poor children *up* from the water's edge. When Allmers questions her motives and suggests that she isn't suited to such a task, she says that she will "opdrage" (raise or rear) herself, through *oplæring* (education) and *opøving* (training) (*LE* 77). Finally, Allmers expresses hope that they will receive glimpses of loved ones "opad" (above or upward) (79). Note the repeated use of the prefix *op* (up), of which these examples do not comprise an exhaustive list.

Significantly, as Ewbank suggests, downward movements and attractions counter-balance the drama's references to finding and/or letting go of one's self (vocation and identity) and others (lost loved ones) by going or looking up. Allmers himself identifies his desire to return to the

heights with the lure of the depths. In Act One, he says that he understands the Ratmaid's explanation for why the rats *"must"* follow her to
their (sweet) death in the fjord: "Just because they don't *want* to": "Actually, I can understand the compelling and luring power that she talked
about. The loneliness up among the treetops and on the great mountain
plateaus has something similar to it" (*LE* 15, 17). Allmers's admission
of sympathy for the rats also makes it clear that the aspirational peaks
are not radically different from the dreaded depths in *Little Eyolf.* The
landscape of Ibsen's antepenultimate play is inverted in two principal
ways: first, through Allmers's suggestion that a person can drown on the
heights, and second, through Rita's replacement project, where going up
also means taking the place of the only (drowned) son. Both inversions
involve combinations of external (setting) and metaphoric features and
suggest that going up/down might actually mean going back and forth
or represent a failure to advance.

   The first act of *Little Eyolf* stages a homecoming that appears to be
provisional, taking place in a moment of suspension or shuttling between unfinished projects. When Allmers enters the stage for the first
time, Asta asks him about his book manuscript, and he is forced to confess that he has not written a single line. Rita, who has been unpacking
his bag, exclaims, "Of course! I couldn't understand why all the paper
in your suitcase was untouched" (*LE* 8). Allmers's startling announce-
ments from the first half of Act One—that he will give up the book, that
writing does not matter—are further explained in the second half of the
act, when we hear in some detail about his new paternal mission in life.
Discussion of this mission leads to Rita's own scandalous admission of
profoundly ambivalent feelings toward anything that prevents complete
possession of her husband, including the book, her sister-in-law, and her
son. Even in Allmers's moment of return and professed renunciation,
he conceives of his son as an interim task, a human obligation enabling
eventual escape—or freedom from nagging and gnawing responsibility
(something the Ratmaid too promises, yet cannot really deliver).

   Allmers's mingling of two forms of continuance—creative and
procreative—introduces *Little Eyolf*'s somewhat implicit reproductive
metaphor: book and boy alike are *opgaver* (tasks or assignments) (note,
again, the prefix *op*). Asta associates Allmers's positive mood with progress on the book project, and he acknowledges that his happiness once
depended on such progress. However, he now wholly dismisses the value
of writing in a move that Frode Helland designates "a radicalization of
the primacy of thought," rather than an actual abandonment of theory
in favor of practice (*Melankoliens spill* 248):

> ALLMERS   [...] I've been so dumb, you see. To think, that
>   brings out the best in a person. What ends up on
>   paper doesn't matter much.

ASTA (*shouts out*)
        Doesn't matter! [...]
EYOLF (*looks up at him, trusting*)
        Oh yes, papa. What you write, it matters.
ALLMERS (*smiles and strokes his hair*)
        Yes, yes, when you say it, then—. But believe you
        me,—someone will come after me and do it better.
EYOLF   Who would that be? Oh, say it!
ALLMERS   Just wait. He'll come and make himself known.
EYOLF   And then what will you do?
ALLMERS (*seriously*)
        Then I'll go to the mountains again—(*LE* 9)

Asta's startled reaction to Allmers's dismissal of the value of the book project suggests that a complete about-face in priorities has taken place. As Helland argues, however, the mode of the act—a replacement planned but not yet undertaken, forever paralyzed by belief in the arrival of a superior future—can make all of Allmers's plans appear dubious, childish, and subject to forces that he cannot or will not control. Although Allmers describes his new mission in terms of practical responsibility, he is preparing so that he might give into the lure of going up. The first trip to the mountains was taken to find focus, for the sake of health and work; the imagined, future trip is associated with death and release.

After Eyolf exits, following the Ratmaid, Rita demands that Allmers explain his comments about "the compelling, luring power" of loneliness, and the three adults sit down in the child's unnoticed absence to discuss the "liden omvæltning" (minor upheaval) that Allmers experienced while in the mountains (*LE* 17). Allmers's preamble emphasizes the fairy-tale life that he has lived with Rita, and he appeals to Asta to confirm his gratitude, given that she shared his impoverished life preceding the marriage. Throughout the conversation, Rita, "*half laughing, half displeased*," tries to change the topic, but Allmers ignores her, stating, "And now I sit here in wealth and glory. I've been able to follow my call. Been able to work and study,—everything after my own desire" (*LE* 18–19). Despite the luxury of being able to practice his calling, the "great, incomprehensible happiness" that Allmers describes and claims he owes to "dearest Rita" has become insufficient under the increasing suspicion that he was actually wasting his time and neglecting his talents by working on the book (*LE* 18). Rita's wealth gave him the chance to start—and never finish—what Asta calls his "life work" (*LE* 19). Lack of dedication and lack of control, or the drive to follow a call that is not desirable from a rational perspective—seeking death in the mountains, for example—is one element of rat-ness, a living toward death with the sneaking feeling that one might be indistinguishable from other pests.

In "Kindermord and Will in *Little Eyolf*" (1965), James E. Kerans claims that Allmers's inversion of the landscape attends his muddling of life and death through a renunciation of will: Allmers dooms the living boy by pronouncing the book project dead. He is incapable, according to Kerans, of practicing the human responsibility that he has been try-ing (and failing) to write about: "the result is that the book drags on, as crippled—almost exactly, we might hazard—as his son" (195). Kerans even asserts that father and son are "identical" in *Little Eyolf*, being equally damaged by the Oedipal desires that manifest as the failure of marriage (no mature sexual bond) and other forms of "disability" (205). As with Ejlert Løvborg's book about the future in *Hedda Gabler*, we don't know much about Allmers's writing project, beyond its broad subject mat-ter. Nonetheless, we know that it is unfinished and has been abandoned, and we know that the paternal project never really gets under way.

In Act Three, Allmers finally offers Rita a more specific and explicit explanation of his sympathy for the rats. He got lost while walking in the mountains, when he was forced off the trail by a "large, lifeless moun-tain lake" and had to make his way around (*LE* 74). He began to be-lieve he would never find his way home. Rita assumes that his thoughts were with her and Eyolf during this time, but Allmers tells her that he did not think at all, and only felt distant from his loved ones, including Asta. Moreover, he felt no angst, because death seemed to be a "good traveling [companion]" (*LE* 74). Paradoxically, this night of exhaustion, withdrawal, and resignation inspired Allmers to reconnect with his son. He was too late, however, as Rita states, because the traveling com-panion then came for the son, and the peace and pleasure that Allmers experienced when close to death became horrible, causing him to cling to life. Kerans describes this experience and the decision that Allmers takes as an explicit "inversion of the drowning," "apparently noble and serene" but actually "disturbing": "Sinking into the depths becomes a climb along the dizzy precipices; being lost in the timeless constancy of childhood becomes being lost in the special wilderness of solitude and a premature acceptance of death" (202). According to Kerans, "life and fulfillment," as reproductive future or via the child, cannot result from Allmers's immaturity: he doomed his only son "when he renounced his will and his work" (202). The landscape of *Little Eyolf* clearly implies that "going up" can sometimes be flipped on its head. Rita reminds All-mers that he could not live on the heights, and he responds, "I am drawn up there just the same now" (*LE* 73). Death waits on high *and* down below in the depths.

After dwelling on the "'vertical' structure" that communicates "the intense inwardness of the protagonist's viewpoint," Ewbank acknowl-edges that Ibsen's plays also manage to "modify and correct" verticality: "An Ibsen play always knows more than its protagonist, and keeps telling us so by various means" (64). Audiences are shown how the protagonists openly "slice through and wreck other lives, as well as their own," while chasing dreams of ascension (Ewbank 64). Ewbank also insists that the "vertical thrust" of the plays is countered by the "voices" and "silences" of other characters, naming Agnes (*Brand*), Gina (*The Wild Duck*), and Ella (*John Gabriel Borkman*) (64). In Keran's account, failed maturation and the unfinished book—the latter being an outward manifestation of the former—modify verticality in *Little Eyolf*, turning the heights into timeless, infantile depths. In my reading, the protagonists' interest in going up is countered by alternative trajectories through the landscape of the play: the Ratmaid travels around the countryside and out across the water; the body of the drowned son is dragged down and out; Asta eventually flees with Borghejm from the Allmers estate on the steamship heading south; Eyolf goes down so that Rita can plan to bring the poor children up.

The resolution of *Little Eyolf*, its final scene of hope and planning for a future in which empty rooms will once again be filled, takes place on the overgrown high point in the garden. Immediately following Eyolf's death, Allmers and Rita begin to imagine methods for coping with their grief and envisioning a meaningful and bearable future, while blaming themselves and one another for the painful situation in which they find themselves. The charitable replacement project on which they finally settle in Act Three is thus one of a series of proposed methods. In Act Two, after Rita and Allmers determine that they don't dare to kill themselves, Rita suggests that they might try to forget their sorrow in some way. Allmers rejects her proposal that they might travel, as well as her suggestion that they could "run a great house," opening the estate to guests: "That kind of life isn't for me.—No,—then I'd rather try to take up my work again" (*LE* 53). This dialogue gestures to that fact that Rita is another isolated Ibsen heroine, a woman who never exits the domestic setting— extended in this case from the bourgeois parlor to the grounds of the estate—although she is neither suited to, nor satisfied with, her domestic role. In Act One, Allmers's replacement project motivates Rita to confess her uninterest in the identity and practice of motherhood. She rejects his declaration that she means everything to him "through our child": "I was capable of *becoming* a mother to the child. But not of *being* a mother because of it" (*LE* 27). At this point, Rita has yet to come up with the idea of taking in the poor children and of raising herself to the task. When she does, she describes the process as a second chance to become a mother. She tells Allmers that the changes taking place in her are painful, "like a kind of birth" (*LE* 70). Allmers revises her non-vertical description, turning her reproductive simile into one of resurrection and conversion to a higher state: "That it is. Or a resurrection. A transition to a higher life" (*LE* 70–71). Although Allmers and Rita both take to the high point and insist on an upward trajectory, their final attempt to go up involves staying put on the estate.

Class and Fantasy

Little Eyolf ends with upward aspirations, but the directional structure and movement of the drama is more accurately described in terms of drag, which can mean pull, current, and friction, evoking the compelling and fascinating, the lure of death, the ebb and flow or circularity of re-placement and reproduction, as well as the undertow that is imagined to carry a child's remains away from the knowable landscape. The category of class can also be used to explore and describe landscape and move-ment in *Little Eyolf*. In *Ibsen: The Dramaturgy of Fear* (1999), Michael Goldman writes, "Rita's wealth gives the play its social dimension. Her fortune has enabled Eyolf to lord it high above the other children in the play, who are damaged by poverty and beaten by their parents" (103). The rich reside on high, above the poor and abused children who live down by the shore. When the children are brought up into the estate, will this level the playing field? The recuperative aspects of the play, or the way in which it refuses to release Allmers and Rita into the larger world and can make room for an entire mischief of poor fosterlings, might make us wonder whether what Rita proposes in the final act of *Little Eyolf* will not turn out to be a third, figurative drowning—after the rats, after Eyolf—in the bourgeois home.

A form of (benevolent?) class blindness is found in the main char-acters' disregard for the families of the poor children and in critical readings of the play that insist Rita's charitable replacement project represents a kind of universal humanism. In "Fantasy and Realism in Henrik Ibsen's Little Eyolf" (2014), Toril Moi argues that *Little Eyolf* advances in the direction of realism, as fantasies are stripped away and characters facing loss and other forms of destabilization strive to "estab-lish community": "To live with others [...] they will have to stop being afraid of change and give up their alienated self-images in order to find some kind of freedom" (202). The play of fantasy and realism in *Little Eyolf* might be more ambiguous than Moi allows, however, given than Rita's dream of a new form of community will take place as a new form of isolation.[6] Moi admits that Rita and Allmers are "not necessarily well equipped to carry out their project," and that Ibsen himself ex-pressed doubts regarding "Rita's persistence and resolve": "But even if we share Ibsen's doubts [...] it doesn't follow that she is wrong to try to lead a life of charity and compassion" (198). Without dismissing Moi's sympathy and respect for the good intentions of Ibsen's characters, we might take into account that the "others" with whom Rita and Allmers propose to live comprise a rather restricted form of community: a group of poor children who will be separated from their families. To call Rita's replacement project another drowning might be more pessimistic than the ending of the play allows; yet it is necessary to counter-balance the claim that what Rita and Allmers do is unambiguously "attempt to free [themselves] from illusions and turn toward the world with something like a realistic spirit" (Moi 206). The emphasis on inversion elsewhere in *Little Eyolf*, the implicit association of little boys with vermin, and the recuperative aspects of the play mean that going up is no guarantee against going down.

Moi asserts that Rita and Allmers are trading superstitious fear of change as magical transformation for an acceptance of more realistic forms of change as *Little Eyolf* ends. In *The Quintessence of Ibsenism* (1913), George Bernard Shaw also suggests that *Little Eyolf* progresses in the direction of realism, or at least that a more normal relationship to labor will lift the negative enchantment from the Allmers estate. Shaw reads *Little Eyolf* as a tale of entrapment and release that shows what happens when the ideals of home and marriage are pushed too far, tested under near-fantastic conditions of idleness: "This home clearly cannot be a working-class home" (Shaw 178). He describes the working-class home as a mere "roof under which" a man "sleeps and eats," a place where a wife labors, cooking and cleaning and caring from children "when they are neither in school nor in the streets, or who at least sees that the servants do these things [...]" (178). These conditions, he asserts, do not allow for testing of the "home ideal" (Shaw 178). According to Shaw, the notion of home as a space of sacrifice, honesty, and true relationships, which is almost always being tested in Ibsen's plays, is under "full strain" in *Little Eyolf* (178). The Allmers estate constitutes a world isolated from what continues to be the reality of most people: a life determined by the demands, burdens, and rewards (or lack thereof) of labor—or at the very least by management of the labor of others. Under the strange, overly unburdened conditions of her class, Rita becomes a kind of evil enchantress, who "snatches [Allmers] from his work as a school-master and imprisons him in their house" (Shaw 179). In his isolation, Allmers becomes a "male sultana," who "takes himself very seriously indeed" (Shaw 179). The exceptional class conditions depicted in *Little Eyolf*—which must be magical, given that there are no domestic servants in this play—make for a world shot through with fairy tales, involving not only invasion (the Ratmaid, the supernatural, the "oriental" attitude of the sultana) but also "total isolation" (ten years of marriage under Rita's spell of wealth, with no relationship to other people who live nearby) (Shaw 182). These class conditions do not change over the course of the play.

In *Shaw's Ibsen* (2018), Joan Templeton draws our attention to Shaw's discussion of *Little Eyolf* and altruism, defined as identification with vulnerable members of the community. She argues that Shaw "embraces and celebrates the extravagant, reconciliatory Ibsen of the plays of 'the last quartet,'" moving toward the final resurrection of *When We Dead Awaken* (272–273). While this description suits Shaw's broad take on Ibsen's last dramas, his specific rhetoric concerning Rita's replacement project suggests a higher degree of ambivalence. He refers, for example, to the insincerity of charity work directed at the poor from the heights of snobbery, for the sake of self-soothing; and there is definite sarcasm in his claim that Allmers's deliverance occurs because his wife will now be kept busy cleaning up and managing "dirty little wretches" (182–183). Moreover, Shaw's insistence that Rita's plan is "at all events more respectable than the day before"—when she threatened to "throw herself away on the first man she met if Allmers dared to think of anybody but her"—is not exactly high praise (Shaw 183). Finally, his description of the arrival of a form of realism repeats one of the most fantastic cliché phrases of all: "And so they are delivered from their evil dream, and, let us hope, live happily ever after" (Shaw 183). Although "happily ever after" might sound like the beginning of a new regime of fantasy, Shaw is simply insisting that Rita's proposal allows the Allmers estate to take on its "natural aspect" (183). Still, the happiness that will hopefully be permanently secured will emerge from a future in which Allmers is spared the obsessive attentions of his wife: Rita will now have "something else to do than torment him with passions that devour and jealousies that enslave him" (Shaw 183). Again, I am not arguing that the ending of *Little Eyolf* is implausible or must be read ironically, but rather that the drama can also enable us to question the harmlessness and benevolence of this replacement project, looking askance at the disregard for alterity that takes place in a phrase like "After all, [these children] too are little Eyolfs" (Shaw 183).

Even if we do not doubt that Rita and Allmers are capable of leading lives of charity, we might still ask whether bringing these children into Eyolf's rooms can serve to lift the enchantment. Might it not imprison the children in turn, making them into little sultanas, or more likely, isolating them as outsiders-within, making them beholden to a family and class structure they cannot fully join? What if they remain paler (but also "better") copies of the only (lame) son who drowned, or are treated as mere reflections of Rita and Allmers's self-understanding as philanthropic foster parents? Some might regard these questions as overly speculative, but the inverted or invertible character of the world of *Little Eyolf*, its replacement projects, and the relatively obscure status of these poor children and their families, invite us to ask what *going up* means beyond the privileged commencing and recommencing of life's missions that Allmers embodies and seems to have inspired in Rita.

Significantly, moving on from the phenomenon of inversion and out from the upper-class estate also means moving away from verticality. The Ratmaid's primary movement pattern, for example, is circular. This explicit fairy-tale figure is also a traveling saleswoman, who shows up in a variety of places, summoned by those who need her exterminating services. "Always on the go," the Ratmaid's territory is much wider than the Allmers's (*LE* 16). When she arrives at the estate in Act One, she is "out on a round trip" and does not know when she will return to "these parts again" (*LE* 13). Her movements, as well as her entrance, connect her to the subtle but significant class tensions in *Little Eyolf*, while reinforcing the idea that the estate is centralized and isolated. Her summoning provides Ibsen with the opportunity to highlight Eyolf's innocence, or his combined naïveté and wisdom, as well as his status as an indulged yet neglected and bothersome child. It also highlights Allmers's distain for the poor children who live by the wharf.

The summoning of the Ratmaid in Act One begins after Eyolf insists that he *"must"* be a soldier when he grows up.[7] This insistence pains Allmers because it is proof of the lack of harmony between Eyolf's desires and his abilities, so Asta distracts Eyolf by being the first to name the Ratmaid:

> Just think, Eyolf—I have seen the Ratmaid.

EYOLF   What! Have you seen the Ratmaid? Oh, you're just teasing me!

ASTA   No, it's true. I saw her yesterday.

EYOLF   Where did you see her then?

ASTA   I saw her on the road, outside the city.

ALLMERS   I saw her too, someplace up in the country.

RITA (*sitting on the sofa*)
> Maybe we'll get to see her then too, Eyolf. (*LE* 11)

The repetitive, fairy-tale-like evocation of "I saw her" might be essential to the summons, but it is not quite enough to make the Ratmaid appear. Before she enters, Allmers tells Eyolf that he should go out to play. Startled by these instructions, because his father has always insisted that he spend his time studying, Eyolf asks whether he should take books with him. Allmers replies, "No, no books from here on out. Go rather down to the shore to the other boys" (Ibsen 11). Eyolf's fancy soldier's play-uniform makes him reluctant to go, although he insists that the "uskikkelige" (naughty) boys do not dare to make fun of him because he will hit them. The adjective *uskikkelig*, which Eyolf applies to the boys first (followed by Rita), suggests naughtiness, vulgarity, and unsuitability, being common, uneducated, and ill-bred. Unlike Rita and Allmers, Eyolf has engaged with and given these boys some thought. When Allmers asks Eyolf *"with suppressed anger"* if he knows why the boys tell him he cannot be a soldier, Eyolf explains, "They are probably jealous of me. Because, papa, they are so poor that they have to go around barefoot" (*LE* 12). Eyolf's words again cause Allmers pain, due to the dissonance between the child's dreams and abilities—but also, apparently, due to the truth, because the poor boys correctly state that Eyolf cannot be a soldier. Insensitive to the complex context of envy and sympathy, lack and class difference that Eyolf's comments (naively) invoke, Allmers puts the final touch on the Ratmaid's summons: "(*slowly, tormented*) Oh, Rita—how this gnaws at my heart, this here! [...] (*Threateningly*) But those boys, they will soon feel who the masters are down at the shore!" (*LE* 12).

The final, magic word of the summons turns out to be "masters," or "herrer" in Norwegian, and the entrance of the Ratmaid should remind us that a national folk culture and the realities of peasant life surround and can break through the fine culture of the Allmers estate.[8] Now Asta hears a knocking at the door: enter the Ratmaid, who wonders whether "herskabet" (the gentry) has anything in the house that "gnaver" (gnaws) (*LE* 12). A synonym and "audible echo" of Allmers's verb *nage* (worry or pester), the Ratmaid's verb *gnave* draws attention to the fact that Eyolf is like a rat, a nagging source of irritation, guilt, and ambivalence in Rita and Allmers's house (Helland, *Melankoliens spill* 256). The words "herrer" and "herskabet" (masters and the ruling class) are also related. Allmers invites the Ratmaid to sit and rest. She is tired from having worked all night to de-infest the islands, and she proceeds to explain her method to a fascinated Eyolf: she takes three turns around a house with her dog, the pug Mopsemand; she plays on a small jew's harp to draw the rats out of their hiding places and down to her rowboat; and then she rows out, followed by her swimming dog, who is followed by the drowning rats. She does not take three turns around the Allmers's garden room. She has been circling the surrounding countryside, however, and she now uses her dog, and perhaps some magic words of her own, to seduce the master's only child. Perhaps larger circles are necessary for larger prey, for masters and "småpuslingerne deres" (their little babies), who "are hated and persecuted so mercilessly" according to the Ratmaid (*LE* 15, 13).

Moi has also recognized that the Ratmaid represents something more than a fantastic interlude in *Little Eyolf*. She addresses the irony of this character, an explicitly fantastic figure who "looks at Eyolf with more reality than his parents": "In the self-deluded Allmers household, the Rat Wife represents the awful irruption of reality, for she is the embodiment of suffering, ageing and death, the incarnation of the law of change, a constant reminder of human finitude" (200). Together with Shaw, I add class to the categories (suffering, aging, death) that Moi defines as essential to the "irruption of reality." Although the Ratmaid only appears on stage for a few moments, her significance in terms of class difference runs across the entire setting of the play. She has been circling the surrounding countryside; she has been out on the islands; and now she comes to the very heart of the dramatic landscape. She is mistakenly turned away, because Allmers and Rita are as of yet unable to face the fact that they *do* have a creature in their home whose existence gnaws at their consciences.

The Ratmaid, Eyolf, and Asta all exit from the wharf, which happens to be a marker of class difference, death within, and escape from the estate. Un-described in the stage directions, the activity on the wharf is first heard by audiences, just before we learn that a child has drowned. Asta, Borghejm, Rita, and Allmers wonder what the "[d]*istant, confused screams and shouts*" down by the water might mean (*LE* 32). Allmers suggests that it is "[p]robably those street urchins making mischief again" (*LE* 32–33). When Asta looks out, she sees what we hear: a whole crowd of onlookers, one of the few reminders that other people surround the Allmers's estate. Rita and Allmers's charitable focus on "street urchins" will eventually obscure these other people. During Act Two, Allmers describes what the boys witnessed: Eyolf standing "at the very end of the dock," dizzily staring after the Ratmaid rowing out across the water, and then falling (*LE* 36). Later in the act, Rita adds the following details: he was not swept away at once; the boys saw him lying face up at the very bottom of the clear water, with open eyes: "And then something came and took him outward. They called it an undertow" (*LE* 46). The force of the undertow, described with a nautical word apparently unfamiliar to Rita ("strømsætning"), is an oddly foreign presence. Mysterious and purposeful rather than natural and neutral, it *came and took* Eyolf. His open eyes, or an imagined version of them (given that she did not see them herself), will become a central figure in Rita's grief. Eventually, she will see accusing eyes everywhere. While the body of the drowned son is dragged down and out from the wharf and into the open sea, and while Asta leaves with Borghejm on the steamship, the "street urchins" remain, to be used in a circle game of replacement that reopens the question of inversion and resists the never in Never Land (never never).

As Helland has also argued, *Little Eyolf* clearly indicates that these anonymous children are conceived of as copies and placeholders. In Act Three, Allmers responds to the screams and shouts from the wharf: "The whole waterfront should be cleared away. The men have now come home. Drunk, as usual. They beat the children. Listen, listen to the boys scream! The women howl for help for them—" (*LE* 75). When Rita questions whether someone should help them, Allmers reminds her that they failed to help Eyolf and then doubles down: "All the old shacks should be torn down," and the poor people who live in these shacks will simply have to find someplace else to live (*LE* 76). When Rita asks about the children, Allmers responds, "Does it really matter where they go to die?" (*LE* 76). Startled by his callousness and believing he will soon leave her, Rita now describes her own replacement project. Given that she is not temperamentally suited to the task, Allmers wonders what Rita will do with the children. He is incredulous when she insists,

RITA   I want to take them to me.
ALLMERS   *You* want that!
RITA   Yes, I want that. From the day that you have left, they
                   will be here, all of them,—as if they were my own.

ALLMERS (*dismayed*)
      In our little Eyolf's place!

RITA   Yes, in our little Eyolf's place. They'll get to live in Eyolf's rooms. They'll get to read his books. Get to play with his toys. They'll take turns sitting in his chair at the table. (*LE* 77)

The dialogue here is repetitive, formally supporting the interchangeability of these children, who are a group of uncertain number, yet Rita will "take" them all. Although they will have access to more and nicer things than before, the children cannot expect things or a place of their own. They must take turns sitting in Eyolf's chair (*LE* 77). Is Rita's replacement project a gift, or another form of revenge, or both? Goldman calls the plan "a kind of fantasy version of the modern social project," wherein "[c]lass warfare [...] will be assuaged by a program of education, love, and generous subvention" (105). Rita and Allmers seek to make up for having been both neglectful parents and landlords. The project, however, could continue class warfare by other, perhaps more benevolent, means. It appears, for example, to use the needs of poor children to enable a displacing of poor adults.

Class, age, and gender complicate the assumption that Rita's replacement project could be pure fantasy, unshaped by material conditions. The phrase lost boys works in the case of the children that Rita longs to foster because the lost boys of *Peter Pan* are also severed from familial and social contexts, and because the poor children are generally gendered male in *Little Eyolf*.[9] When Rita describes her project, she cites Eyolf's earlier use of the adjective *uskikkelig*, specifying that she has all "the naughty boys" in mind (*LE* 77). Allmers too designates boys when the screams drift up from the wharf for the second time. This focus makes sense because of Eyolf's rather ambivalent relationship with these boys. In addition, it might be realistic—meaning conventional, in this case—to focus on the futures of little boys while forgetting poor mothers, fathers, and especially little girls. It is certainly conventional to assume that a wealthier life is a better life, and that poor parents are bad parents. In *Little Eyolf*, however, the rich boy and the poor boys alike have received the wrong kinds of attention from their fathers: cold schooling and beatings, respectively. In Act One, when Rita is explaining her jealousy and lack of desire to live for motherhood to Allmers, she tells him that she did not so much adore Eyolf as pity him, because Allmers "made him live on bread and cold water. Just let him read and study. Almost didn't see him at all" (*LE* 127). Perhaps Allmers will manage to be a more affectionate and attentive foster father, after his encounter with death and the loss of Eyolf. But what will the poor boys' mothers and fathers be doing while the "naughty boys"—and their sisters?—play with Eyolf's toys? For the moment, Eyolf's parents have yet to consider such details. They are overwhelmed by Rita's "transformation" and looking forward to the "demanding workday" ahead of them, shot through with moments of "Sunday silence" (*LE* 78).

Neither Rita nor Allmers mention seeking or needing consent from the poor children or their parents. In *When Wendy Grew Up: An Afterthought*, Wendy and her daughter Jane (whom Peter will soon fetch) discuss the fate of the lost boys, who have been sent to school and must now be grown like Wendy's brothers: "John has a beard now" and "Michael is an engine driver" (Barrie, *Peter Pan* 158).

> JANE   Did they ever wish they were back in the
>   Never Never Land?
> WENDY (*hesitating*)
>   I—I don't know. (158)

Significantly, it is a little girl who asks the question about the lost boys' desires. Grown up Wendy had yet to consider it, although she now hesitates and admits to uncertainty. The stated goal of Rita's project is to "soften—and improve" the fortunes of the poor children (*LE* 78). Rita and Allmers are not given an afterthought in which to consider what these children might wish for. Nor do they hesitate on their behalf. It does not occur to them that their journey up, in terms of landscape as well as class, might also be a kind of drowning in the ambivalent, circling currents of replacement.

Looking at the Child

The Ratmaid breaks through, seducing Eyolf with the help of Mopsemand, whom she carries in her black bag: "(*nods and waves to Eyolf*) Come closer without fear, little wounded warrior! He doesn't bite. Come here! Come here!" (*LE* 14). She does not return within the confines of the play; but Rita, who is sometimes understood to be an inverted version of the Ratmaid, insists that she will bring the poor children up.[10] How will she lure them, and will their new lives represent a surfacing or a drowning? Peter Pan also "Breaks Through," seducing Wendy before taking all three of the Darling children away (Barrie, *Peter and Wendy* 1). Peter is a figure of recuperation because he empties and refills a nursery. He is also an exile, barred from the nursery, "another little boy sleeping in [his] bed" (Barrie, *Peter Pan* 132). Peter returns the children in the end, only to return for Wendy's daughters and granddaughters, so that the Never Never Land and its adventures are framed, but not fully contained, by a more realistic world. Despite the realities that the Ratmaid and Eyolf's death usher in, and despite Ibsen's highly realistic portrayal of grief (ambivalent, impossible, inevitably unfaithful to the deceased), *Little Eyolf* is not simply a "return-to-reality" play (Gilead 278).[11] It remains, instead, a dramatization of fantasies that function as both life raft and undertow, showing us how Allmers and Rita continue to *"alle-gorize* their lives and their surroundings" (Helland, *Melankoliens* 33). As we have seen, one of these fantasies involves "making good" by offering Eyolf's space to other children. Jacqueline Rose uses Peter to critique the myth of innocence as a fantasy of origins and fresh starts. She insists that *Peter Pan* "shows innocence not as a property of childhood but as a portion of adult desire," arguing that the significance of Barrie's play "lies in what [it] demonstrates about a fantasy of childhood, with children's literature as just one of the arenas in which this fantasy is played out" (1984, xii and 138). Reading *Little Eyolf* with lost boys in mind confirms that the scholarly reception of this drama at our own turn of the century is another arena in which such fantasies play out.

Whether or not Allmers and Rita manage to complete her proposed replacement project changes neither its class-blind and substitutive characteristics nor the ideologies of innocence that even pessimistic or doubtful readings of the play's conclusion tend to reproduce. I have thus far defined lost boys by the ways in which they counter verticality and by their isolation from familial, social contexts; but lost boys are also made by death, failure to grow up, and neglect. In Act One of *Peter Pan*, Peter explains to Wendy that lost boys "are the children who fall out of their prams when the nurse is looking the other way. If they are not claimed in seven days they are sent far away to the Never Land" (Barrie 101). This casual and somewhat absurd description evokes the oddly menacing character of neglect, as well as the potentially banal causes of child disappearance and death. Nurses simply look the other way, thus overlooking their duties. Then, these nurses or other guardians fail to claim the baby boys. After the Ratmaid leaves in *Little Eyolf*, Rita and Allmers and Asta simply look away: "*Rita goes out on the veranda and fans herself with her handkerchief. Shortly afterward, Eyolf goes out to the right, cautiously and unnoticed*" (LE 16). While *Peter Pan* allows readers to follow the children to Never Land, readers, critics, and spectators of *Little Eyolf* remain behind with the parents, who must try to learn to live with their guilt.

Unlike Peter, Eyolf does not return in person, so his character and embodied figure take no part in the Never Never Land that the adults begin to reconstruct in Acts Two and Three. Eyolf really dies, making him absent and irrecuperable—except in the stories that the adults tell about him. What do we look at, and what do we fail to see, when we tell stories about Eyolf as representative of the innocent child, or praise the use of his death as inspiration for a replacement project, without attending to the ambiguities of this project? In *Ibsen's Women*, Templeton argues that Rita, like Gina in *The Wild Duck*, "looks at the child," while Allmers, like Hjalmar, "thinks of what the child's life means to him" (283). Helland, conversely, finds that Rita sees only "figural, private meaning" in the world, performing further allegorization of her own failure to see, after Eyolf's death (291). Whether or not Rita sees reality when she makes her final plan for coping with Eyolf's death, it is clear that looking at the child is a "[risky]" business, or that it can never be an innocent act (Lesnik-Oberstein and Thomson 45).[12]

As other scholars working in critical child studies have noted, the figure of the child is often *out of play*, a "theoretical exile" that "[drags]" "the dynamics of [the] narratives" in which it is found "to virtual standstill" (Lesnik-Oberstein and Thomson 35–36), a "ground zero for the edifice that is adult life and around which narratives of sexuality get organized" (Bruhm and Hurley xiii). Even Ibsen scholars who emphasize the "ironic underside" (Goldman 105) of Rita's project rather than reading it as a positive example of redemption through charity—the project that means Eyolf did not die "in vain" (*LE* 77)—tend to place the figure of the child in a kind of exile, outside the dynamics of their critique. In *The Dramaturgy of Fear*, Goldman refers to Rita's project as "comprehensive, progressive in its outlines but tainted at its root," with a "dubious likelihood of success" (105–106). Nonetheless, he describes the child as a kind of all-seeing, centered and pivoting mechanism, like a spotlight:

> Fueled by *Little Eyolf*, we may think of Ibsen's theater as the seeing place for a child's vengeance, where the force of the action is a kind of seeing vengeance *on* the adult world. We see with the eyes of the child, and at the same time we feel the child's gaze directed at us. The unblinking focus of the claim *against* us is reinforced by the sweeping assault on the elders and masters by whom we are limited and denied. (94)

Little Eyolf definitely enables a painful critique of the adult(erated) world; we are perhaps encouraged to remember our own childhood traumas and vulnerability, the neglect to which our "elders and masters" have subjected us. But even though Goldman begins with the phrase "a child's vengeance," the child's gaze is not a child's gaze in this passage. It is rather the child within the adult, whose look is informed precisely by knowledge of blame and corruption.[13]

In "Petrified Time," Helland describes Rita's project as a theft, in which the boys are conceived as mere placeholders: "When all is petrified and near-dead, everything at the same [time] becomes fleetingly interchangeable—the one child can be in the other's place, they can all 'take turns at' being Eyolf" (142). Despite his critique of interchangeability, Helland defines the child as "the future, the new [...] change, transformation" (135). These metaphors imply that a child who does not guarantee a better future is less a child than a sign of adult blindness and failure:

> Having children turns things around, negates the given in such a way that 'past life' receives new meaning [...] Eyolf's appearance on

the stage of life changed nothing. The child stayed invisible as such, the parents never saw its individuality and the legitimate demands for change on their part that the child constituted. (140)

The question remains whether Helland himself see the child's "individuality," or whether he accepts an alternative form of *not* seeing by labeling the child as "legitimate demands for change." Both Goldman and Helland insist that versions of innocence could be solutions to the problem at hand; and yet they define innocence in adult(erated) forms: taking vengeance for assault (loss of innocence) and giving the past new meaning, respectively.

Before his death, Eyolf is definitely an "occasion of pathos," or a sweet and innocent yet wise boy, whose trusting attitude and ambivalent, naïve sympathy for the poor boys might deepen the sadness that we feel when we discover that he has drowned in the fjord (Lesnik-Oberstein and Thomson 35). Ibsen contrasts Eyolf's paralyzed leg and physical weakness with his "beautiful, wise eyes" (*LE* 8). Moreover, as we have seen, when Allmers disparages the value of writing, Eyolf "*looks up at him, trusting*," and says "Oh yes, papa. What you write, it matters" (*LE* 8–9). Eyolf's faith in and admiration for his father, as well as his awareness of the poor boys' bare feet, differentiate him from his shoulder-shrugging parents, who later admit that they have given the poor boys by the shore only minimum consideration.[14] Eyolf's trusting certainty is also framed by Allmers's understanding of the future and of his parental role in its creation. The modern understanding of the self as achievement makes accidental drowning into wasted potential, a canceled narrative, meaninglessness, even if it can be reincorporated into narratives of judgment, vengeance, and eventual redemption.[15]

Whether living or dead, Eyolf's character is forced to function as the pivot around which all manner of ambivalent feelings swirl. Before he drowns, Rita and Allmers's disagreement over the nature of their relationship and what should satisfy Rita's desires—living through one's child and accepting the natural course of change in life—culminates in Rita's jealous accusation that Allmers has betrayed her with Eyolf, that she "could almost be tempted to wish that—well!" (*LE* 30–31). She insinuates that Eyolf has managed to play a trick, cursing all romantic attachments, including a possible match between Asta and Borgheim, whose absence from the scene enables her to confess scandalous feelings. When Borghejm and Asta return, Borghejm states that it will be their "last walk together" (*LE* 31). Rita responds, "Do you hear that, Alfred? (*Turns to Borghejm*) I'm willing to bet that evil eyes have played a trick here" (*LE* 32). Borghejm questions whether Rita holds such a superstitious belief, and she shocks Allmers by confirming and specifying, "Yes, I have started to believe in evil eyes now. Mostly in evil children's eyes" (*LE* 32). The first evidence of Eyolf's drowning is now heard, drifting up from the wharf. Rita's guilt and obsession with her son's eyes can be traced to this moment, in which she curses herself by daring to speak so scandalously, in a desperate attempt to get Allmers to take her desire seriously.

In Act Three, after Asta and Borghejm run down to catch the steamship, Rita and Allmers see the ship coming in to dock at the wharf, with its red and green lights like "glowing eyes" that "stare and stare out from the darkness.—And into the darkness too" (*LE* 69). Rita is horrified that ships will continue to dock where Eyolf's body momentarily rested before disappearing to a place that she cannot, and would not choose to, go. Although his body by this point has been swept far away, the end of the wharf and the clear waters that surround it remain significant for Rita, because the last material evidence of his presence, his neglect, and his disability surfaced there: the crutch. Rita and Allmers agree that life continues, "ruthlessly," as if nothing had happened (*LE* 70). Thus, they express a question familiar to the grieving: how can the world go on after the death of a loved one? Significantly, Rita's rejoinder communicates some impartial self-awareness: "And nothing has really happened after all. Not to the others. Just to the two of us" (*LE* 70).

It is clear that Eyolf embodies much more than trusting innocence: he is also a minor character, an assignment, an excuse, a rat (to Peter's bird), a stranger, a dead-end, and a figure for temporal and emotional drag, or the dynamic standstill of desire and repression (circling, going to and fro, never progressing). He is "damaged goods," and so represents a contradiction for his father, who believes that he can cultivate "all the rich possibilities that are dawning in his child's mind," while also insisting that Eyolf must capitulate in some sense to his disability (*LE* 20). Eyolf's status as "the fulfillment of [Allmers's] family line" remains a permanent to-come, a forever-deferred future (*LE* 21). When Allmers sits down with Rita and Asta to explain his motivations for abandoning the book and dedicating himself to fatherhood in Act One, the boy is already heading for, leaning out over, falling into the water at the end of the wharf. In Act Two, Allmers mourns the fact that Eyolf was standing at the threshold of a "spiritually conscious life," that his son was supposed to fill his life with happiness, and that an old maid's "luring game" took all future happiness and achievements away, for no comprehensible reason (*LE* 35–36). In *Feminist, Queer, Crip*, Alison Kafer notes that normative discourses mark disability as the "agreed-upon limit of our projected futures" (27). Even as Allmers insists on Eyolf's preciousness—"Such a precious life! Such a precious a life!" (*LE* 33)—*Little Eyolf* seems to reproduce and/or submit to the normative understanding of disability as the sign "of a future that no one wants" (Kafer 46).[16] In fact, Ibsen's drama depicts a family that has long been engaged in anticipatory, melancholic mourning: a father desperate to make good, a mother seemingly resigned concerning her child, but clinging to and idealizing the early, erotic days of her marriage, an aunt whose role includes distracting both the boy and his father from their pain.

In Act Two, Allmers and Rita discuss the moment when Eyolf was injured in the first fall. Allmers blames Rita for making him forget the baby while in her arms: "In that moment, you sentenced little Eyolf to death" (*LE* 50). When Rita asserts that Allmers must take some of the blame, he insists that the meaning of Eyolf's death is "gengældelsen" (reprisal), or a judgment passed on their failure to love and see the child while he was living (*LE* 50). Suggesting that they fall short of the ideal of true mourning, he now insists that their pain is "samvittighedsnag" (conscience-remorse) rather than "sorrow and loss" (*LE* 50–51). When Rita laments that this state of affairs can never be remedied, Allmers tells her about his dream from the night before, in which Eyolf ran up from the wharf, alive and able-bodied. He admits, without uttering the proper name, that he almost thanked God, which causes Rita to rebuke him for having made her doubt her own faith. This conversation touches, if cursorily, on teleological thinking—perfect-ability, a fantasy of healing that cannot be relinquished, but also doom or negative and unchangeable fate—which persists despite the references to (imperfect) renunciation of faith, and makes apparent the mourning that preceded Eyolf's mortality, a mourning that can be traced to the earlier "death" of laming.

Are we to imagine that Rita's final replacement project sustains, or breaks with, *Little Eyolf*'s established pattern of false starts and deferred futures? Eyolf is a minor character that we barely get to know, a boy who enters the stage for a few moments and then passes into obscurity. Unlike *Peter Pan*, *Little Eyolf* lets its dead child go; but Rita's final replacement project also contains the kind of movement that Peter suggests: a loss or escape recouped through circularity and replacement, a boy barred from the nursery whose barring enables a deferred fantasy of nurseries re-filled.

Asta: The First Lost Boy

Poor children are not the only figures in *Little Eyolf* that Rita and Allmers imagine might take their son's place. Before Rita conceives her plan for repurposing Eyolf's rooms, Allmers and Rita ask Asta, a grown but unmarried woman, to stay on: "Oh, Asta [...] Stay here and help us! Replace Eyolf for us" (*LE* 68). Because Eyolf dies in Act One, he is the first lost boy that we meet in *Little Eyolf*. In the subsequent acts, however, we learn that Eyolf was already a replacement for others, including the able-bodied child that he could have been, and a lost boy who is no longer a boy. In Act Two, Allmers and Asta's conversations reveal that little Eyolf was a kind of replacement for another Eyolf: the little sister-brother who came before. Goldman writes, "At this point we may begin to wonder just which damaged child stands at the center of the

drama" (97). Asta, it turns out, was both the first to be called Eyolf and
is the first to be asked to take Eyolf's place. Although she is a replacement child herself, who once acted out the lost hopes and desires of her
big brother, Asta will stand in for the first lost boy in this chapter.[17]
She is an excellent figure for the impossibility of an "ultimate beginning
where everything is perfect or can at least be made good" (Rose 138).
She has played at embodying the longing for what should have been;
she is a boy who was "never here nor anywhere" (Barrie 135).[18] Asta
also momentarily disables Allmers's memorialization of Eyolf-as-ideal
by enabling him to dwell on a past that exceeds any possible idealization
of the lame son.

Allmers and Asta's closeness is based on some of the essential ingredi-
ents for making lost boys: neglect, death, and isolation. Allmers states,
for example, that he always felt he owed Asta compensatory kindness
for his father's lack of kindness toward her. Asta's status as a lost boy
who is a woman, but once played at being a boy, becomes particularly
apparent when we learn of her former nickname in Act Two, as she sews
a mourning flower on Allmers's hat and sleeve. She did the same on his
student cap after Allmers's father died, when she was supposedly still too
little to remember, and then again for her mother: "And then we were
alone in the world, we two" (*LE* 38):

ASTA   [...] It was really a lovely time for us, all things consid-
            ered, Alfred. The two of us alone.
ALLMERS   Yes, it turned into one, despite all the struggle.
ASTA   You struggled.
ALLMERS (*more lively*)
            Oh, you struggled just as much in your way, you
            too,—(*smiles*) you, my dear, faithful Eyolf.
ASTA   Uh,—don't remind me of that ridiculous nonsense
            with the name.
ALLMERS   Well, if you have been a boy, you would have been
            called Eyolf.
ASTA   Yes, *if*. But when you began university—. (*Smiles in-
            voluntarily*) To think that you could be so childish, all
            the same.
ALLMERS   Was I the one who was childish!
ASTA   Yes, I really think so now, when I remember it. Be-
            cause you were ashamed not to have a brother. Just a
            sister.
ALLMERS   No, it was really you. *You* were ashamed.
ASTA   Oh yes, a little bit, maybe. And I almost felt sorry for
            you—
ALLMERS   Yes, you certainly did. And so you took out my old
            boy's clothes—

ASTA   Those nice Sunday clothes, yes. Do you remember the
             blue blouse and the knickers?

ALLMERS (*lets his eyes linger on her*)
             How well I remember you, when you put them on and
             walked around in them.

ASTA   Yes, but I only did that when we were home alone
             together.

ALLMERS And how serious and important we felt. And I called
             you only Eyolf. (*LE* 38–39)

Asta's nickname is the name of a boy who was never born, a longed-
for son and brother. The sibling's memories of the nickname and the
dress-up game are disconcerting but apparently not unpleasant. Asta
is clearly embarrassed and somewhat hesitant to speak, but she "*smiles
involuntarily*" while doing so.

This dress-up game is sometimes read as a suppression of heterosexual
desire, by means of disguise, or as a sign of latent homosexual desire.[19]
Instead of insisting on this veiled, either-or structure of desire, we might
take a moment to "linger on" its queerer surface characteristics: that
the memory of gendered shame is shared but perhaps mis-remembered,
that "childish" display felt "serious" and "important," that it involved a
child dressed up in big brother's old clothes and a university student, in
a time when the siblings are alone together. I use the term "queerer" here
to refer to the peculiar aspects of the game, and to insist that its memory
evokes a variety of complex tensions and desires, rather than to insist
that it was an explicitly erotic encounter.[20]

Although this is sometimes overlooked, both parties were not children
when they played this dress-up game. Allmers was in a later stage of
adolescence, while Asta was still a child or in the early stages of adolescence. The game itself might be "childish," but given the siblings' age
gap (approximately eleven years), it might also be described as mixed
age.[21] The "lovely time" that Allmers and Asta shared, joined together
by struggles as well as joys, adds another fairy tale aspect to *Little Eyolf*,
a world of idiosyncratic behaviors and pleasures, isolated from the larger
world, free from parental supervision. Although the early days of Allmers and Rita's marriage are also described as "dejlig" (lovely), Allmers's
time alone with Asta appears to trump all other periods of loveliness.[22]
Later, Allmers describes it as "a single, high holy day from first to last"
(*LE* 57).

Whether or not Eyolf-the-son was a replacement child for Asta—the
absent boy/little brother Allmers could never have but will continue to
desire (as what could have been and what will not have been)—Eyolf/
Asta came *before*, and so would seem to threaten any dream of ultimate
beginnings. In many ways, Allmers and Asta remain partners during the
play, distinguished from Rita by intra-bourgeois class difference and by

their shared interest in the life of the mind. When Allmers attempts to explain his gratitude to Rita in Act One, he states that both he and Asta owe their happiness to her wealth. It is significant if subtle foreshadowing that Allmers uses "we" in this context (*LE* 18). Ibsen uses the context of recent loss to open the past for reconsideration only to seal off the future, making the sibling's union and their apparent desire for one another into a current (im)possibility, or a "what might have been."

In Act Two, Ibsen makes Allmers and Asta's closeness apparent before limiting its future potential by introducing the possibility of (non-taboo) sex. As mentioned, Rita proposes a series of modes for moving on after Eyolf's death, including opening the house for social events and traveling. Allmers's initial idea for moving on involves a return to the idealized past, or to the "days of yore" when he and Asta were alone, playing dress-up games and sharing the joys and struggles of his intellectual work (*LE* 57). Toward the end of the act, he tells Asta that he intends to leave Rita in order to return to her: "I *must* come home to you again. Home to you to be purified and perfected from cohabitation with—" (*LE* 56–57). Allmers insists that his relationship with Asta cannot be compared to his relationship with Rita, because the bond between a brother and sister is unique, not subject to "the law of transformation"—a phrase that he uses on several occasions when insisting that erotic love must be expended and sublated through procreativity (*LE* 57). However, Asta now informs him that the letters she carried with her when she arrived in Act One prove that they are not biologically related. Allmers *"half defiantly"* insists that this changes nothing about their "holy" relationship, but Asta insists that they too are subject to the unchanging law of change (*LE* 58–59). Asta now offers a bundle of lilies to Allmers. These flowers grow in the brackish water, where a lake flows out to meet the fjord, and Asta describes them as shooting up from the deep. They might remind us of the play's verticality, or of its character's longing to mark rising/going up as the proper, ethical and progressive direction; yet they also symbolize a threshold space: the meeting place between fresh and salt water, brotherhood and sexuality, a moment of departure from a past unmarked by knowledge of Asta's illegitimacy, a confusion of two Eyolfs, little and big. Asta intends the lilies as "a last goodbye" to Allmers from "little Eyolf" (*LE* 59). Allmers asks, "From Eyolf out there? Or from you?"; and Asta responds, "From us both" (*LE* 59). Act Two ends on this point of impending departure and confusion. Before he follows Borghejm, Rita, and Asta up the path to the gardens that surround the estate, Allmers whispers the last line of the act, which iterates the three names of two lost boys: "Asta. Eyolf. Little Eyolf—!" (*LE* 59).

In Act Three, just before Rita and Allmers beg Asta to take Eyolf's place, Allmers suggests that he now regards Asta as the true, lost companion of his life. He tells Borghejm that it is for the best that he will not have a traveling companion when he leaves, implying that Borghejm is lucky that Asta turned down his proposals. Borghejm is taken aback, but Allmers assures him, "Yes, because you never know who you might meet afterward. On the journey [...] the true travel companion. When it's too late. Too late" (*LE* 67). In a confused and rapidly paced dialogue, Rita begs them not to leave her alone, referring to her fear of the dark and the accusing eyes that stare at her, Allmers tells her that she should not be afraid of those eyes and begs Asta to stay, Allmers again insists that his and Rita's grief is not sorrow and loss, but rather resentment and torment, Rita exclaims, "From here on out, you will be *our* Eyolf, Asta! Eyolf, like you were before" (*LE* 68); and Allmers adds, with "*concealed emotion*," "Stay—and share life with us, Asta. With Rita. With me. With me,—your brother!" (*LE* 68). The desperation of their pleas might distract audiences from the unsettling ways in which they trouble identity and evoke the persistence of symbolic incest, regardless of the revelation of parentage. Rita's words enclose Asta between Eyolfs, clearly marking her as Rita and Allmers's hoped-for replacement child. Allmers's words both double and separate him as man and as brother.

Templeton reads Asta's decision to escape with Borghejm as an "attempt to bury her love for Alfred," as the moment in which she chooses her own replacement project, "exchang[ing] ethics [the subject of Alfred's abandoned book project] for engineering, one man for another through which to live" (286).[23] It is also a refusal of the replacement-child role and an alternative trajectory. Although Ibsen makes it difficult to believe in any exit but death, it is an exit, for the time being, from the fairy-tale world in which her brother has been living and working and from the vertical and circular movements suggested by the immediate setting of the play (the Allmers's own neverland).

Postmortem

Analyses of class and fantasy, patterns of movement through landscape, and innocence and replacement can provide a means of thinking about forms of (in)fidelity to a dead son. Ibsen kills *a child*—with the help of that child's parents and the Ratmaid—in order to use *the child* as the pivot around which family drama will continue to turn. *Little Eyolf* also depicts a child's passing into obscurity, which might help us to question idealizing habits and gesture toward respect for the "alterity" and "infinite remove" of the dead, which is the work of ethical ("impossible") mourning according to Jacques Derrida (6).[24] If we "interiorize within us the image, idol, or ideal of the other who is dead," do we also refuse their indefinite singularity, emphasizing instead replace-ability and perpetuating forms of neglect (Derrida 6)? This chapter has worked through a variety of metaphors and modes of looking at *the child*. It now concludes by trying to resist that category, welcoming the unseen and unseeing elements of *Little Eyolf* and letting Eyolf slip away, contrasting his status as *a dead child* with the child's status as figure for innocent potential, vengeance, and redemption.

My final aim is to emphasize a child's final exit. Eyolf will never return to his rooms. Unlike Peter, he is neither "a dream of immortality come true" nor a plague to the other, unseen children in the play—except perhaps in memoriam (Gilead 286). Both *Little Eyolf* and *Peter Pan* are morbid works that recognize replacement and adulteration at the heart of a certain understanding of childhood. Never growing up means more than the end of memory and interpersonal connection; it also means death. When Peter fights with Hook in Act Five, he is youth and joy, "a little bird that has broken out of the egg" (Barrie, *Peter Pan* 145). But he is also *"less like a boy than a mote of dust"* (145), and when he arrives in Act One, dressed in "autumn leaves and cobwebs," the nursery darkens (97). In "Replacement Children," Gabriele Schwab writes, the "replacement child confronts the bitter irony that the ideal child is a dead child" (281). The ideal child that Schwab describes is a child that never really was. Dead children do not embody the ideal while living; nor do they achieve such embodiment simply by dying, but instead through processes of postmortem idealization. Despite Peter's morbid qualities, and although he does not fall short of the ideal of an endlessly deferred future, he is too alive to be completely ideal. Eyolf, on the other hand, disappears under the surface of the water. He becomes "boy eternal" by providing inspiration for his parents' charitable and/or vengeful replacement and redemption project (Gilead 286). He cannot take active part in the work of mourning that Rita suggests is motivated by his eyes. Can we bring a child back into critical play, not as an all-seeing, judging eye or a fantasy of beginning anew, but instead as a character momentarily strung out between originality and replacement, life and death, innocence and adulteration (just like the rest of us)? Alternatively, can we leave Eyolf out of play in way that does not re-invoke the pathos of innocence and freeze him in un-theorized territory?

After Act One, Eyolf is invisible and untouchable in a stricter sense even than Peter.[25] When Act Two opens, Allmers stands in the trees by the shore, staring at the fjord. In a state of near shock, unhearing and slightly disoriented, he describes the surface water to Asta: "How merciless the fjord looks today. Lying so heavy and drowsy. Blue-gray—with golden glints—, and reflecting the rainclouds [...] On the surface, yes. But in the depths,—the violent undertow runs *there*" (*LE* 34). Asta begs Allmers twice not to look at or think about the water, but he reminds her that Eyolf is already far away from the estate: "You probably believe that he's lying here, right outside? But he isn't Asta. You mustn't believe it. Because you have to remember how furiously the current flows outward here. Right to the sea" (*LE* 35). Allmers asks Asta to calculate how far the currents must have swept the body out to sea in

"twenty-eight—twenty-nine hours," recognizing the vast distance between his deceased son and "the rest of us" (*LE* 35). After they discuss
the apparent meaninglessness of the loss, they distract one another with
memories of their life alone together in the past. When Allmers returns
to the present moment, he is horrified that he managed momentarily to
forget his son: "He slid out of my mind. Out of my thoughts. I didn't see
him before me for a moment, while we sat and talked. Forgot him entirely for the whole, long moment" (*LE* 40). Asta urges Allmers to accept
this forgetting as a necessary moment of rest in the midst of grief, but
Allmers insists that it is evidence of his failure to love Eyolf sufficiently,
claiming that he has neither the "right" nor the "heart" to rest (*LE* 40).
He insists that his thoughts must follow Eyolf's body, as it drifts in the
deep, and he states that he will take the boat out (*LE* 40). Asta holds him
back and compels him to sit with his back to the water.

Not only is Allmers's grief realistic, complete with uncertainty, confusion, and anger, but Ibsen also shows us, through Asta, that the living
simply must turn their backs on the dead, seeking moments of rest in
grief, support from others, and sustenance. Allmers and Asta's conversation turns again to his father and her mother, to their shortcomings
when it came to treating both Asta and one another with proper love and
respect. Knowing more than Allmers about her mother's infidelity, Asta
"*rises up*," "*fighting tears*," and begs Allmers,

	Oh, dear Alfred,—let them rest,—those who are gone. [...]
ALLMERS (*stands up*)	
	Yes, let them rest. (*Wrings his hands*) But they, those who are gone,—they don't let *us* rest, Asta. (*LE* 43)

One might ask whether the infidelities of turning one's back on the scene
of death and wondering what will be served for dinner are worse than
accusing the dead of haunting and tormenting the living. Allmers's accusation makes the notion of vigilant grief look like a form of vengeful
culpability, a payback demanded by the dead and the living alike.

Relying on the Freudian distinction between mourning and melancholy, Helland takes a moment to question his own description of Rita
and Allmers's grief: "sorg uten grunn" (mourning without grounds or
reason) (*Melankoliens spill* 260). He wonders whether the appropriate
term for their grief might be mourning rather than melancholy: "Should
not [...] the play be understood as a movement out of melancholy's repetitive blindness to a true work of mourning, whereby the son becomes
visible, maybe for the first time, as the object of mourning?" (260). His
answer to his own question is no. Eyolf's death enables Rita and Allmers
"to see the invisibility that they cast over" the child, but they continue
to construct their grief only out of this failure to see, which means that

their failure is the actual object of their mourning, rather than their son (270). Although I agree that *Little Eyolf* does not depict a movement toward "true mourning," I also resist the concept of "genuine grief" (Helland 270). Attempts to see the dead involve infidelity, regret, and narcissism, or incorporation of what is (not) other into the self. Mourning cannot evade melancholy because the dead do not remain; yet we can only focus on what remains: a memory, a projection, a name—which, as Ibsen makes explicit in the case of *Little Eyolf*, was already severed from the singularity of its bearer, in any case.[26]

Little Eyolf itself depicts—and should therefore caution against?—judging and blaming others when it comes to the work of mourning. It is clear that Rita and Allmers point fingers at one another to cover up their mutual need to eschew guilt and responsibility. According to Shaw, Rita gets her almost stated wish to be rid of little Eyolf, so that she can have Allmers all to herself. The "result," he writes, "may be imagined":

> They are soon at it hammer and tongs, each tearing the mask from the other's grief for the child, and leaving it exposed as their remorse: hers for having jealously hated Eyolf: his for having sacrificed him to his passion for Rita, and to the schoolmasterly vanity and folly which sees in the child nothing more than the vivisector sees in a guinea-pig: something to experiment on with a view to arranging the world to suit his own little ideas. (181)

Shaw appears to mimic the reproachful tones that Allmers and Rita use with one another, while remaining critical of using the living child as a means of recreating the world in the image of one's own beliefs. Each spouse accuses the other of having failed to love Eyolf enough or in the right way. Allmers says to Rita that she has gotten what she wished for, but she now adamantly denies ever having wished for such a thing: "Never in the world have I wished that! That Eyolf didn't stand between us two,—*that* I wished for" (*LE* 47). Rita then alleges, in kinder tones than Shaw's, that Allmers's motivations for making "a boy-wonder out of poor little Eyolf" were his diminishing love for her and his self-doubt, rather than love for their son: "Because you had begun to doubt that you had any great calling to live for in this world" (*LE* 49). After appearing to accept Rita's allegations, Allmers indicts Rita for seducing him away and dooming Eyolf to an early death: "*You* are to blame for what he became! It's *your* fault that he couldn't get himself out of the water" (*LE* 50). Feeling or inspiring (too much, the wrong kind of) desire is a prime mover in *Little Eyolf*. Rita is to blame for having been desirable, for having "lured" Allmers away from his duty as a father (*LE* 5). Allmers has not only desired Rita; he has also confided to Rita his nickname for Asta during that "all-consuming, lovely moment" in which they first neglected Eyolf, "dooming" him to fall (*LE* 55). Rita reminds Allmers of his confession now, and he can only recoil in horror, exclaiming "I remember nothing! Will remember nothing!" before uttering again the watchword of Act Two, the concept that he first denies and then claims: reprisal (*LE* 55).

The prelude to Eyolf's death is longer and slower than either the summoning of the Ratmaid or Rita's insistence on Eyolf's evil eye (while he is living) might at first imply. This prelude exceeds the bounds of the play's present, emerging for audiences through Ibsen's retrospective technique. Allmers and Rita's grief can be traced to Eyolf's first fall—his laming or disabling—and to a failure to cultivate a relationship with the boy that they now realize has been a stranger. Significantly, this realization constitutes a rallying point for husband and wife, a shared moment of agreement between accusations:

> ALLMERS (*looks thoughtfully at her*)
> If it's really as you think, then the two of us have never really owned our own child.
> RITA   No. Not fully, in love.
> ALLMERS   And just the same we walk around and grieve him so bitterly.
> RITA (*bitterly*)
> Yes, isn't it strange to think about? Walking around and mourning like this for a boy who was a little stranger. (*LE* 49)

Helland reads this moment as proof that Rita and Allmers have not loved their son, that they continue to talk about something abstract when using words like "owned." Their dialogue might also be read as honest and openly ambivalent. Although one might like to believe that parents know their children, and although Rita's realization does nothing to ameliorate Eyolf's life (because he is dead), recognizing that children too can be strangers can indicate a form of respect for alterity. This is perhaps not quite what Rita intends here. Nonetheless, she certainly gestures in this direction, while Allmers can only exclaim in resistance, "Oh, don't call him a stranger" (*LE* 49). The idea that Rita and Allmers could have and should have "owned" their child "fully in love" strikes me as a component of the innocence ideology, with its dreams of perfect starts.

Ibsen's characters, and many audience members, might cling to the ideal of an unconditionally and wholly loved child, but *Little Eyolf* is poised on the verge of letting this ideal go. In Act Three, Rita admits to Allmers that her plan to take in the poor children is not motivated by love "yet," but rather by the lessons about human responsibility she has learned from listening to Allmers and Asta's conversations, and by her desire to get in good with "the large, open eyes" that signal her grief and guilt (*LE* Ibsen 78). This revivification of Eyolf's eyes is a definite infidelity to the dead son in the form of negative idolization; yet it also emerges from an admirable admission of feelings that do not resemble idealized love.

Eyolf's remains go where even Peter and the Darling children do not go: into the threatening depths far below their flight to the Never Land in *Peter and Wendy*, under the surface where the mermaids who like to drown children live, and over which "a threatening change has come" in Act Three of *Peter Pan*, sending *"all the wiser mermaids to their coral recesses"* (Hook and his pirates are arriving) (Barrie 119). Wendy just barely manages to escape the clutches of a "mermaid who has dared to come back in the stillness," and Peter now recites his most infamous line: "(*with a drum beating in his breast as if he were a real boy at last*) To die will be an awfully big adventure" (Barrie, *Peter Pan* 124–125). A primary difference between the children of *Peter Pan* and Eyolf lies in both the Darling children's evasion of the depths and in Peter's immortality: Eyolf's death is no prelude to a great adventure. It is a disappearance into the depths, where neither growing up nor transgenerational visions of vengeance or dreams of redemption are possible.[27] Scholars might imagine what lies beneath. Kerans, for example, suggests that "lethal, vindictive sexuality" and "incestuous threat" lie beneath the sea's calm, regressive surface, with its "soothing constancy" (201). But no one has seen what lies beneath and lived to tell of it.

Why do we need to pursue Eyolf's body with our theories of perversion? Helland asserts that the effect of the Ratmaid's entrance in *Little Eyolf* "lies, to be sure, in the striking *break* with the reader's expectations" for a realist drama (*Melankoliens spill* 253). She has also served as bait for "interpreters of the text," who are rendered "in the image of the rat" when they look for her deep, symbolic significance—and thus "drown" in "the depths of meaning" (255). The Ratmaid herself makes it clear that she lures not only rat babies but also their parents and other adults to the depths (*LE* 15). Helland urges readers to consider the Ratmaid's meta-dramatic function as well as her symbolic meaning, respecting "that which is other/foreign about her," the way in which she can draw our attention to the limits of realist illusion (*Melankoliens spill* 254). Readers and characters alike can suffer from distinct forms of "kinship with the rats" (Weinstein 295): living and reproducing as animals, following in the footsteps of their forbearers, being drawn to the depths, being perceived as a nuisance or treated as vermin, invading or being unwelcome in a house, looking under the surface or drowning. Rather than pursuing Eyolf as the sign of failure and perversion, we might attempt to respect that which is other about him, not in the sense of marking childhood as other—an island; a realm apart; a mode of being that *should* mean transformation—but instead by acknowledging his indefinite singularity, his alternative trajectory, his horizontal exit from the vertical world of *Little Eyolf*, and the limits of his ability to look back.

The Eyolf who is reanimated as a seer after death is not the Eyolf who has exited the estate by drowning. Looking at, looking with, and feeling looked at by *the child* can also mean looking away from the death of *a child*. The final replacement project of *Little Eyolf* appears to ask us to imagine mourning and charitable progress as the shift from Eyolf's eyes to ghostly and accusing eyes to the eyes of all children: "Eyolf dies, so that the children may live" (Weinstein 316).[28] This move is generalizing, violating an indefinite singularity that might be untenable if the deceased character were not a child. It overlooks the problematic class dynamics of the final project. It also reproduces the interchangeability that Rita clearly expresses, or the poor boys' status as replacements for Eyolf. Just like other dead loved ones, a lost child is radically unique (irreplaceable) and radically indefinite (unfixed and inaccessible). Even if childhood is a category that asks us to look back, demanding that we judge, regret, and justify our actions and our adult-ness, a dead child cannot look back. There is an unseen and unseeing element to Ibsen's portrait of Eyolf that might make us critical of any insistence on "the eyes of the child" and "the child's gaze" of vengeance (Goldman 94).[29] Goldman emphasizes the visual aspect of the final moments of drama, staged or imagined as staged: "the long last look," the "afterimage" sharpened even by "a quick blackout" (108). The unseen spaces of the landscape of *Little Eyolf*, which might also influence staging, include underwater locations, the fjord and the deepening shelf of the North Sea, places that no one in the world of this drama can see—the place where Eyolf's unseeing corpse is nonetheless understood to go, sweeping down and horizontally away from the heights to seaside landscape in which his parents remain.

In the next and final chapter, I move from dramatic emptiness and dreams of future fulfillment to forms of historical fullness, by returning to the nursery at the folk museum (already occupied in the Prologue) and consulting advice manuals that describe the nursery, nanny, and ideologies of child-rearing at the turn of the century in Norway. This fullness, it turns out, does not prevent the nursery from remaining a fitting figure for innocence: a space of anxious potential that triggers fears about the future.

Notes

1 I dedicate this chapter to my nephew, Levi H Watanabe (2003–2014). The decision to consider a work of children's literature and to compare *Little Eyolf* with *Peter Pan* has been part of my (interminable) work of mourning for Levi, who also drowned and will never grow up. In *For Derrida*, J. Hillis Miller describes his chapters on mourning as his "way of discovering that Derrida was right when he said that mourning is 'impossible,' 'absolute,' 'endless,' and, in the end, only with difficulty to be distinguished from melancholy" (326). I modify Miller's final words from "Absolute Mourning: It

is Jacques You Mourn For (*In memory of Rosie, a cat*)": "If my chapter is a work of mourning for [Levi], it hasn't worked" (326).

2 Fjelde translates the appellation *Rottejomfrue* as Ratwife, which might obscure the fact that "frøken Varg" (Miss Varg, varg meaning wolf) is an older woman who has never married. An alternative translation might be Rat-spinster.

3 Both Peter Pan and Lewis Carroll's Alice are central and exceptional figures in Anglophone children's literature and child studies. In *Child Loving*, Kincaid refers to Barrie's and Carroll's stories of Peter and Alice as "dramas of perpetuation": "No figures are more consistently Other, more adept at resisting satisfaction, blocking fulfillment, keeping the chase and desire alive" (276–277). Regarding Peter specifically, he expresses surprise that

> the charge of sentimentality is brought against a figure that is antithetical to syrup, who is so unsoft and unfurry as to bite all those who try their hand at petting [...] Peter's toughness is vitally connected to his innocence, an innocence nowhere more relentlessly tied to ignorance. (281–282)

Significantly, innocence is not yielding or sweet or aware and self-sacrificing in *Peter Pan*—all adjectives that can be applied to the depiction of Eyolf's innocence in Act One of *Little Eyolf*.

4 My consideration of the landscape of *Little Eyolf* (as well as the attention that I pay to the minor spaces of nurseries) is inspired in large part by Elinor Fuchs's and Una Chaudhuri's work on theater and landscape. See Fuchs, "EF's Visit to a Small Planet: Some Questions to Ask a Play" and Fuchs and Chaudhuri, *Land/scape/theater*.

5 For another consideration of Ibsen against the vertical grain, see Ellen Rees's "Problems of landscape and representation in Ibsen's *Når vi døde vågner*".

6 Moi finds that the recent trend of focusing on childhood and sexuality in *Little Eyolf* is too limiting, "marginalizing the character of Borghejm and generally leaving too much of the play in the dark" (188). This might be the case (Borghejm certainly remains peripheral to my own reading). Then again, I find that Moi's universalizing reading of Ibsen's play leaves significant counterevidence out of play. If focus on the child can obscure the forest for the trees, focus on broad themes, such as will or love, can obscure the trees for the forest.

7 According to Moi, this "must" is a reference to conscription, which means that Eyolf's parents have yet to discuss his disability with him (10).

8 For a discussion of folk culture references and symbolism in Ibsen, see Nina S. Alnæs *Varulv om natten* (Werewolf at Night). See also Moi's discussion of the possible influence on Ibsen of illustrations by Arthur C. Payne and Harry Payne in a German translation of Robert Browning's poem adaptations, "The Pied Piper of Hamelin: A Child's Story" (1842) (129–131).

9 There are no lost girls in *Peter Pan*. According to Peter, girls "are much too clever to fall out of their prams" (Barrie 101).

10 Arnold Weinstein, for example, writes that we see the "Rat Wife again in the werewolf Rita, who is strangling her husband in a frenzy of hunger" (313).

11 In "Magic Abjured," Sarah Gilead analyzes types of "return-to-reality closural frame[s]" in children's fiction, finding that *Peter and Wendy* "acts in a tragic mode that reveals, without an assuring sense of mediation, both the seductive force and the dangerous potentiality of fantasy" (278).

12 Referring to the risky business of looking at the child in "What Is Queer Theory Doing with the Child?" Karín Lesnik-Oberstein and Stephen Thomson write, "We are not suggesting that there is a safe way to invoke the child, but rather that this can only be risked in an acceptance of its full danger.

That is to say, it is a matter of assuming the responsibility self-reflexively for the figure and what it might entail" (45).

13 See also Weinstein's reading of the child in *Little Eyolf* in "Metamorphosis in Ibsen's *Little Eyolf*." Weinstein defines Eyolf as a "prop, a 'crutch,'" who, "grotesquely enough, allowed his parents to maintain their equilibrium and personae" (302). Like Goldman (and unlike Helland, who insists that Rita and Alfred never manage to see Eyolf), he insists that "the child's own vision is discovered and vindicated in this text," but defines this child as "the prying light of consciousness itself" (303).

14 In *Melankoliens spill* (*The Play of Melancholy*), Helland also notes that Rita and Allmers share a gesture of indifference in Act One: the "shoulder shrug" (*LE* 7). Rita shrugs her shoulders regarding parenting, leaving such matters firstly to Allmers and secondarily to Asta. Allmers shrugs his shoulders twice, when his book is first mentioned and then again when he and Rita are fighting toward the end of Act One, after Eyolf has wandered out unnoticed, but before they realize that he has drowned.

15 For a historicizing discussion of this understanding of the self as achievement (and its impact on our understanding of death in childhood), see "Too Soon: Representations of Childhood Death in Literature for Children" by Reynolds and Yates.

16 Kafer asks, "how might a feminist/queer/crip–informed analysis expand or complicate queer theoretical texts that rely on a trope of mobility for their analyses or that tend to allegorize rather than analyze disability and disabled bodies?" (18). Although I do not claim to analyze disability in this chapter, I am pointing to the ways in which Ibsen's play allegorizes disability.

17 There is, of course, no first lost boy. Even prominent, truly lost boys come after and are themselves versions of, or replacements for, other lost boys. In one sense (and in the sense of one sentence) a truly singular figure—"All children, except one, grow up"—Peter too goes on and after (Barrie, *Peter and Wendy* 1). There is, for example, a series of biographical boys, including Barrie's dead brother, David, and the boys that Barrie later adopted, and there is a series of literary and theatrical depictions of Peter and other figures of the Never Land. See Mavor 2007, 177–178 and 201–203.

18 The boy who never was is introduced in Barrie's stage directions: "*He is dreaming, and in his dreams he is always in pursuit of a boy who was never here, nor anywhere: the only boy who could beat him*" (Barrie 135).

19 Templeton notes that while John Northam and Errol Durbach have read the dress-up game as a repression of the siblings' attraction or desire for one another—an "innocent incest"—it could just as easily be read as a repressed "homoerotic fantasy" (Northam qtd. in Templeton and Templeton 283).

20 Kincaid warns against "reducing to simple perversity the difference of the past" by over-gendering or by applying contemporary ideas to the dress and activities of children of the past (*Child Loving* 65). He notes that Richard von Krafft-Ebing (1840–1902), for example, argued that children were neuter in terms of both gender and sexuality before puberty. When it comes to gendered dress, Kincaid writes, "Our own view of the matter tends, significantly, to be more edgy: we look back and see not neutrality but some kind of cross-dressing" (65). In *Strange Dislocations*, Carolyn Steedman similarly argues (while cautioning against the erasure of feminization from the scene of being watched) that one mistake "in watching the child being watched, is to think that her audience always thought it important that she was a girl (thought her 'girlness' to be important in the way we now think it important)" (8–9).

21 The chronology suggested is somewhat unclear. When the play opens, Asta is 25, Allmers 36 or 37. Allmers has been married to Rita for ten years.

Allmers' father died when Asta was big enough to sew but little enough not to remember, perhaps around 5 years of age, making Allmers around 17 at the time. This would mean that ten years passed between the father's death and Allmers' marriage. The time between Allmers's fathers' and Asta's mother's death was two years, so the siblings' dress-up game could have taken place anytime (the whole time?) during the remaining eight years. In Norwegian, "student" could mean a person studying at university or someone who had completed the *examen atrium*, an entrance exam. The quoted dialogue suggests that Allmers had passed the exam when his father died (because he had a student cap), and that the game began when he began studying.

22 "Dejlig," a frequently used adjective in *Little Eyolf*, has a range of meanings, from lovely to charming to beautiful to delicious. Some examples: Eyolf uses *dejlig* to describe the Ratmaid's dog, Mopsemand; Borghejm uses it to refer to love and other wonderful things; Allmers uses it to describe Rita's appearance on the night of his return (dressed in white with loose hair flowing down her back), when she failed to seduce him; Rita uses it to describe Allmers' return from the mountains and erotic relations.

23 Helland acknowledges that *Little Eyolf* provides plenty of evidence to indicate that Asta and Borghejm's match is not ideal, but he insists that these two have a better chance of taking part "in the game of life" than Rita and Allmers (*Melankoliens spill*, 279). He asserts that Asta does not have "the same regressive wish to stop time" as Allmers (279). Unlike Templeton, then, he insists that this couple, at least, "enters their relationship with open eyes, and with somewhat more realistic expectations" (Helland 279).

24 Questions of mourning, mortality, and survival are addressed in a wide variety of Derrida's essays and books. For introductions to mourning in Derrida, see Michael Naas's introduction to *The Work of Mourning* and J. Hillis Miller's "Touching Derrida Touching Nancy" and "Absolute Mourning: It Is Jacques You Mourn For" in *For Derrida*.

25 When Wendy attempts to embrace Peter because he does not have a mother, he tells her that she must not touch him, that no one ever touches him, and he does not know why (Barrie, *Peter Pan* 98).

26 See Naas' Introduction to *The Work of Mourning* and "Fors," Derrida's Foreword to *The Wolfman's Magic Word* by Nicolas Abraham and Maria Torok.

27 For an adaptation of *Little Eyolf* that allows its dead boy to return to the stage from the water (and that might evoke questions about the cultural specificity of my universalizing descriptions of death here), see Hiro Kanagawa's *Indian Arm*.

28 After associating Rita's proposal with "selfless love" and "maturation," Weinstein suggest that the poor children "may even play with [Eyolf's] crutch" (316–317). With this last phase, Weinstein appears, knowingly but indirectly, to return to more ambivalent territory, where "what must remain pure is foul(ed); what must remain innocent is diseased" (298).

29 See also "Ibsen's *Little Eyolf*," wherein Barry Jacobs notes that Ibsen describes his character's eyes with particular care in *Little Eyolf* and repeatedly emphasizes looking in his stage directions, making the play read "more like a twentieth-century film script than a late nineteenth-century play" (607).

4 Unfaithful Authenticity
Going Backstage in the Bourgeois Home

In *A Doll House*, Nora Helmer insists that children's space and child's play are the backdrop and (faulty) foundation of her marriage and family life: "our home has been nothing other than a playroom. I have been your doll-wife here, just as I was papa's doll-child at home. And the children, they have been my dolls" (*Du* 87). Both Nora's playroom metaphor and Ibsen's neologistic title, *Et dukkehjem* (literally *A Dollhome*), suggest that the Helmer world is somehow miniaturized and estranging, that playrooms and childish practices can threaten mature personhood and the quest for freedom.[1] They suggest Torvald and Nora are themselves childlike, playing house and playing dolls, and that Nora and her children have been played with as if they were dolls, uncanny copies of children living out an inauthentic existence. After Nora stops playing and starts making demands, Torvald informs her that she is childish and does not understand the world in which she lives. She responds, "No, that I don't. But I will make a go of it now. I have to try to figure out who is right, society or me" (*Du* 89). Many critics have considered the extent to which Nora's prior mode of living—keeping secrets and longing for the day when her husband will realize that she has made a great sacrifice for him and rescue her in turn—can initiate the revolutionary demands that she makes before leaving. Torvald's appraisal implies that Nora can be associated with the child until the end. She leaves behind the role of doll-wife, playing house in a world apart, only to inhabit a differently childish mode of utopian (and, Torvald implies, unrealistic) demands for access to universal personhood, justice, and a better future. It is difficult, it seems, to shake both childish habits and accusations of childishness.

This book has explored the return of the children's room in three of Ibsen's late dramas, which I have called "the empty nursery plays": *Hedda Gabler* (1890), *Bygmester Solness* (*The Master Builder*) (1892), and *Lille Eyolf* (*Little Eyolf*) (1894). The metaphorical playroom never materializes as a mimetic room in dialogue or stage directions in *A Doll House*. Nora's three children are simply sent away from the parlor and into the *"room to the left"* (*Du* 26). In the empty nursery plays, Ibsen's childless characters discuss unused children's rooms and make plans to fill them up, a pattern that has enabled me to explore and resist some conventional conceptualizations of reproduction and innocence. In the Introduction, I acknowledged that these rooms are little more than traces, even in these late plays. In fact, none of the dramas extend into the more private spaces of the home with the mimetic ease found in "A Doll House—1879," the apartment-installation inspired by *A Doll House* at the Norsk Folkemuseum (the Norwegian Museum of Cultural History). The material authenticity of "A Doll House—1879" represents, I argued, a faithful faithlessness, because it aims to offer an accurate staging of a petit bourgeois home by fleshing out the world that can be assumed to surround, but is not actually described in, *A Doll House*.

Because they are naturalistically peripheral in the dramas, Ibsen's children's rooms are most effectively explored through their figuration of absence and absenting, maintenance of emptiness, and disregard for children. At the same time, playrooms and nurseries remain traces of the diversely classed worlds of childhood and women's reproductive labor—from birth to domestic service—which are mostly offstage in Ibsen's dramas and un-staged in theatrical productions. Marginalization of women's labor is not particularly surprising, in Ibsen's oeuvre or elsewhere. Nonetheless, it remains curious that nurseries are named and establish a pattern across three consecutive dramas when Ibsen is less interested in incorporating minor roles for servants, and when he begins to be particularly interested in failure, aging, and the ends of (pro)creative possibilities.

I have attended, thus far, to Ibsen's interest in emptiness, while also making an attempt to queer that emptiness by looking toward implied non- or post-procreative futures. I now take a greater interest in nurseries and women's labor in more explicitly material and historical senses. This chapter brings this book full circle before opening a can of worms: it returns to the apartment-installation at the folk museum and then consults archival materials to consider things that take place just beyond Ibsen's dramatic line of sight, in the offstage world of the nursery and nanny. This world can also serve to define an outer limit of Ibsen's interest in women. Although he gives the bourgeois wife center stage, he also includes maids, nannies, and other working women in his character lists; and yet women's *labor* cannot be described as playing a major role in his dramatic visions of vocation, creativity, survival, and mortality. By focusing on nurseries and nannies, or by going backstage in order to flesh out forms of emptiness and minimalism, I perform my own faithful faithlessness. I break faith, that is, with the general dramatic status— peripheral, figurative, empty and so disposed to being refilled—of children's rooms in the empty nursery plays, expressing more interest in offstage spaces and figures than might be deemed appropriate in a study on Ibsen. This interest might be described as a meeting point of respect and disregard for (looking away from) the playwright's vision.

In the first section of this chapter, I describe my theoretical and literary-critical motivations for breaking faith, engaging with the frequent contention that antisocial queer theory is insufficiently materialist and exploring Franco Moretti's claim that class conflicts are largely absent from Ibsen's oeuvre. Inspired by criticisms of Lee Edelman's abstract and ahistorical Child and Moretti's claim that *A Doll House* "doesn't really *believe* in the public sphere," I argue that thinking about nurseries should eventually lead us back to the question of women's labor, not only in *A Doll House* but also in the empty nursery plays (Moretti 186). Nurseries cannot be fully stripped of their class identity, no matter their emptiness—an emptiness that is, after all, enabled by wealth, or by the ability to maintain spaces of memorialization. In the next section, I return to the apartment-installation at the museum in order to work my way from the frontstage to the backstage of the bourgeois household. While the playwright makes visible the theatricality of bourgeois life via semi-private settings such as the parlor, the museum both emphasizes the parlor and puts some offstage and fully private spaces on display, including the nursery. In the third section, I use Norwegian scholarship and primary sources available in Dano-Norwegian at the turn of the century—mostly advice manuals from the period 1890–1920—to consider ideologies of child-rearing and proper development surrounding nurseries and nannies, while offering a glimpse of what remains behind the scenes. Perhaps paradoxically, it is the fully private spaces in the bourgeois home that open to a wider world of class conflicts legible at the limits of Ibsen's dramatic worlds.

In both its empty and offstage dramatic form and its evocation in advice manuals, the nursery remains a fitting figure for innocence, because it is a constructed, classed, and contingent space of potential, filled with anxious expectations. Ibsen wrote his dramas during the "nanny chapter," an era of profound negative influence on the home and family according to one advice manual from 1902: "Yes, one could certainly say quite a bit about the nanny chapter. What they have inflicted on our homes in terms of the corruption of decency cannot be ignored. Morally and physically" (Selmer 47). Ibsen was profoundly interested in skewering ideas like "the corruption of decency." As I have tried to show, he did so not only through the bourgeois family and its semi-private spaces, but also by means of peripheral play with empty spaces that figure and trouble innocence and the deferred future. Inspired by Ibsen's displacement of the child and by the limits of his dramatic vision when it comes to women's labor, I have taken on the project of skewering "the corruption of decency" by means of *another room in the house*, a space that the playwright both conjures and neglects, three dramas in a row.

Materializing Emptiness

The antisocial queer theory that has influenced this book is sometimes criticized for being insufficiently materialist and unaware of the ways in which it reproduces specific representations of race, gender, sex, ability, and class. José Esteban Muñoz, for example, has argued that Lee Edelman's polemical treatment of the Child in *No Future* (2004) makes it appear as if "all queers" are the "stealth-universal-white-gayman" and as if "all children" are the "privileged white babies to whom contemporary society caters" (Muñoz 94). According to this critique, Edelman's "gayman" is "stealth-universal" because *No Future* proceeds without expressing awareness of privilege or acknowledging those who might disidentify, and its children are white or racially unmarked because *No Future* does not consider how processes of racialization challenge the symbolic and material operations of innocence. Edelman's primary aim is to oppose queerness to identities and social institutions, but he also acknowledges that different people have different lived relationships to power and politics. He insists, relatedly, that "the image of the Child" is "not to be confused with the lived experiences of any historical children" (11). In response, many critics have asked the question, given here in Alison Kafer's formulation, "How does the Child differ from historical children?" (34). Edelman includes a preemptive response in a footnote in *No Future*, in which he confesses that he has little sympathy for such criticisms, given that they do not recognize the ways in which they themselves "represent the compulsory norm that [*No Future*] is challenging" (157). They are unable, Edelman implies, to recognize that their politics also pivot on the Child and its deferred future.[2]

In "Reproduction and Queer Theory" (2017), Anca Parvulescu revisits *No Future* because it has been so influential within queer studies and because interest in the figure of the child is still going strong.[3] She insists, however, that Edelman's approach is no longer a "theoretical model to be cultivated and reproduced," while also implying that the Child is a misleading or limited figure for thinking about reproduction (87). Parvulescu makes note of the congratulatory and triumphant use of the term non-reproductive to describe queer lives and wants to point to "risks inherent in this trend" (87). There are no non-reproductive lives, she reminds us, because all lives are dependent upon labor and capital.[4] Parvulescu's major criticisms of *No Future*, anchored in her reading of J. M. Coetzee's *Slow Man*, are that it fails to theorize reproduction and that it fails to acknowledge how its "queer man" remains dependent on women's labor (89). She writes,

> *No Future* told a necessary but partial story about reproductive futurism, because Edelman worked with a narrow concept of reproduction as procreative heteronormativity tethered to heterosexual sex. The book left untold the other story of reproduction: our daily reproduction in the service of capitalism. (Parvulescu 89)

Reproduction in Ibsen's oeuvre is certainly "tethered to" figures of heterosexual procreativity, but I have attempted to draw attention to some of the ways in which Ibsen problematizes this tether. After all, every future in the empty nursery plays takes place in a post-procreative horizon (after the death of the child), and each drama provides material for troubling the notion of innocent origins. Moreover, stories and performances of the reproduction of class differences *are* present in Ibsen's oeuvre, if peripheral.

In many ways, this chapter is inspired by these and related critiques of Edelman, and the broader challenges that such critiques pose to antisocial queer theory. I do not, however, take the side of historical children against the Child or seek to reinforce binaries like symbolic/material or abstract/real in any strict sense.[5] Instead, I make strategic use of the fields of tension that such binaries repeatedly open, in queer considerations of the Child/children and elsewhere. Edelman's Child is, among other things, a figure for a particular emptiness in political rhetoric, which hails a normative subject, cannot tolerate (or does not need to bother with) the realities of reproduction and its uneven impacts on people, and refuses to acknowledge how its reality relies on a wide variety of un-masterable fantasies. In *No Future*, Edelman also emphasizes the power of the parent, or their good fit with the rhetorical reproduction of political values. I focus instead on the moving parts of parenting, particularly the vulnerable and much less visible—in politics and elsewhere—"mother-surrogate" (Vammen 21).[6] Of particular interest to me in Parvulescu's critique of Edelman are her references to today's nannies, who often leave their children behind to care for other people's middle-class offspring. I am using Ibsen's dramas as a springboard for thinking about this particular story of reproduction in turn of the century Norway.

In *A Doll House*, the nanny is an essential, enabling feature of the "playful" situation that Nora describes in her final conversation with Torvald. Toward the beginning of the second act, Anne-Marie, Nora's former nanny and the current mother-surrogate for Nora's three children, describes a rather less idealizing approach to family, identity, and survival than is found in Torvald's ideology of womanhood or in Nora's romantic dreams of rescue and revolutionary demands for freedom. Later, Torvald tells Nora that her "holiest duties" are to her husband and children, but she rejects this in favor of her duty to herself (*Du* 88). Anne-Marie had to leave her own "illegitimate" child to become Nora's caregiver, and she considered herself lucky to get the job (*Du* 40). Nora asks her whether she wanted to be a nanny, and Anne-Marie responds, "When I could get such a good position? A poor girl in unfortunate circumstances must be happy for that" (*Du* 40). Torvald and Nora can rely on Anne-Marie to care for their children while they deal with the crises in their lives. In the realist imagination, Anne-Marie watches Ivar, Bob, and Emmy when they are not in the parlor. In the theatrical imagination, she waits for them in the wings, while Nora plays with them on stage.

In the naturalist (and perhaps also materialist-feminist) imagination, she works in the nursery and kitchens to tidy and clean and prepare food for the children, caring for them under the course of Nora's metamorphosis. She will presumably stay on to care for them after Nora slams the door.

As I have stated, and although Ibsen gestures to this particular class conflict in *A Doll House*, the question of women's labor in the bourgeois home is primarily peripheral in his oeuvre. By the time we get to the empty nursery plays, there are definite references to procreative labor: Hedda Tesman is clearly valued as a carrier for the Tesman family's expectations; Aline Solness gave birth to twins and then insisted (ironically, murderously) on fulfilling her maternal duty by nursing them herself, even when she was ill and her milk posed a threat; Rita Allmers refers to enduring the "unspeakable pain" of childbirth "with jubilation and joy," for her husband's sake (*LE* 27). But there is only one servant in the empty nursery plays: Berte, the maid of *Hedda Gabler*, who also cared for Tesman when he was a boy. These plays make figurative use of children's rooms, but they do not emphasize the divisions in procreative and domestic labor of which nurseries are often signs. What would it mean to insist upon the relevance of this particular story of the reproduction of class, which appears briefly on Ibsen's stage before withdrawing to the wings, yet remains fully relevant to the performance of bourgeois life?

In *The Bourgeois* (2013), Franco Moretti asserts that the bourgeois settings, characterizations, and conflicts in Ibsen's plays represent both the potency and limits of Ibsen's critique. He opens "Ibsen and the Spirit of Capitalism," the last chapter of this book, by describing Ibsen's "broad bourgeois fresco"—"shipbuilders, industrialists, financiers, merchants, bankers, developers" (and the list goes on)—and then expresses some surprise at the lack of workers, "except for a few house servants" (169–170). Moretti quickly offers an explanation for this "strange" lack of laborers, however: "No workers, because the conflict Ibsen wants to focus on is *internal* to the bourgeoisie itself" (Moretti 170). He specifies that this conflict, more accurately labeled as a "dissonance" given its internality, is not simply the contradiction between "good *Bürger*" and "unscrupulous financier" found in George Eliot or George Bernard Shaw (178, 186). What Ibsen stages—and Moretti goes so far as to claim that he is the "only" writer who looks this dissonance right in the face (170)—is the triumph of the will of the "creative destroyer" over the best intentions of any bourgeois realist (187).[7]

Moretti gestures to, but does not consider in detail, the ways in which gender or specifically sexed forms of labor might support, alter, or add nuance to his claims. Regarding Ibsen's decision to depict the "realist as a woman," he writes,

> an odd choice, for the times [...] A radical choice, too, in the spirit of Mill's *Subjection of Women*. But also profoundly pessimistic about

the scope of bourgeois 'realism': imaginable within the intimate sphere—as the solvent of the nuclear family and its lies—but not in society at large. Nora's prose at the end of *Dollhouse* echoes the writings of Wollstonecraft, Fuller, Martineau: but their public arguments are now locked inside a living room [...] What a paradox, this drama that shocks the European public sphere, but doesn't really *believe* in the public sphere. (186)

Here, Moretti evokes the public/private binary and its broad strokes gendering as a way of understanding the limits of Ibsen's critique. Of course, Nora's arguments are conceived as a way *out* of the living room in *A Doll House*; and, as Moretti knows, the fourth wall is very public indeed, so Nora's lines are not really "locked inside a living room" but generally take place in and for a specific (generally bourgeois) public at the theater. Nevertheless, it is true that the text of *A Doll House* ends at the limit of the private home and with a good deal of uncertainty concerning Nora's future. The public sphere is an unknowable night in Ibsen's drama because Nora walks out of the parlor and into darkness when she slams the door. It is also imagined as a place of differently gendered labor and struggle via Mrs. Linde's work outside the home. Moreover, the private sphere is depicted as a divider of working-class mothers and daughters, given its ability to employ mother-surrogates like Anne-Marie. Is Anne-Marie another, differently classed "realist as woman," or does this also violate the necessary public-ness of addressing problems in "society at large"? Perhaps Anne-Marie's particular story of class differentiation makes no difference to the grand claim that Moretti makes concerning Ibsen's "enduring lesson for the world today": "the impotence of bourgeois realism in the face of capitalist megalomania" (187).

Moretti's discussion resonates with my own, in the sense that I too emphasize the intensely bourgeois character of Ibsen's dramatic worlds and am interested in the lengths and limits of his capacity to use those worlds to produce a broader critique of systemic delusions and inequities. One thing that differentiates my consideration of class from Moretti's is the following question: What happens if we reject a simplistic division of public and private, taking variation within the bourgeois home into closer consideration (and insisting that sexed and gendered lives are reproduced under patriarchy and from within capitalism)?[8] Focused as Moretti is on the professions, he cannot take women's labor into account. He does cite Nora's playroom metaphor, describing it as the pivot on which she turns from playing house and waiting for miracles to being "serious" and inhabiting prose (181). Prose is "Ibsen's idea of freedom," according to Moretti, "a style that understands the delusions of metaphors, and leaves them behind. A Woman who understands a man and leaves him behind" (181). Of course, this is also the moment when Torvald accuses Nora of being childish in another sense: not as the passive doll-wife, an apparently willing participant in Torvald's rather conventional game of playing house, but as the naïve and demanding child. Is this really prose—"I have to try to figure out who is right, society or me?" (*Du* 89)—or must we look to Anne-Marie for a prosaic realism that is more instructive when it comes to the ways in which class is also sexed, gendered, and racializing? Perhaps the marginalization of sexed and gendered forms of domestic labor—in Moretti as well as Ibsen—is another sign of realism's at once "indispensable" and "unthinkable" status (Moretti 186).

What makes Ibsen's oeuvre both profoundly bourgeois and able to stick with dissonance, according to Moretti, is the very briefness of the serious turn to prose followed by the swift return or multiplication of metaphors. Moretti compares passages from *Pillars of Society* (1877) and *John Gabriel Borkman* (1896) to illustrate the "so-called 'symbolism' of the late Ibsen," when prose is "overrun by tropes," capitalism "de-materialized" (Moretti 181–182). The empty nursery plays are from Ibsen's late period, when "there are no Noras left, to counter Borkman's and Solness's destructive metaphors; the opposite: Hilde, inciting '*my* masterbuilder' to his suicidal hallucination" (Moretti 186 and *BS* qtd. in Moretti). Although Nora appears to use and then leave her playroom metaphor behind, Moretti knows that in "Ibsen's world," "*nothing* disappears" (170). In the empty nursery plays, the playroom too returns, in a contested mode of materialization no less. Or perhaps it never really went away.

As I have proposed, it is curious that the nursery emerges as a figure when Ibsen begins to dramatize impotence and resistance to impotence, in the double sense of powerlessness and sexual-reproductive dysfunction, while also more or less erasing "house servants" (Moretti 170). Again, *Hedda Gabler* is the exception to the servant-less rule in the empty nursery plays. Ibsen describes "the faithful servant Berte," Tesman's former nanny and current maid, as a member of the harmonious unit that is the Tesman family (*Speeches and Letters* 299, trans. Sprinchorn). Neither *The Master Builder* nor *Little Eyolf* include servants in their character lists. Perhaps we might imagine that Aline does most of the housework in the former drama, given that she is so interested in "duty" (*BS* 28). It is suggested that she prepares the middle nursery room for Hilde, but she is also somewhat delicate or sickly, and she appears to have time to sit in the sun contemplating her losses. Who has prepared the food, and who will serve it when she calls Solness and Hilde to the table? *Little Eyolf* mostly places questions of class difference outside the stately home, but we might wonder who cleans Eyolf's rooms, who cooks his meals and washes his clothes, who cares for him when his parents are not with him? Perhaps it is intended that audiences will assume the house is staffed, in which case the total absence of servants would represent a form of mimetic minimalism in the drama. Perhaps it is Rita who does the work. She is unpacking Alfred's suitcase when the play opens, work that is performed together with the maid in *Hedda Gabler*. In Act Three, however, when Allmers questions why Rita grieves Eyolf's loss so deeply, he suggests that she was not burdened with the daily tasks of childcare while Eyolf was living: "You went entire half days without having him before your eyes" (*LE* 70). Was Eyolf with Alfred during these half days, or simply on his own? Why would a boy with rooms of his own not have a nanny or a governess?[9]

Whatever questions we ask or do not ask concerning labor in Ibsen's households, it remains the case that there are children's rooms and no servants in *The Master Builder* and *Little Eyolf*. This curious combination—more rooms and fewer servants—might trigger our imagination in other ways. Ibsen's treatment of empty nursery rooms is also "*internal* to the bourgeois itself" (Moretti 170), but it is so deeply internal that thinking about it can take us out the other end, where even abstract figures of reproduction demand that we consider women workers.

The persistence of Nora's playroom metaphor, or its reemergence as a series of traces in the empty nursery plays, might lead one to reverse Moretti's claim that Ibsen's dramas do not *believe* in the public sphere, asking instead whether they *believe* in the private sphere. After all, the children's rooms of *Hedda Gabler*, *The Master Builder*, and *Little Eyolf* are less public and more marginalized in Ibsen's domestic-dramatic worlds than the parlor in *A Doll House*. How can we take Nora's realism seriously if we do not compare her ability to "[understand] a man, and [leave] him behind" with Anne-Marie's ability to understand her own life choices, which necessitated that she leave her daughter behind to rear other people's children (Moretti 181)?[10] Perhaps paradoxically—although it is only paradoxical if we take Moretti's differentiation of the public and private seriously—more private rooms can serve to open our awareness to a more diversely classed world. That is, nurseries are signs of the ways in which the supposedly isolated and limited sphere of the parlor relies on women's labor, in both senses of the word: giving birth and working. Of course, this opening to a wider world is one of the reasons why such spaces are kept hidden. Keeping up appearances generally involves hiding the help.

Back to the Museum

The Norsk Folkemuseum employs a common metaphor—the bourgeois-home-as-theater—to describe "A Doll House—1879," the apartment-installation inside Wessels Street 15, a reconstructed building in *Gamlebyen*, the old city section of the open-air museum. The museum's website reads: "We will present the late 19th century bourgeois home as a female sphere in a male world, with the front stage where the master and the mistress entertained guests and the back stage where the servants worked and the children usually were hidden way."[11] This description not only makes use of the common concept of gendered separate spheres, wherein the private home is "female" and opposed to the public or "male world," it also observes how the private home is itself divided between a dual-gendered, semi-private place of entertainment, on the one hand, and more private spaces and persons, on the other. I now return to the museum in order to re-approach the drama of reproduction, working my way from the frontstage to the backstage, from the parlor to the nursery.

"A Doll House—1879" is a theatrical space, in the sense that it is inspired by a drama and conceptualized in relationship to the performance of bourgeois private life. Nonetheless, and as discussed in the Prologue, this apartment-installation leads me to ask, What remains of theater and Ibsen's dramatic text at the museum? In *A Doll House*, characters come and go; they enter other rooms or the wider world by exiting one of four doors. The stage directions describe only the space that is visible to the audience: the semi-private, highly theatrical world of the bourgeois parlor.[12] I call this room highly theatrical not only because it is a space for display, visitors, and keeping up appearances, but also because it was, and generally is, the staged space in many of Ibsen's realist dramas. The most significant remainder and reminder of Ibsen's text in the museum is thus the setting of the parlor, a room in which the bourgeois wife performs and from which she escapes—but to which she will return, again and again, in subsequent stagings and adaptations. The modes of display and the arrangement of rooms at the museum evoke a variety of issues that matter to this book, including the postmodern spectator's relationship to a dramatized and/or (un)staged past, the politics and performance of the family and private home, and the classed and gendered characteristics of domestic spaces and practices. At the same time, "A Doll House—1879" can enable one to consider the lengths and limits of Ibsen's dramatic worlds. Ibsen gives more attention to the performing wife and her semi-private space than to nurseries and their proper occupants. The museum, on the other hand, both stages the nursery and maintains its status as backstage, less visible, marginalized.

As is well known, *A Doll House* makes the connections between bourgeois life and theater explicit, in part by means of its performance in the parlor. In Act Three, Nora executes a dance within the drama, a tarantella performed rapidly and confusedly in order to distract her husband and keep him from the mailbox, where the blackmail letter revealing her forgery waits. This tarantella expresses Nora's understanding of her husband's desires: that he longs to be her teacher and guide, that her enacted helplessness turns him on. It also represents a particularly dynamic phase in her metamorphosis from doll-wife to rebel. In *Ibsen and the*

Birth of Modernism (2007), Toril Moi spends several pages analyzing the tarantella scene and its meta-theatrical implications, concluding that

> The striking theatricality of the tarantella—the fact that it is such an obvious theatrical show-stopper—reminds us that we are in a theater. Ibsen's modernism is based on the sense that we need theater—I mean the actual art form—to reveal to us the frames of concealment and theatricalization on which we inevitably engage in everyday life. I do not base this claim only on Nora's dancing. By placing two kinds of spectator onstage during the tarantella, Ibsen tells us that only the audience is capable of seeing the whole picture: seeing both the temptation to theatricalize others [Torvald and Dr. Rank's spectatorship] and the possibility of understanding and acknowledging Nora's suffering [Mrs. Linde's spectatorship]. (241)

According to Moi, Ibsen uses metatheater to point to quotidian forms of theatricalization and concealment that take place outside the theater. Her "we" in the audience—the "we" in need of theater—sounds rather universal, and it is undoubtedly true that many forms of life are theatricalized, in senses concealing as well as revealing.

I am interested, by contrast, in the particularly bourgeois flavor communicated by Ibsen's parlor setting, and in those aspects of "the whole picture" that remain marginalized and de-materialized in Ibsen's oeuvre (Moi 241). Again, Nora describes her family's entire (in)authentic life, including the theatricalization of others and any performances or sensations of embodied authenticity, as taking place inside a "playroom," a space that is classed and contingent, or dependent on wealth and excess and created to house a certain phase of life. The embodied performance in *A Doll House*—a dance of desperation, in which Nora's hair comes down[13]—is necessarily absent from the apartment-installation at the museum, where the only embodied occupation involves museumgoers. On the other hand, the museum also allows visitors to go backstage, occupying more private spaces with distinct relationships to household theater.

In an article for the museum's magazine, *By og Bygd* (*Town and Country*), Janike Sverdrup Ugelstad acknowledges that the curators of "A Doll House—1879" began with Ibsen's play, but have aimed to represent "more of the period's dwelling customs," adding Helmer's office (offstage, but named and occupied during the action of the drama), a dining room, kitchen, servants' bedroom, and the nursery, and decorating each space with materials appropriate to the era and social class (134).[14] The captions on the wall just inside the front door also refer to Ibsen's stage directions as a "point of departure" before naming sources beyond these directions: "traces" in the original building (paint as well as wallpaper), "[d]escriptions of interiors by Norwegian authors from the period, like Camilla Collett and Amalie Skram," and "photographs and books containing plates for furniture upholsterers and cabinet makers." One caption addresses the semi-private status of "Nora's drawing room," acknowledging that it was a place for receiving guests "whilst guarding the privacy within," or while guarding the spaces in which "the housewife was in charge of the children and the maidservants."[15] When Sverdrup Ugelstad mentions the partitioning of the bourgeois home into semi-private and private domains, she makes a wide-ranging claim about the gendered significance of these divisions and decorations, which suits Ibsen's depiction of home and marriage as trap:

> She, the woman and mother, had highly restricted zones, but her domains were, in return, over-filled with things, as if in compensation. The well to do, over-decorated home compensated for the world from which she was locked out, the real world, where life actually took place. (140)

This rhetoric of gendered separate spheres retells a familiar story of false recompense, of an "over-filled" façade hiding deeper, sparer truths, of an unreal life of acting or make-believe, as in the theater, as in a playroom. It might also perpetuate bourgeois-centric associations of the real world with masculinity, of masculinity with employment and labor, encouraging an overly sweeping feminization of private life, further ignorance of the characteristics of both childhood and women's labor, further conflation of women with "the woman and mother" who is like Nora.[16]

"A Doll House—1879" effects a rather different experience of realist temporality than a period staging, although both seek to offer imagined access to the past. Theatergoers watch from a time and space apart, sitting in the audience. Museumgoers, on the other hand, can enter the rooms of the apartment-installation, stepping right up to and looking through the Plexiglass barrier—perhaps feeling like a fly on the wall, or like an uncannily quick interloper in a world of ghosts. Sverdrup Ugelstad notes that the family that occupied this apartment in the mid- to late 1870s was a remarkably suitable real-life counterpart for the fictional family in *A Doll House*. Like Torvald Helmer, Jacob E. Dybwad was a lawyer who had recently become director at a bank. He lived in the apartment together with his wife, Alice, their son, and two women servants (134–135).[17] Unlike the empty and mostly undescribed children's rooms in the empty nursery plays, the display-nursery in "A Doll's House—1879" enables postmodern visitors to begin to imagine how children's space might have functioned for members of a similar household, including parents, children, and servants. The reconstructed nursery contains a bed, cradle, dresser, and a variety of toys; it is decorated with framed illustrations and a display dollhouse; and it can be accessed from the hallway, the dining room, and another room (behind a closed door; perhaps the parents' bedroom). The curators have employed what Mark Sandberg calls "missing person display," a technique developed for world fairs and folk and open-air museums, setting up a home for people (or characters) who are not present (*Living Pictures, Missing Persons* 2). Museumgoers can use their own embodied experience and visual access to the nursery to imagine children sleeping in the bed and cradle, playing with the toys on the floor, wandering through the door into the dining room, or down the hall into the kitchen, where the nanny or maid was likely to be found, working to keep the household running smoothly.[18]

Neither Sverdrup Ugelstad nor the captions describe all the rooms in the apartment-installation in equal detail. The objects, furnishings, and architectural dimensions of the nursery and the sparsely decorated kitchen and servant's bedroom, both with walls painted salmon-pink—a common color for servants' rooms, according to Head Curator Kari Telste—must do most of the talking for themselves ("Tjenestepiken" 14). I have argued that empty nurseries are located at the limit of Ibsen's realist vision. Despite its concrete staging in Wessels Street 15, the nursery also appears to be located at the limits of the curators' interest—or at least at the limits of the story that they are able to tell in this particular apartment-installation. A bourgeois family must think of how it represents itself to the wider world by means of its semi-private spaces, just behind the windows and just visible from the street, while keeping other spaces, activities, and individuals hidden behind the scenes. Things and persons hidden and disregarded in daily life often leave fewer traces in the archive.

While the nursery is not described in the captions at the museum, Sverdrup Ugelstad mentions it twice in her article: first, when she refers to the division of space between "representative" and "private areas of the residence" (135), and again, before she concludes her article by referring to Nora's decision to abandon both the security of her material world and her children:

> The nursery in the apartment is furnished with Helmer's three children in mind: Ivar, Bob and Emmy. They have diverse, historically correct toys, wooden blocks, dolls and books. We have placed a dollhouse [*dukkestue*] inside the nursery—a real dollhome [*dukkehjem*]. The museum's dollhome [*dukkehjem*] is from the early 1800s and from Kristiansand. The dollhouse [*dukkestuen*] contains all the elements that Ibsen most likely saw before him when he came up with the title for his play. (140)

Sverdrup Ugelstad assures us that the objects placed in the nursery are historically correct and then turns her focus to the dollhouse, an object more broadly evocative of Ibsen's dramatic text. She plays with the difference between the word for a dollhouse in Norwegian, *dukkestue*, and the neologism that Ibsen created for his title, *dukkehjem* (dollhome), using the two terms interchangeably. The dollhouse at the Norsk Folkemuseum is one example of a common decoration in the nursery room, found mostly in upper-class homes before the era of mass-production.[19] This large item—"more likely to be a substantial piece of furniture than a toy" (Sandberg, *Ibsen's Houses* 72)—is also a mise-en-abyme. That is, it is a representation of a home whose hinges indicate that it was once sealed in behind glass-paned doors, inside a representation of a home sealed behind Plexiglass, inside a building "that is itself like a giant, walk-in dollhouse" (74). Sandberg writes, "the material characteristics of these objects [nineteenth century dollhouses in Norway and Sweden] had a strongly observational and representational function for family life. They encouraged an analogy between careful display and family structure" (74). At the museum, whether we zoom in to the nursery and the miniature world of the dollhouse or zoom out to the life-sized world surrounding Wessels Street 15, we remain on "strongly observational and representational" territory.

The actual backstage of the bourgeois household, on the other hand, was—or was supposed to be—silent and concealed, performing neither for visitors nor for passers-by on the street. Telste uses the home-as-theater metaphor to describe the position of domestic servants in this household, while shifting our focus from the parlor to the wings:

> Servant girls were not to be heard; they had to keep to the wings, in the backstairs, in the kitchens, which, similarly to the girl's room, faced the backyard. In the representative rooms, facing the street, the "master and mistress" were supposed to put themselves on display. The backstairs made it possible to keep the different functions of the house separate. ("Tjenestepiken" 17)

The backstage was, in other words, non-theatrical yet essential for performances taking place out front. While the emptiness of nurseries belongs to Ibsen's childless and bereaved or parentally unfit main characters (and to broader anxieties, fears, and hopes concerning the future), their fullness was once the domain not only of bourgeois mothers and children but also of women "in the wings": domestic servants from the countryside or urban working classes who sought their livelihood and the experience necessary to set up households of their own.[20] Both *A Doll House* and "A Doll House—1879" indicate that the conditions of possibility for the performance of bourgeois life are reliant on sexed and gendered forms of labor, even if these forms of labor do not occupy center stage in Ibsen's dramas. Although children hardly ever take center stage in this book, children's spaces and their caretakers take on a more centered presence below. More centered does not mean fully centered, of course. As Telste's metaphor suggests, the story of the nanny must be told, at least in part, through acknowledgment of absence, silence, and marginalization.

Backstage

My foray into the Norwegian nursery relies on scholarship by curators and historians and on archival sources from the period 1890–1920, predominantly but not exclusively in the form of advice manuals. Advice manuals are useful because they address the nursery and nanny explicitly and in greatest detail. They help me begin tackling the curiosity that offstage and un-described nurseries have created in me, and perhaps in my reader. What were these room "really like"? What did they mean to people who lived in Norway at the turn of the century? Advice manuals are also highly normative, showcasing how things *should be* rather than how they were in practice. Especially in the first decades of the twentieth century, when such books appear to proliferate, purveyors of advice were responding to what they considered to be errors of the recent past—the damage done by the "nanny chapter" (Selmer 47)[21]—and looking toward a better, more properly reared future in the new century. A more complete study of the Norwegian nursery and nanny would cover a longer period of time and consult a broader range of sources, as well as pay further attention to counter-narratives, considering the many passing references to nurseries and nannies in memoirs and literature, and offer a more detailed exploration of material culture and practices of employment. Most advice manuals are concerned, first and foremost, with healthy development enabled by proper occupation of nursery space. Their representations of the child-nursery-nanny configuration nonetheless conjure up a foundation that serves to undermine, a place of propriety that houses potential threats to decency and decorum. Although I move away from the limited description and figurative emptiness in Ibsen's dramas and toward a description that suggests historical fullness, the nursery remains, for many, a sight of anxiety concerning improper occupation.

Neither the nanny nor the nursery are cultural touchstones in Norway, as they are in Britain and (to a lesser extent) the United States. This is probably owing to two major factors. First, Norway's national identity is constructed around images of peasant and farm life. Second, Norway's middle classes developed rather late in the European context and represented a small percentage of the population.[22] According to some accounts, nearly ninety percent of the Norwegian population remained in the countryside until the middle of the nineteenth century (Sogner et al.), with primary economic social divisions being worker, farmer, and tradesmen. Despite the nursery and nanny's lack of prominence in Norwegian culture, they were certainly features of middle-class life in Kristiania, the capital city renamed Oslo in 1925. Although I do not consider parks and other public spaces here, Telste notes that parks and park benches in the capital were often full of nannies pushing baby carriages or socializing with soldiers during their free time ("Tjenestepiken" 16).

Research on the demographics of Kristiania, and on what might be called the intended demographics of architecture, allows one to read the classed landscape of the city through variations in employment. In the coffee table book, *En historiebok i tre etasjer: Boskikk i byen, 1865–2002* (*A History Book in Three Stories: Dwelling Customs in the City*), authors Morten Bing, Torgeir Kjos, and Birte Sandvik describe turn-of-the-century Meyerløkka, the neighborhood in which Wessels Street 15 was originally located:

> In the decades before and after 1900, Meyerløkka was a petit bourgeois bastion, certainly with some workers, but with just a few representatives from the upper middle class. Widows were numerous, and craftsmen, many functionaries, and merchants were to be found, but rather few academics. (19)[23]

According to Bing, sixty servant girls were employed in the homes along Wessels Street in 1900, another marker of the neighborhood's petit bourgeois status when we compare it, for example, with Markveien, where only eleven servant girls were employed, or Oscar's Street, where 144 were employed ("En liten verden" 54). The original plans for Wessels Street 15 show that each apartment in the building included a servant's bedroom, which means that the architect assumed that the building's tenants would employ at least one woman (Bing, "Tjenestejenter" 13).

In "Tjenestepiken i hverdag og fritid" (Every-Day and Free-Time for the Servant Girl), Telste informs us that these bedrooms were, in fact, occupied by domestic laborers: "The census from 1875 shows that ten women were in service in the apartment building at the time" (15). Two households employed both a nurse/nanny and a maid (15). The majority of these women were under thirty years of age and had migrated to the capital from neighboring districts or other small cities in the eastern part of Norway, while a few individuals came from Sweden (16). The Dybwad family that occupied the Wessels Street 15 apartment reconstructed as "A Doll House—1879" employed "Johanne Gurine Sørensen from Mandal and Emma Christine Olsen from Sweden" (Bing, "Tjenestejenter" 38). No domestic servants lived at Wessels Street 15 after 1940—although this does not mean that au pairs and other domestic laborers are not employed at the address today.[24]

Despite differences in the historical development and size of the middle classes in Norway and England in the nineteenth and early twentieth centuries, historical research on the middle-class family suggests that there were significant similarities between practices of child-rearing in England and Scandinavia, including the employment of nursemaids, the existence of distance (material and/or emotional) between mothers and fathers and their children, and the division of reproductive labor among mothers and mother-surrogates. In *Material Relations* (2012),

Jane Hamlett shows how the "common use" of the nursery "among middle-class families in the second half of the nineteenth century" in England shaped the very form and function of middle- and upper-class families (111). The nursery's material culture and its repurposing throughout a lifetime (first as a school room for older children and then as a sitting room for young women) shaped the family and its relationships through dynamics of distance (from the parents) and closeness (to the servants, especially the nanny), discipline (changing expectations regarding obedience and distinct expectations for gendered behavior), and resistance (free interpretation of didactic materials, tomboy-play or appropriation of boys' toys). Hamlett notes that while "[a]ssistance with childcare [...] had long been a privilege of the rich," by 1850 only "those in the least well-off middle-class families do not mention a nanny or nursemaid" in their autobiographies (111–112).[25] She also claims that the "practice of having a specialized nanny was distinctively British" (119). Hamlett describes this specialized practice as involving primary responsibility for "physical care": "Although mothers occasionally performed some tasks, nannies performed the lion's share of the work [...] Such constant contact often meant that a strong bond of love was formed between the nanny and the child" (119).

I have more than once encountered resistance to the idea that nursery rooms and nannies could be a significant topic for Norwegian literary and cultural studies, generally emerging from the assumption that Norway did not have a child-rearing culture similar to that found in Britain. British and Norwegian cultures of child-rearing should not be conflated in a simplistic fashion, but there *are* points of literary and historical overlap. These points are reflected in *A Doll House* and *Hedda Gabler*, as well as in historical research on the family in the Norwegian context.[26] Both Nora and Tesman break rank, in the former case to seek wisdom from Anne-Marie about what it might mean to leave one's children behind, and in the latter case to insist on Berte's status as a member of the family. When Hedda expresses concern that Tesman's excitement over her pregnancy announcement will be overheard by "the maid," Tesman tells Hedda calls her amusing and insists that he will tell Berte the news himself (*HG* 93). These dramatic moments suggest that bonds of love and trust have been formed between Nora and Tesman and the minor characters who once served as their caregivers.

In *I gode og vonde dagar* (*In Good and Hard times*) (2003), Sølvi Sogner et al. describe a conflict between a dominant romantic ideal of the loving mother and practices among the "higher social classes," from 1900 until the interwar period:

> Motherhood was also celebrated with the breakthrough of the new understanding of the child around 1900. This movement emphasized the special responsibility of the mother for childcare, but it

would be a few decades before middle class mothers themselves took over the practical care of children. Paradoxically enough, it appears that the distance between parents and children in bourgeois environs and in the civil class increased even though familial attachments were promoted to a greater degree than before. It was not just father who was a relatively distant figure for the children, but also mother. Her responsibilities were to orchestrate social life, go visiting, and direct the servants in their work. The servants had a central place in children's lives, because the middle class kept servants, later called "house help," all the way up until the interwar period. "The girl" generally slept in the same room with the smallest children, so that mother was spared disturbance in the night. During the day *the girl* was responsible for things like potty-training, she clothed them, and she minded them both in public and at home. Among the wealthy, it was common for the servants to eat together with the children who had not learned to eat "prettily," so that the family was spared the job of teaching them table manners. In a sense, one bought freedom from the very task of giving everyday care to one's own children. (194–195)

This description certainly implies correspondence between English and Norwegian practices, while evoking a variety of issues relevant to an understanding of parenting in Norway in the decades around 1900, including a strong interest in combatting the negative influence of the nanny by placing the mother at the heart of parenting (an interest not necessarily abided by in practice) and a particular division of labor: bourgeois wives gave birth and then performed social duties and management, while nurses and nannies did the "lion's share" of quotidian care (Hamlett 119). The description also acknowledges variation in practices among different levels within the middle class—variations that we might imagine mapping onto the different neighborhoods and streets of Kristiania, with their differing numbers of nannies employed.

The subjects and settings of early Norwegian children's literature appear to support the claim that the nursery is not a cultural touchtone in this national context. The national romantic features of early twentieth-century picture books also render them somewhat misleading when it comes to representing rural/urban and working/bourgeois divisions within Norwegian childhood. In "Nasjonsbygging og barndomsideal rundt hundreårsskiftet" (Nation-building and the ideal of childhood around the turn of the century), Marit Hassel notes that the collecting and writing down of children's songs and tales involved a "bourgeoisification" of childhood (46). The authors and artists who created children's literature came from the civil and middle classes, and their depictions of childhood were normativizing, making the early stages of life look naïve and innocent (Hassel 46–47). While these authors and artists "looked for the roots of Norwegian-ness among the farmers and in the villages," their depictions did not, according to Hassel, agree with the laborious realities of farm and village life for children: "in picture books either we see bourgeois children who are visiting [the countryside] or we see farm children through the eyes of the bourgeoisie" (46). Hasselt closes her discussion of "Childhood in the country: the bourgeois version" by noting that Lisbeth Bergh's paintings for her children's book *Setesdal* (1919) were modeled on interiors from the Norsk Folkemuseum: "She creates, in truth, an ideal museal image of the Norwegian freeholder" (47). In "A Doll's House—1879" at the folk museum today, the title of the book on the dresser in the nursery is not legible from behind the Plexiglass. Nonetheless, one might imagine a mother reading national romantic picture books to her child in this nationally uncharacteristic and differently normativizing room. Or one might imagine a nanny telling (less naïve and innocent?) tales from her home village.

According to the archival sources that I refer to here, the space of the nursery and the figure of the nanny were repositories for a variety of anxieties concerning childhood and the future, both in Norway and in Northern Europe more broadly. An editorial from 1911, signed S. B. and published in the Danish weekly, *Hjemmet* (distributed in Norway from 1911), opens by addressing both the remembered contents of the nursery and the beloved nanny, whose stories could sometimes be slightly menacing:

> The dear old nursery, whitewashed walls, red-painted pine-table, hard chairs with matching backs, with a low ceiling, but—wonderful space for all kinds of games [...] And old Anna the nanny, who came for the second to youngest and then grew attached, until a late marriage induced her to detach herself—yes, she was no educated nanny—but how she could talk to children and tell them stories. It must be confessed right away: she told dreadful ghost stories, which caused the children to glance in angst in all directions when they had to walk down the dark hall [...]. (306)

Old Anna brings all manner of stories into the "dear old nursery," not only ghost stories but also old fairy tales and her own compositions, "taken right out of the life of a child" (S. B. 306). She is remembered as a figure of imagination, giving "her own and our fantasy free reign," while young mothers are pictured sitting in their finely decorated parlors, at some distance from the children who make trouble when they play in improper spaces, such as the dining room (S. B. 306). S. B.'s editorial aims to answer the question, "Where should the children be?" (306). The author emphasizes the significance of maternal involvement in managing children's free time, especially in an urban context, where safe and appropriate spaces to play freely are limited. One paragraph begins by acknowledging the common nervousness of the bourgeois mother and closes by insisting that children must have the opportunity to move and play if they are going to grow up to be healthy adults in mind and body (unlike their mothers, it is implied). S. B. thus reproduces the perspective, common among many advice-givers in the decades surround 1900, that the mother should be the central figure in the child's life in the new "Century of the Child" (306).[27]

S. B.'s editorial evokes several of the main concerns and beliefs stated in advice manuals: not only the insistence on the centrality of the mother, but also the possibility of education in the sphere of child-rearing, proper furnishing of the nursery, and concerns about how to handle the permeability of intimate space. While *Forældre og børn: en bog om hjemmets oppgaver af forældre og barnevenner* (*Parents and Children: A Book about the Duties of the Home by Parents and Friends of Children*) (1902) treats "opdrageren" (the person who rears the child) as an interchangeable figure—listing "mother, father, nanny" as possible individuals that might take on the general task of child-rearing—the majority of the sources that I have consulted insist on the special status of the mother (358). S. B. also suggests that unlike old Anna, some nannies were educated, and thus that specialization was possible. In *Barnestel: en liden bog for unge mødre* (*Childcare: A Little Book for Young Mothers*) (1903), Olaug Løken insists that one of the greatest expectations of the new century are "Schools for Childcare" (7). She warns new mothers that they have much to learn and cautions them against assuming that "a clever nanny will manage well when the child comes," given that, "for the first thing," very few nannies have had any reliable training, and "for the second," "both the child and the mother are happiest when the mother herself is the nanny—or at least the head nanny" (7). By referring to "wonderful space" for games in the nursery and to play in improper spaces, S. B.'s editorial evokes the prominent insistence in advice manuals that one should furnish and maintain nursery rooms with thoughts of physical health and correct child-development in mind. By referring to Old Anna's ghost stories, the editorial evokes a very mild version of a commonly expressed anxiety concerning the fact that the presence of the nanny meant the presence of an outsider in the urban, middle-class family. The practicalities of childcare are rarely inconsequential or neutral in advice manuals. The nanny is a locus both for nice memories and bad feelings, or affections made perilous by transgressions of the boundary between the spheres of intimacy and employment.

When it comes to proper maintenance of nursery space for the health of the child, advice manuals emphasize how important it is to avoid furnishings that might lessen opportunities for free movement, or otherwise compromise physical development. The Norwegian co-author of *Husstel og Madstel* (*Arranging the Home and Cooking*) (1890), a translation and revision of the sixth edition of a German language text by Maria Clima, insists that "so-called children's chairs, where one ties down the little one for long periods of time in order to be rid of it," should never be found in nurseries because they can damage both the child's posture and its ability to learn to be clean (27). In *Når man skal sætte bo* (*Setting Up a Household*) (1892), the anonymous author insists that the ideal nursery is modestly furnished, the humbler the better: "Our refined parlors filled with thousands of 'necessary items' are not suitable for children's movements" (66). This author also acknowledges the possibility that a family might not be able to obtain an extra room for children. They recommend, in this case, that the family decorate the dining room or a bedroom "as practically as possible" for its double function of eating and play or sleeping and play, so that both caregiver and child are spared the distress of limited movement and constant scolding (68). Regardless of which room is designated for child's play, a separate bed is deemed essential. The loving mother, who might otherwise enjoy sleeping beside her child, has a duty to keep it safe and so must make this sacrifice. New knowledge of infectious diseases, especially tuberculosis, which is often mentioned in literature addressing nannying and nurseries at this time, makes it imperative that adults and children never sleep together.

Advice manuals also insist that nurseries and playrooms be well-ventilated and kept immaculately clean. In *Spædbarnet, Dets udvikling og stel* (*The Infant, Its Development and Care*) (1891), Dr. Chr. Døderlein insists that an infant's more delicate constitution necessitates that the "largest, airiest, and best room" in the apartment be the nursery (133). Such rooms must be "light and warmed by the sun, which means that the windows will ideally face south or southwest" (133). It would be preferable, according to this "practicing doctor in Kristiania," if two rooms could be dedicated children's space, so that each room could be aired "several times a day," and "in the winter a fire can be laid" without needing to remove the child from the nursery space altogether (133). Døderlein also warns against smoking, cooking, washing, ironing, or hanging clothes to dry in the nursery. In *For barnepiger og mødre, veiledning i barnestel* (*For Nannies and Mothers, Guidance in the Care of Children*) (1905), Løken (supervised in this text by the Pediatrician Dr. L. W. Schibbye) speaks to the nanny directly: "A nanny can never be too clean. But she can certainly be too slow in her work. Accustom yourself to doing everything with rapid rather than slow movements, and you will manage to be both clean and swift" (49). Everything in the nursery room, from objects such as washing bowls and toilet buckets to children in diapers, should be constantly cleaned and refreshed, day and night. The nursery should never smell of dirty things, and "if a child is not completely clean during the night when it is one-year old, then only the nanny is to blame" (Løken, *For barnepiger* 48). This judgment, Løken tells her reader, comes from "an experienced old doctor who had twelve children himself and had trained with gusto both the nanny and the children"—in part by knocking on the wall to wake the nanny when he heard a child stir (48). When it comes to cleanliness, children's rooms are clearly exceptional spaces: Løken insists that in the nursery, "'saturday-washing' should be done every day" (49). The very life of the child can depend on the washing of bodies and rooms.

Such practicalities quickly make way for bad feelings, given that the nanny's duties are clearly tied to propriety, with its dual implications of personal respectability and physical and moral cleanliness. Løken not only urges the nanny to be quick and clean but also informs her that it "is extremely unfortunate, it is a shame for the nanny, if the child is not clean" (*For barnepiger* 48). The consequences of failing to keep proper standards of cleanliness in the nursery can include the nanny's loss of "honor," as well as threats to the child's moral health (48). In *Vore børns sedelige op-dragelse* (*Our Children's Moral Upbringing*) (1902), Ågot Gjems Selmer insists that the "natural consequence" of an unkempt child are sores on the skin and a strong desire to scratch them: *"It is quite often precisely this that first instigates masturbation"* (46). Selmer's causal logic makes the link between dirty bodies and "perverse" sexual behaviors explicit. Masturbation, in this case, is the result of conditions that are dangerous for one's general health. The child scratches its itches and happens upon body parts that are equally itchy, but more consequential, lending themselves to habits of "inappropriate" touch. Selmer insists that children are "trained up" in this way to habits that cannot, in the end, be mastered (46).

Concern over perverse possibilities appears to be a primary motivator for the increasing emphasis on the biological mother's role, or her place in the nursery as a preventative measure.[28] In *Slægten som kommer: en bog for forældre og for dem, som vil blive det: det seksuelle prob-lem i barne opdragelse* (*The Generation to Come: A Book for Parents and for Those Who Want to Be: The Sexual Problem in Childrearing*) (1913), Hans Wegener sandwiches a description of the nursery between two admonitions: first, "breast is best," while wet nurses are a "foreign influence that cannot be controlled"; and second, "the mother belongs in the nursery. Not the *personnel*!" (90).[29] Wegener's emphasis on the term *"personnel"* is likely intended to suggest the bad fit of the non-private matter of employment with the private space in which the children of the family sleep and play. Protections that only a mother can provide are essential for insuring the sanctity of the nursery itself, that "little world in which the child first grows up":

We always associate this word—nursery—with thoughts of picture books, rocking horses, and tin soldiers. We understand the nursery's meaning for the child's waking life and consciousness best of all when we look at ill-mannered people who have not had a nursery. Those people who gather their descendants around them in the nursery always have the future before them. (Wegener 90–91)

Wegener's description suggests that our association of the nursery with picture books and toys underestimates the significance of the child's "little world." Not only is the nursery essential for the rearing of well-mannered people, but those without a nursery (the working class and rural poor, for example?) also risk their very future. In this context, the phrase "little world," which on its own suggests both miniaturization and totality (a small realm unto itself), contains the same exaggerative link between the nursery and generational futures that reproductive futurism uses, as Edelman has demonstrated, to bind the future to the Child.[30]

Wegener also appeals to mothers to understand their irreplaceability, which appears to result from their natural-moral and cultural (class) superiority when it comes to forming the sexual health of their own children. He insists that cow's milk is preferable to "hvilkensomhelst" (any old) wet nurse-milk because it is "personally neutral" (Wegener 90). He then asks the imagined reader, "Do you really believe that the nanny or the governess can be for the child what the mother can be?" (91). Because mother-surrogates are uneducated and inexperienced—being childlike and curious themselves, it is implied—they find sexual subjects to be "piquant" and play on their "forbidden" nature, which means that "too much intimacy" with servants is a "danger, precisely, for the child's sexual development" (Wegener 91). Especially dangerous situations involve bathing and sleeping in the same room with children, the latter of which Wegener totally advises against. A "secretive confidentiality" between the nanny and the child might arise from such intimate sleeping arrangements, threatening proper intimacy between the child and its parent and potentially costing them "the happiness of family" (Wegener 92). Such concerns might represent the beginnings of the "modern fascination with the sexual abuse of children," which "is quite new," according to Carolyn Steedman, and which would become "one of the most commonly told stories of the late twentieth century in Europe and the US" (165).

Both *The Generation to Come* and *Our Children's Moral Upbringing* openly ask and offer answers to questions that James R. Kincaid would recognize as regressive, resulting from the strange yet familiar association of sexuality and "'innocence'" (78): Where might we locate the sources (or cradles) of immoral behavior? And what might happen in the nursery managed by an all-too intimate nanny and a distant mother? If risky forms of self-touch are deemed a potential result of a dirty nursery and child, even more dangerous forms of touch are recounted as the result of letting nannies have too much free reign. Selmer offers anecdotes clearly intended to make mothers aware of the dangers that lurk in admitting a nanny into one's home, while emphasizing the irony of the fact that these "girls" are hired to help the mother and lessen her duties:

> one does not only need to watch over the child, but truly just as much over those who have been hired to watch it, because it is

certainly incomprehensible—yes, terrible, what nannies can allow themselves to do with children—due to ignorance, indifference, or irresponsibility. (46)

One terrible allowance involves a nanny who opens her charge's under-clothes so that he might "play with himself" while he eats (Selmer 47). When the mother happens across this scene and asks the nanny "why in the world" she would allow such a thing to take place, the nanny explains that he likes it and "will not stay still when he eats otherwise" (Selmer 47). Selmer insists that "everyone can certainly imagine what this kind of behavior can lead to for the child" (Selmer 47), which seems to suggest either that the nanny herself knew what she was encouraging, but did not have the moral sense to care, or that "everyone" excludes the nanny, referring only to the "stealth-universal" bourgeois subject (Muñoz 94). Selmer also tells of a nanny who seduced her ten-year-old charge "to outright immorality" (47). Lack of trust between mother and child resulted in the boy confessing his shame and misery to an older sister (Selmer 47). In this case, the nanny and the mother share in the blame for corruption of the innocent child. Even in a "good and happy home," depravity can take root in the nursery, especially when the mother is withdrawn and fails to keep watch over employee as well as child (Selmer 47).

I have suggested that the anxiety that surrounds the nursery in Ibsen's dramas is related in part to its emptiness, its status as an unoccupied space to fill. Strong forms of anxiety clearly persist, even when the nursery is occupied by children and nannies. Advice manuals for mothers available in Norwegian from 1890 to 1920 clearly respond to the troubling association of innocence and sexuality. They also appear to play a role in reinforcing the union of opposites—of that which is vacant and that which fills vacancy—that Kincaid describes:

> One could say that innocence is more than a blank, that it takes on substance by feeding off its polar opposite, which we might call depravity, a word with plenty of substance [...] It takes little maneuvering to make depravity (corruption, evil) the superior term in this opposition; innocence is the absence of it. (78)

In making his argument for depravity as the "polar opposite" of innocence, Kincaid takes issue with the OED's antonym, evil, given that evil is more readily opposed to good, that we associate innocence with "passivity" rather than action, and that the "tendency over the last two centuries" has been "to narrow 'innocence' to a sexual meaning" (78). Kincaid's basic idea is that "[a]bhorred vacuums get filled up," but he also insists that depravity has a special relationship to that which is childish, infantile, regressive: "As we regress, push back to the child, we find the foulest depravity" (Kincaid 78). This process of filling emptiness with depravity is somewhat more literal in the case of the nursery, given that we are talking about a figure of domestic space rather than the figure of the child. On the other hand, it is both the unsupervised space in the home and the emotional distance created by the moving parts of bourgeois child-rearing that constitute a space in which the nanny can transfer her uncultivated relationship to sexuality to the blank and impressionable child, thus filling its future with her own perverse childishness.

While anxieties and disagreeable feelings appear to dominate advice and editorial genres—often in senses more menacing than old Anna's ghost stories—other sources can suggest nice feelings, even idealization. In a biographical essay titled "Lykkens dager" (Days of Happiness), Haakon Shetelig, whose family lived in Wessels Street 15 in the 1880s, provides a brief portrait of life in the nursery.[31] Rather than describing the full layout of the room, its contents and activities, Shetelig emphasizes specific sensual moments, experiences that brought pleasure or pain on a daily basis:

> How I remember from early years that little world which was the apartment on Wessels Street. The morning in the nursery when I woke before dawn and lay still and waited while the first rays of the sun began slowly to appear, filtering in from behind the dark shades. How I studied the rose of plaster on the ceiling with the lamp hook in the middle and its crown of acanthus leaves. I could not understand what they were supposed to represent, almost believing they were a kind of owl like the ones I had seen in picture books. And then came voices and footsteps from the neighboring bedroom, light came in and mother's smile over the bed as she leaned over me. Simultaneously I began to dread what was coming, not the morning wash, which I remember went quickly and roughly, but when my hair was put in order. I had curls, which were *dadas* [nanny's] pride and caused me torment with screaming and tears every morning. But afterward the maple tree fluttered like quiet happiness in the parlor while mother dusted and gave the flowers water, while the sun played through the prisms of the chandelier and shone in rainbow colors on the walls and furniture. (221)

Shetelig remembers not "picture books, rocking horses, and tin soldiers" most of all (Wegener 90), but rather the decorative ceiling of his childhood room, the play of light and sound throughout the house, his mother's smiling presence in the nursery upon waking, and daily grooming rituals. It is Shetelig's mother who wakes him and works, dusting and watering plants, while his *dada* seems a slightly more distant and possessive figure in this description, with her pride in his curls. Similarly to the term nanny, *dada* is a pet-name for a servant engaged for child-care. Perhaps it was *dada* who did the quick and rough washing and the hair combing. All of Shetelig's subsequent references to his *dada* involve memories of regular afternoon walks. Unlike authors of advice manuals, Shetelig does not dwell at length on questions of cleanliness and health, on the proper role of the mother, the education of servant girls, or the moral safeguards and hazards of the nursery.

Shetelig focuses on specific details that linger in lasting memory, while other aspects have either disappeared from memory or are simply not shared with the reader. Photographs of the nursery and nanny from the same period available at digitaltmuseum.no and oslobilder.no also evoke disappearance or absence in the midst of preservation, providing seductive proof of the nanny and nursery's material existence while supporting the idea that this room and person are rather undocumented and marginalized in the Norwegian context. Photographs featuring nurseries mostly support the idea, reflected in the nursery in "A Doll House—1879" and recommended in advice manuals, that Norwegian nurseries were of modest size and decoration. Excluding formal portraits, the majority of photographs featuring nannies are taken out of doors, in parks and gardens, or on porches. Many show nannies pushing buggies or holding or watching over small children at play. A photograph by Oscar Hvalbye, titled "På St. Hanshaugen" (circa 1900), shows a nanny seated on a bench in the park, a straw cap on her head decorated with a wide ribbon and large feather.[32] She holds a toddler dressed in white on her lap, and a child seated beside her is dressed in what appears to be a sailor suit. The toddler rubs one eye with the back of his hand; the little boy tilts his head down at a slight angle; the nanny looks at the camera with a serious and direct expression on her face.

Only one photograph from these online collections, titled "Saturday wash in the nursery" by Anders Beer Wilse (1904), shows women engaged in the labor of childcare in the nursery.[33] A child is being scrubbed in a small galvanized washtub by a young woman on her knees. She is wearing a full, checkered apron and matching sleeves to protect her black dress from the wash-water. An older and more finely dressed woman, wearing a silky jacket and skirt covered in a white half-apron with embroidered detailing, brushes the long hair of an older child. A third child, the oldest judging by size, waits in a chair, bundled in towels from head to toe. It is not absolutely certain that these women are employed as domestic servants, but the room is definitely a nursery, with three beds for the three children and paper decorations fastened to the wall featuring drawings of children and young ladies. Other photographs of children's rooms by Anders Beer Wilse include one of two older boys playing with a train set on the floor at Christmastime and one of two small girls having a tea party, surrounded by their toys and an enormous canine *dada* (like Nana in J. M. Barrie's *Peter Pan*).[34] In the latter case, two small beds with large white head- and footboards are separated by a small dresser, on which three dolls sit side by side. A third bed appears to be tucked into the corner of the room. Perhaps this is where their nanny slept?

The following caption attends one photograph, possibly taken between 1920 and 1930: "photo of five children out in nature sitting on a little crag, probably in Roligheten in Kristiansund. We can see the houses in Langveien in the background. Possibly a nanny standing right by?"[35] The five children on the crag are the grandchildren of Georg Sverdrup, a Norwegian statesman listed as the likely photographer. A woman dressed for domestic labor stands to the right of the group of children, who all appear to be under the age of five. A third of her body, one foot, and most of her face are outside the frame of the photograph. One plain leather shoe and parts of her white apron and plaid shirt are visible, as are her bare forearm, chin, and the beginnings of a mouth. She might be a nanny; she might be young; she might be smiling; but she stands at the limits of both the photograph and oslobilder.no's ability to identify her.

Back to the Future

Throughout this book, my "modern eye" has been "drawn irresistibly" to the absences and silent "spaces in the text," to the domestic rooms, people, and activities that are not named—or are named only in passing, and then withdraw from view (Steedman 163–164). This mode of reading silences probably makes this book's engagement with traces of the past a contribution to the "history of the present," especially because I am less interested in the past than in using it to estrange contemporary assumptions about childhood innocence (Kincaid 62).[36] Ibsen leaves his characters and audiences with many unfilled nurseries at curtain. I have filled up many pages while trying to stay faithful to that emptiness, while also making it speak; and I have filled up some more while giving in to the desire to flesh out the historical Norwegian nursery, especially by means of advice manuals that convey ideologies of proper child-rearing from the period 1890 to 1920. The dramatic and archival traces of this nursery and its ruling yet marginalized figure—the nanny—have performed for the demands made on them from a future. They have also been redeployed as a means of analyzing and critiquing claims made by means of the figure of the child in examples of Ibsen criticism from our own turn of the century, 1980–2019. In addition to contributing to child studies by means of a queerer discussion of innocence in Ibsen—via the decentered or absented child and its empty spaces—I hope to have made a small contribution to denaturalizing motherhood with this chapter.

In her Editor's Introduction to *Ibsen's* Hedda Gabler: *Philosophical Perspectives* (2018), Kristin Gjesdal asks, "What kind of world [...] is staged in Ibsen's drama? [...] Is it the world of nineteenth-century Norway? Of nineteenth-century Europe? Or a global state of art at that time? And, further, is this world still ours?" (20). Whatever worlds we find, or long to find, in Ibsen's dramas, we read, stage, and teach them in our own. I have stressed that Ibsen's empty nursery plays do not include detailed depictions of children's spaces from the 1890s. Nonetheless, a return to contemporary ideas about nurseries might help us to connect Ibsen's dramas with a world that still belongs to us: a world in which anxieties over threats to innocence as the future persist, in which we continue to reproduce heteronormative and classist divisions of life, and in which issues of labor and visibility remain supremely relevant.

My visit to the turn of the century Norwegian nursery leaves me with a variety of questions. For example: How might nurseries matter for the postfeminist theater and classroom? How might they inspire imaginative readings, stagings, and adaptations? For now, I leave these questions open, posed to future scholars, teachers, theater practitioners, and to my future self. Having made my way back to the cusp of another future, I conclude this book with a short Epilogue addressing Ibsen's last two dramas, *John Gabriel Borkman* and *When We Dead Awaken*. Not only do these dramas lack the pattern of emptying and (dreaming about) re-filling children's rooms, but they also involve survivors: a grown son and a world-famous masterpiece. The Epilogue thus provides me with an opportunity to consider, in brief, what difference survival might make to Ibsen's dramatization of reproduction.

Notes

1 In *Ibsen's Houses*, Sandberg notes that the Norwegian word *dukkehjem* is not to be found in present-day Norwegian dictionaries. Moreover, the definition given in the older *Riksmål* dictionary refers to Ibsen's play: "'an apparently idyllic home where the husband spoils the wife, but doesn't treat her as an independent personality'" (qtd. in Sandberg 70). Sandberg comments, "In other words, the dictionary definition of the word *dukkehjem*, when it is listed at all, has no real referent beyond the context of Ibsen's play, and the word *dukkehjem*, for all its current fame, remains mainly an Ibsenien term" (70). Working through various implications of the two parts of this estranging word, with the original reception of *A Doll House* in mind, Sandberg finds that "'doll' trumps 'home'" in Ibsen's play (77).

2 Edelman's argument relies on concepts from Lacanian psychoanalysis as well as close readings of political, literary, and cinematic rhetoric. Like many of his critics, I am probably oversimplifying by sidestepping his claims about queerness and the death drive (while racking up my own debt to psychoanalysis). For a critical reading of *No Future* that focuses on Edelman's particular engagement with psychoanalysis, see Tim Dean's "An Impossible Embrace."

3 Concerning continued interest in the figure of the child, Parvulescu writes,

> The multifaceted conversations around *No Future* have shaped queer theory, which in the last decade has become the dominant institutional framework within which we theorize sexuality in universities in the United States. The sustained interest in the figure of the child, as evidenced by special issues of *Women's Studies Quarterly* (Chinn and Duane [2015]) and *GLQ* (Gill-Peterson et al. [2016]), and the recent focus on normativity and antinormativity, as evidenced by the 2015 special issue of *Differences* (Wiegman and Wilson), can be explained as reverberations of the Edelman debates. (87)

4 Parvulescu's research also addresses the contemporary global traffic in women in Europe, which involves the unequal participation of non-Western-European women in domestic and care-labor (including elder care and sex work) and new industries of regenerative technology. The European nuclear family and other institutions rely, disproportionately, on Eastern European women's bodies and reproductive labor when it comes to blood and organ donation, "adoption, egg donation, surrogacy, stem-cell tissues, and clinical trials" (91). See also Parvulescu's *The Traffic in Women's Work*.

5 Karín Lesnik-Oberstein and Neil Cocks have drawn attention to the ways in which analyses of the child within queer theory (including Edelman's) tend to locate a real child in an apparently stable location outside their theorizations. See, for example, Lesnik-Oberstein's "Childhood, Queer Theory, and Feminism" and "What is Queer Theory Doing with the Child?" (co-authored by Stephen Thomson) and Cock's *The Peripheral Child*.

6 I borrow the term mother-surrogate from *Rent og Urent: Hovedstadens piger og fruer, 1880–1920* (Clean and Unclean: Girls and Wives of the Capital) by Tinne Vammen. Vammen uses the word "modersurrogater" (mother-surrogates) as a label for domestic laborers, including wet nurses and nannies, who helped to define bourgeois motherhood in Copenhagen (21). She writes, "These mother-surrogates, who were generally of 'lower' social origins, made it possible for well-to-do women to withdraw from larger or smaller parts of the care and rearing of infants and small children" (21–22).

7 See also Terry Eagleton's "Ibsen and the Nightmare of History," which comes to some similar conclusions but is not cited by Moretti.

8 In "The Sexonomics of *Et dukkehjem*," Anna Westerståhl Stenport also takes variation within the bourgeois home into consideration, arguing that *A Doll House* "clearly seeks to challenge the gendered conventions of production and consumption, and of public and private spheres" under the "liberal and capitalist market system" (343). She is particularly focused on the ways in which the play is haunted by the "specter of prostitution," a haunting that relies on blurred boundaries between public and private spheres (347). For further consideration of the history of parenting's moving parts, with sustained critiques of the public/private binary, see also Jørgen Lorentzen's *The History of Fatherhood in Norway: 1850–2012* (Palgrave Macmillan, 2013).

9 As I argue in Chapter 3, class is most certainly relevant in *Little Eyolf*, despite this lack of servants. The Ratmaid, for example, is a traveling salesperson, who penetrates the stately home and poses a major threat to the master and mistress (*LE* 12). The poor boys who live in shacks by the shore also pose a threat: having teased Eyolf, they fail to rescue him from drowning. At the same time, they are conceived as a means of rescue, since the planned entry of these boys into the stately home—their proposed occupation of Eyolf's

empty rooms—is supposed to represent Rita and Alfred Allmers's surfacing from the undertow of grief, as well as their entry into reality and happiness by means of labor, according to George Bernard Shaw. See Chapter 4 for a discussion of Shaw's reading of class and realism in *Little Eyolf*.

10 How can we take Nora's realism seriously if we do not consider the fact that bourgeois women themselves represent a form of "conflict between capital and labor" (Moretti 170)? As Stenport notes in "The Sexonomics of *Et dukkehjem*," matrimonial laws in Norway "gave a husband almost complete legal authority over his wife's possessions," while "inheritance and means to trade or make money were not modified until 1888" and "only in 1927 was the husband's authority over the joint estate repealed" (343).

11 See https://norskfolkemuseum.no/en/the-dolls-house

12 Sometimes the stage directions describe a world that is audible to the audience: for example, the sound of the feared blackmail letter in the letter box, or of Krogstad's steps heading down the stairs in Act Two, or the slamming of the offstage door at the very end of the play.

13 Moi notes that Nora's loosening hair probably "invokes the theatrical convention of 'back hair,' which in nineteenth-century melodrama handbooks signifies the 'onset of madness.' As her hair comes down, Nora no longer listens to Helmer's instructions" (238).

14 The title of Sverdrup Ugelstad's article is "Lerkefugl og pomponger" (Lark and pompoms). The lark-bird, or "lærkefuglen" in Dano-Norwegian, is one of the nicknames that Torvald uses for Nora (*Du* 5). Pompoms refer to the popular Victorian design element.

15 The caption also tells about the derivative and excessive style of the era—eclecticism or *klunkestil* (clunky style), popular from 1870 to 1910—which has since been subject to distain for lacking individuality:

> The Victorian Age has been criticized for its mingling of items from different periods and styles; A stylistically 'confusing' period, lacking a style of its own [...] Nora's drawing room, even more 'rococo,' more voluminous and pompous than its prototype from the 18th century.

The last sentence of this description appears to clash with Ibsen's stage directions: "A comfortably and tastefully, but not expensively, furnished living room" (*Du* 5). Perhaps Ibsen did not realize the gaucheness of his own era—or perhaps we are simply carried away by our rhetoric?

16 In *The Wild Duck*, Ibsen has Gina, a former domestic servant, comment on the tendency to collapse all women into "woman." When Old Werle's housekeeper and fiancée, Mrs. Sørby, announces that women get along best by being open-hearted, Gina responds: "Oh, we ladies are so different. Some are this way, some are that" (*Vi* 89).

17 Morten Bing describes the family in more detail: "merchant class" Dybwad, the son of a banker, was 27 years old; his "English-born wife Alice" was two years younger; the couple had a newborn son, Thomas James, "and in addition two servant girls, Johanne Gurine Sørensen from Mandal and Emma Christine Olsen from Sweden" (Bing, "Tjenestejenter og hushjelper" 38).

18 In "Tjenestepiken i hverdag og fritid," Telste describes the extensive tasks of servant girls, which often began before other members of the household stirred and continued after they had retired for the evening.

19 According to Sverdrup Ugelstad, mass production began in the last decades of the 1800s, or just after *A Doll House* was written (131).

20 Telste notes that marriage and labor were intertwined for most women who worked in service: "time spent in service was a form of investment that was

supposed to secure a future. Time spent in service was for learning and preparation for marriage" ("Tjenestepiken" 14). She supports her claims with similar conclusions found in the works of Norway's first sociologist, Eilert Sundt (1817–1875): "'young men from the lower social classes did not necessarily fall for feminine youthfulness, grace and beauty, but instead sought out a woman who was a talented housewife, cook, and dairymaid; yes, she had to do her part to build a household and unify a household'" (Sundt qtd. in Telste, "Tjenestepiken" 14).

21 Selmer is presumably referring to the second half of the 1800s, although other forms of mother-surrogacy, such as wet nurses, were of course employed in earlier periods. For a short history of the wet nurse in Norway, see Ida Blom's "Ammestuehistorier: glimpt gjennom noen århundrer."

22 The broad term bourgeoisie is a good fit for the wide range of non-worker characters in Ibsen's oeuvre. They might also be described, depending on their specific circumstances, as ranging from petty to haute bourgeois, or as members of the lower, middle and upper middle classes. Their financial independence and jobs range from struggling photographer to hopeful academic to successful builder to wealthy landowner to world-famous artist. The term middle class, in singular form, could be misleading in the case of Ibsen, whose characters also include members of the wealthier trade and civil classes. The middle class proper—as an urban class distinct from the working and the wealthier trade and civil classes—began developing in the 1800s and grew rapidly over the course of the twentieth century in Norway. For an analysis of the rather complex and semantically evasive history of the middle class in Norway, see "The Middle Classes of Norway, 1840–1940" by Jan Eivind Myhre.

23 As one turns the pages of this coffee table book, photographs of Wessels Street 15 from 1897, 1904, 1984, and 1999, just before it was pulled down and then relocated to the folk museum, show deterioration of the façade and the addition of loft apartments (not re-created at the museum), suggesting reconfigurations of classed dwelling through time and space, as Oslo grew and became increasingly urbanized. "A Doll House—1879" has been installed in the largest apartment in the building, in the corner of the top floor, which has a balcony. It represents both the oldest time period and the original, petit bourgeois class context, while other installations represent homes from 1905, 1935, 1950, 1965, 1979, 1982, and 2002.

24 Although they are less focused on nannies than maids, Telste and Sølvi Sogner cover the history of women in domestic service in Norway in the 1800s, as well as the dissolution of this occupation in the first half of the twentieth century, in *Ut å søkje teneste* (Out looking for service). Sogner et al. notes that industrialization created more diverse employment options for working-class women, and that the difficultly of hiring domestics contributed to the decline in the Norwegian birthrate by making large families less desirable (*I gode og vonde* 53).

25 Hamlett refers to Gathorne-Hardy's study, *The Unnatural History of the Nanny*, as "a popular account," which somewhat inaccurately represents the nanny "as an upper-class ideal, a matronly figure who has been with the family her entire life and is retained in old age" (118). She cites Theresa' McBride's study, "'As The Twig is Bent': The Victorian Nanny" (from *The Victorian Family: Structures and Stresses*. Ed. A. S. Wohl, 1978) as offering a "different picture that is more accurate for the middle classes in this period": McBride shows that the nursemaid was commonly the only servant in the middle-class home, that these women "were often young

and untrained, and that there was a high turnover" (Hamlett 118–119). Although Gathorne-Hardy might offer a more compelling portrait of the nannies of upper class children, he is, in fact, aware that employment of nannies and other domestics was common, even among the lower middle class. See the section in Gathorne-Hardy's book, "Changing Attitudes to Child Upbringing; Influence of Nursery Training Colleges; Number of Nannies" (174–187).

26 Although Ibsen set all of his plays in Norway (with the exception of the fourth act of *Peer Gynt*), he lived abroad in Italy and Germany for twenty-seven years. As Sandberg notes, Ibsen's "metaphoric source domain had likely become wider than that of many of his readers or viewers," not only because he "wrote about his Norwegian home culture" from a distance but also because "he and his family constantly shifted domiciles throughout his time abroad" (*Ibsen's Houses* 11). I do not wish to wade into the nationalist debate concerning Ibsen's Norwegian-ness, but simply to acknowledge that the nursery is arguably an aspect of European middle-class culture, broadly speaking.

27 *The Century of the Child* is also the English title of Swedish feminist Ellen Key's best-known study, *Barnets århundrade*, which was first published in 1900. Key's study expresses similar ideas about free play, proper furnishing of the nursery, and the significance of fantasy to childhood.

28 In order to understand this "increasing emphasis" fully, a complete history of the nanny in the Norwegian context would need to consider, among other things, changes in the relationship between servants and the ruling classes, especially over the course of the second half of the nineteenth century. The changes in this relationship coincided with the end of the dominance of the civil class, which coincided with increasing industrialization and changes in opportunities for employment in Norway—and, eventually, with changes in the birthrate as it became more difficult to hire live-in care for children (see Sogner and Telste). In books such as *For tjenestepiger* (*For Servant Girls*) (1851), writer and self-made expert, Hanna Winsnes, recognized the significance of servants for the smooth running of a household and articulated a strict understanding of their God-given place in the world ruled over by the civil class. Later, she recognized the social changes taking place and the end of starker hierarchies that had secured obedience. For an introduction to Winsnes's life, writings, and philosophy of service, see Kari Melby's "Hanna Winsnes og Stadsinteresse."

29 The title page of Wegener's advice manual announces that it was translated and published for Danish and Norwegian readers in 1913. It does not indicate the original language of the text. The translator, Ragnv. Lexow-Breck, is perhaps Jens Ragnvald Lexow-Breck, who is listed in the 1910 census as an occupant at the Kristiania address 0301. Lexow-Breck was a pastor with two children and one servant, Ingrid Hegge. See https://www.digitalarkivet.no/census/person/pf01036392046642

30 See the Introduction and Chapter 1 for explications of this exaggerative link with reference to Edelman's *No Future*.

31 See also Telste's "Familieklenodiet" (The Family's Treasure) for a study of Ingeborg Christine Gulbrandsen (born in 1835), a servant girl who became a beloved, lifelong member of the Sommerfelt family. Although the Sommerfelt family cannot be the only case, Telste notes that such a position in the family was in no way guaranteed or common. Another striking example of lifelong love and admiration appears to be reflected in Mount Betty, an Antarctic Peak discovered in 1911 and named by Roald Amundsen (1872–1928) after his nanny and longtime housekeeper, Betty Andersson.

32 www.oslobilder.no/OMU/OB.OH516?query=barnepike&count=10&search_context=1&pos=6

33 https://digitaltmuseum.no/011014872819/lordagsvask-i-barnevaerelset

34 https://digitaltmuseum.no/011014873577/lek-pa-barnevaerelset; https://digitaltmuseum.no/011014880530/barnevaerelse-i-thomas-heftyes-gate-2

35 https://digitaltmuseum.no/021016567480/foto-av-fem-barn-ute-i-naturen-sittende-pa-en-liten-berghammer-trolig-i

36 In *Child Loving*, Kincaid uses the phrase "history of the present" to describe the work of French medievalist and historian of childhood, Philippe Ariès, whose methods function to "[de-nature] 'the child,' exposing our own constructing apparatus, freeing us, at least a little, from the tyranny of our own eccentric seeing" (62). Although I believe Kincaid's phrase also suits my project, I do not claim to deploy Ariès's methods. For an example of Ariès's scholarship, see "From Immodesty to Innocence" in *The Children's Culture Reader*.

Epilogue
Survivors

The title of this book refers to Ibsen's late plays, but its core chapters have focused on the first three of the last five dramas, likely leaving some readers with a question: What about *John Gabriel Borkman* (1896) and *Når vi døde vågner* (*When We Dead Awaken*) (1899)? All of the late plays take us closer and closer to what might be called successful re-production, from Hedda's suicide-coterminous abortion, to Solness's dead twin babies, to Eyolf's drowning at age eight, to Erhart Borkman's decision to leave his old, miserable parents behind, to Arnold Rubek's world-famous statue/child, "Resurrection Day," which is already out traveling the world (*Nvdv* 9). While the three "empty nursery plays" pivot on unfinished projects, the loss or absence of children, and parents' plans for refilling nurseries left behind, *John Gabriel Borkman* and *When We Dead Awaken* present us with survivors. *Hedda Gabler*, *The Master Builder*, and *Little Eyolf* tempt us to ask, What would have been different had babies been born or survived, if nurseries were filled with "a flock of children," that sign of happiness according to the master builder (*BS* 68)? Such questions can only be answered in speculative mode, but we might also look to Ibsen's last two dramas to ask what difference survival makes.

This Epilogue briefly introduces each of the survivors, and the state in which they leave their parents, in order to open a new argument about re-production in Ibsen: survival makes no difference. In Chapter 1, I asked whether Ibsen's understanding of creativity and procreativity is in some sense mirrored in his characters' reproductive figures and claims, or whether he wants us to question the parent-child/artist-"child" relationship. Although his dramas sometimes appear to suggest that it is wrong to confuse children with artworks or life-missions, *John Gabriel Borkman* and *When We Dead Awaken* indicate that offspring and artworks are the same, at least when it comes to the parent or artist's desire to mark, master, and live on by means of their progeny. In these last two works, the author—as former banker and sculptor, respectively—is not quite dead; but he dies alongside his ambitions and best intentions (just like the rest of us), while the almost grown son and masterpiece remain outsiders to the biological and aesthetic family.

John Gabriel Borkman portrays, among other things, the departure of a grown son, who does not care to redeem his father's name. According to his mother, Gunhild, Erhart was once the "innocent" child (*JGB* 7). Socially shamed by his father's financial crimes, he was sent away to be reared by his aunt, Ella Rentheim, whose fortunes were spared when Borkman went to jail. When the drama opens, Erhart is living in the vicinity of the Borkman house, where his estranged parents now lead separate lives on separate floors. Throughout the first three acts, twin sisters Ella and Gunhild fight over the only son of the Borkman family. Having understood that she is terminally ill, Ella wants Erhart to return to the west coast with her, to take the Rentheim name and inherit her money. Gunhild wants to use her son as an instrument of revenge, blotting out all traces of his father's life and crimes, while redeeming the Borkman name. In Act Three, Erhart insists four times that he is young and can thrive neither with mother nor aunt, because it's "roses and lavender,—parlor-air, there as here!" (66). When Borkman hears his son reject his sister-in-law's and wife's propositions, he believes for a moment that he might recruit Erhart for his own project of conquering the past, of leaving the realm of dreams and beginning to work again: "come and bind yourself to me [...]! Because life, it's work, Erhart. Come, and we'll go out into life and work together" (68). Although Erhart professes love for both Ella and Gunhild and speaks in a tone of formal respect to his father, he also *"passionately"* exclaims, "I don't *want* to work! Just live, live, live!" (68). When Gunhild questions what Erhart will live for, he names happiness and then brings his lover, divorcee Fanny Wilton, into the room.

Elinor Fuchs asserts that Ibsen depicts the older generation as "vampires" in *John Gabriel Borkman*, desperate to make good by feeding on new life-blood ("Estragement" 71). Erhart refuses to represent or even think about the future, reveling in the privilege of late adolescence: a temporary experience of timelessness, a desire to live for pleasure without (yet) feeling compelled to engage in either planning or "life review" (Fuchs 71). Gunhild insists that Erhart's focus on living for happiness is shortsighted, to which he responds, "I don't care to look forward in time. Don't want to look around in any direction!" (*JGB* 71). Erhart and Fanny now announce that they will leave right away, traveling south to foreign lands with Frida Foldal, a young friend of the family—and, it is implied, a possible future lover for Erhart. Frida will study music, receive tutoring from Erhart, and "give the expedition the colour of respectability" (Fuchs 75). When Erhart leaves, the older generation is denied their dreams of persistence by means of a successor. Ella wishes him happiness, but Gunhild utters the word "childless," and Borkman demands his hat and cloak, leaving the self-imposed exile of his house for the first time in years (*JGB* 73).

The struggle over Erhart lingers momentarily in the opening of Act Four, until the sound of silver bells from Fanny's sleigh fade from earshot. Gunhild decides that these bells have sounded both her own and Erhart's funeral; and then Vilhelm Foldal, Borkman's friend and Frida's father, arrives, bringing with him some comic relief. Covered in snow and limping, Foldal announces that he has received a letter from his daughter concerning her intention to leave. He is hoping to say good-bye in person, not realizing that the sleigh that just crushed his foot, driving him off the road and into the snow, was already carrying Frida away. Although he will not have the opportunity to wish her well, Foldal remains thrilled that his daughter is traveling out into a world that he always dreamed of seeing, especially in such grandeur, to the sound of real silver bells. Unlike Ella, Gunhild, and Borkman, he understands his progeny to be traveling in his name, a living legacy: "It's my—my scrap of poetic talent that has translated itself into music in Frida. And so I haven't been a poet in vain after all" (81). Foldal does not mind, or does not see the irony in, the fact that he has been run over by the coach carrying his own daughter, the girl who supposedly carries his poetic gift into the world. He is only happy that the streetcar is near, so that he can return home quickly to comfort Frida's mother, despite his injured foot. Without the possibility of working side by side with his son for restoration, Borkman can now refocus on his fantasies of industrial empire. He walks up to an open, snow-covered high point in the forest near his house, expresses his undying love for the metal in the depths of the earth, and dies, leaving Gunhild and Ella behind to mourn him, "two shadows—over the dead man" (88).

In *When We Dead Awaken*, the main characters discuss Rubek's one and only masterpiece, a world-famous sculpture that also fails to live up to its "parents," artist and model/muse/mother's, expectations. When the drama opens, Rubek has recently returned home to Norway as a tourist, where he happens to cross paths with his former muse, Irene, at a health resort. Irene inspired an early version of the sculpture, which was supposed to show "the world's noblest, cleanest, most ideal woman, she, who awakes" from the sleep of death unchanged on judgment day (*Nvdv* 26). When Irene thought that the sculpture was finished, she left Rubek, feeling betrayed by his failure to consummate their relationship, to treat it as anything other than a "happy episode"—a failure that she claims made her into a dead-living statue (50). Since that time, both Irene and Rubek have traveled widely, worked, and married. Irene continued to model and perform in the nude, and she insists that she has murdered one husband, driven another insane, and killed several babies. Rubek is currently traveling with his much younger and profoundly bored wife, Maja. He has also continued to sculpt, producing portrait busts praised for their striking likenesses, but revealing the hidden truth of ugly animal features to the sculptor's eyes alone.

"Resurrection Day" has made Rubek both famous and wealthy. Like his busts, however, the masterpiece is misunderstood and misread by audiences. The fact that so many people delight in something "that isn't even there"—something "that has never been" in Rubek's "thoughts"—causes the artist both to mistrust and resolutely affirm its value: "because 'Resurrection Day' *is* a masterpiece! Or *was* one in the beginning. No, it *is* still. *Shall, shall, shall* be a masterpiece" (Nvdv 9). Rubek protests too much, doubting his work for its failure to cohere with and communicate his vision. In Act Two, he admits to Irene that, having become "wise to the world," he significantly altered the original sculpture after she left him, both widening its base and making it "somewhat more various" (48). He decentered the figure modeled on Irene and placed it in a group of figures, dimming the "happy enlightenment" that once shone in its face (48–49). Irene is furious, insisting that Rubek has pronounced a judgment over himself, but then Rubek excitedly tells her (as if this might change the judgment) how he added a self-portrait to the work: "In front of a spring, like here, sits a man weighed down by guilt, who can't quite get free of the crust of earth. I call him regret over a squandered life" (49). This figure tries to wash his fingers in the spring, but he knows that it will never work, that he will never be free—or resurrected, like Irene's figure—that he will remain "stuck forever in his own hell" (49). Rubek's description inspires Irene to call him "Digter" (poet) and a "precious, great, ageing child," a person who attempts to excuse and cover up his own sins (49–50). We are not given further details about the public interpretation of the masterpiece.

Irene claims that her former life with Rubek can have no "resurrection," but they both decide that they can continue to play games together (Nvdv 54). They act out aspects of the sculpture/"child," approaching its attitudes, replaying its figuration in real-life theater. In Act Three, Rubek insists that their love is not dead, that it "seethes and burns" in him "hotter than ever before," but Irene claims that revival only gives one the capacity to see the rigor mortis in life: "Your young, resurrected woman can see all of life laid out like a corpse" (67). Although she never explicitly renounces her identity as a dead-living statue—and although Rubek's passion might not depend on Irene's identity in any case: "For me, you are the woman that I dream of seeing in you"—she agrees to make one last attempt to live with him (67). Having made their way to the heights, they climb higher into the stormy weather, planning to celebrate their spiritual marriage on the peak in the light of the sun. They disappear into the fog and are shortly brought down by an avalanche (perhaps triggered by Maja's song of freedom). Meanwhile, the world-famous masterpiece presumably goes on living a life of its own, telling stories that the artist never authorized, leaving its parents behind to suffer and mourn—and to play and die.

When it comes to (pro)creativity, Ibsen's last five dramas offer a critique of mastery. *John Gabriel Borkman* and *When We Dead Awaken* especially remind us that "one can sign neither a child nor a work. Being a father means having the extremely joyful and painful experience of the fact that one is not the father—that a son or a daughter is someone one does not answer for, who can speak for themselves" (Derrida, A Taste for the Secret 29). With mixed pain and joy, Ibsen's last two dramas undermine lingering hopes that one might guarantee fulfillment of the parent's or artist's vision by means of survival, because survival neither protects against death nor disables queer(er) "threats" to and reconfigurations of family. If it is not already established, a careful reading of *John Gabriel Borkman* and *When We Dead Awaken* can make it apparent that survivors are neither the key to a good future nor the only sign of bad recurrence. Unwilling or incapable of adhering to the parent/artist's vision, existing in a world full of people who cannot (and probably have no wish to) see the author's intentions, a grown child and a renowned work of art are strangers to the father/artist and mother/muse, whose "immensity of conscious experience" lives on to death (Fuchs 77). Ibsen also uses survivors to show that the impossibility of signing one's child or one's statue is no obstruction to the persistence of vision, regardless of diminishing temporal horizons or challenges to potency and creativity. As Fuchs has suggested, Ibsen's last two dramas seem to "require a landscape, staged or told, that itself becomes a place of estrangement or exile [...] Here the limitations of age may terrify, yet a new horizon of old age may open" (77). Like Erhart, Ibsen's parent-artists want to "live, live, live" (*JGB* 68). Like all his characters, they must live with survival, with the "inadequacy in the very idea of paternity" (Derrida 29), and in the wake of their works and dreams.

Works Cited

Aarseth, Asbjørn. *Ibsens samtidsskuespill: en studie i glasskapets dramaturgi.* Universitetsforlaget, 1999.

Adorno, Theodor W. *Minima Moralia: Reflections from a Damaged Life,* trans. by E. F. N. Jephcott. New Verso, 1978.

Alnæs, Nina S. *Varulv om natten: folketro og folkediktning hos Ibsen.* Gyldendal, 2003.

Ariès, Philippe. "From Immodesty to Innocence." *The Children's Culture Reader,* edited by Henry Jenkins. New York University Press, 1998, pp. 41–57.

Bang, Herman. "Hedda Gabler." *Tilskueren,* vol. 9. P.G. Philipsens Forlag, 1892, pp. 827–838.

Barrie, J. M. *Peter Pan and Other Plays.* Oxford University Press, 1995.

———. *Peter and Wendy.* Grosset and Dunlap, 1911.

Bernstein, Robin. *Racial Innocence: Performing American Childhood from Slavery to Civil Rights.* New York University Press, 2011.

Bing, Morten, Torgeir Kjos and Birte Sandvik. *En historiebok i tre etasjer: Boskikk i byen, 1865–2002.* Cappelen Damm, 2011.

———. "En Tidsmaskin." in *By og Bygd,* vol. 42, 2010, pp. 11–31. https://norskfolkemuseum.no/bb-42.PDF

———. "En liten verden på tre etasjer." in *By og Bygd,* vol. 42, 2010, pp. 33–64. https://norskfolkemuseum.no/bb-42.PDF

———. "Tjenestejenter og hushjelper i Wessels gate 15." *Museumsbulletinen,* no. 4, 2006. p. 13. https://docplayer.me/2341369-Tjenestejenter-og-hushjelper-i-wessels-gate-15.html.PDF

Björklund, Jenny. "Playing with Pistols: Female Masculinity in Henrik Ibsen's *Hedda Gabler.*" *Scandinavian Studies,* vol. 88, no. 1, 2016, pp. 1–16.

Blain, Virginia. "Thinking Back through Our Aunts: Harriet Martineau and Tradition in Women's Writing." *Women: A Cultural Review,* vol. 1, no. 3, 1990, pp. 223–239.

Blau, Herbert. "'Hedda Gabler': The Irony of Decadence." *Educational Theatre Journal,* vol. 5, no. 2, 1953, pp. 112–116.

Blom, Ida. "Ammestuehistorier: glimpt gjennom noen århundrer." *KvinneMinne-Bok: til Ida Blom: på 60-årsdagen, 20. Februar, 1991,* edited by Bente Gullveig and Lisbeth Mikaelsson. Senter for humanistisk kvinneforskning, UiB, 1991. pp. 51–56. https://urn.nb.no/URN:NBN:no-nb_digibok_2007082201032

Bloom, Harold. *The Western Canon: The Books and School of the Ages.* Harcourt Brace, 1994.

Bruhm, Steven, and Hurley, Natasha. "Curiouser: On the Queerness of Children," *Curiouser: On the Queerness of Children*, edited by Steven Bruhm and Natasha Hurley University of Minnesota Press, 2004, pp. ix–xxxviii.

Caserio, Robert L. "The Antisocial Thesis in Queer Theory." *PMLA: Publications of the Modern Language Association of America*, vol. 121, no. 3, 2006, pp. 819–821.

Chaudhuri, Una and Elinor Fuchs. *Land/Scape/Theater*. University of Michigan Press, 2002.

Clima, Maria. *Husstel og Madstel*, trans. and edited by Helga Helgesen. J. W. Cappelens Forlag, 1890. http://urn.nb.no/URN:NBN:no-nb_digibok_ 2009120313003

Cocks, Neil. *The Peripheral Child in Nineteenth Century Literature and Its Criticism*. Palgrave Macmillan, 2014.

Dean, Tim. "An Impossible Embrace: Queerness, Futurity, and the Death Drive." *A Time for the Humanities*, Fordham University Press, 2008.

Derrida, Jacques. *Archive Fever: A Freudian Impression*, trans. by Eric Prenowitz. University of Chicago Press, 1996.

———. *Mémoires: for Paul De Man*. Columbia University Press, 1986.

Derrida, Jacques and Maurizio Ferraris. *A Taste for the Secret*. Polity, 2001.

Diamond, Elin. "Realism and Hysteria: Toward a Feminist Mimesis." *Discourse*, vol. 13, no. 1, 1990, pp. 59–92.

Durbach, Errol. *'Ibsen the Romantic': Analogues of Paradise in the Later Plays*. University of Georgia Press, 1982.

Døderlein, Dr. Chr. *Spædbarnet, Dets udvikling og stel*. Aschehoug, 1891. http://urn.nb.no/URN:NBN:no-nb_digibok_2015012208049

Eagleton, Terry. "Ibsen and the Nightmare of History." *Ibsen Studies*, vol. 8, no. 1, 2008, pp. 4–12.

Edelman, Lee. "Against Survival: Queerness in a Time That's Out of Joint." *Shakespeare Quarterly*, vol. 62, no. 2, 2011, pp. 148–169.

———. *No Future: Queer Theory and the Death Drive*. Duke University Press, 2004.

Ewbank, Inga-Stina. "Henrik Ibsen; National Language and International Drama." *Contemporary Approaches to Ibsen*, vol. 6, 1998, pp. 57–67.

Forældre og børn: en bog om hjemmets oppgaver af forældre og barnevenner, edited by Aksel Arstal. Aschehoug, 1902. http://urn.nb.no/ URN:NBN:no-nb_digibok_2010052006001

Fuchs, Elinor. "Estragement: Towards an 'Age Theory' Theatre Criticism." *Performance Research*, vol. 19, no. 3, 2014, pp. 69–77.

———. "EF's Visit to a Small Planet: Some Questions to Ask a Play." *Theater*, vol. 34, no. 2, 2004, pp. 4–9.

———. *The Death of Character: Perspectives on Theater after Modernism*. Indiana University Press, 1996.

Gathorne-Hardy, Jonathan. *The Unnatural History of the Nanny*. Dial Press, 1973.

Gilead, Sarah. "Magic Abjured: Closure in Children's Fantasy Fiction." *PMLA*, vol. 106, no. 2, 1991, pp. 277–293.

Gjesdal, Kristin (ed). *Ibsen's Hedda Gabler: Philosophical Perspectives*. Oxford University Press, 2018.

Goldman, Michael. *Ibsen: The Dramaturgy of Fear*. Columbia University Press, 1999.

Gorceix, Paul, Ed. Introduction to *Maurice Maeterlinck et le Drame Statique*. Eurédit, 2005.

Gunn, Olivia. "Lost Boys in *Little Eyolf*." *On Replacement: Cultural, Social and Psychological Representations*, edited by Jean Owen and Naomi Segal. Palgrave Macmillan, 2018, pp. 47–56.

———. "A Scandalous Similarity? The Wild Duck and the Romantic Child." *Ibsen Studies*, vol. 13, no. 1, 2013, pp. 47–76.

Guy-Bray, Stephen. *Against Reproduction: Where Renaissance Texts Come From*. University of Toronto Press, 2009.

Halberstam, Judith. *Female Masculinity*. Duke University Press, 2018.

Hamlett, Jane. *Material Relations: Domestic Interiors and Middle-Class Families in England, 1850–1910*. Manchester University Press, 2010.

Hassel, Marit. "Nasjonsbygging og barndomsideal rundt hundreårsskifte: Ei samanlikning av nokre norske biletbøker og Norskt barneblad." *Norsk barndom i to etapper*, edited by Harald Bache-Wiig. Fagbokforlaget Hasselbaum, 1999. pp. 41–52.

Helland, Frode. "The Scars of Modern Life: *Hedda Gabler* in Adorno's Prism." *Ibsen's Hedda Gabler: Philosophical Perspectives*, edited by Kristin Gjesdal. Oxford University Press, 2018, pp. 95–111.

———. "Ibsen and Nietzsche: The Master Builder." *Ibsen Studies*, vol. 9, 2009, pp. 50–75.

———. "Petrified Time: Ibsen's Response to Modernity, with Special Emphasis on *Little Eyolf*." *Ibsen Studies*, vol. 3, no. 2, 2003, pp. 135–144.

———. *Melankoliens spill: en studie i Henrik Ibsens siste dramaer*. Oslo: Universitetsforlaget, 2000.

Hoel, Ane. "Det Provoserende Svangerskapet i Henrik Ibsens Hedda Gabler: Et Spørsmålstegn Ved Traderte Sannheter." *Nordlit*, no. 3, 1998, pp. 267–284.

Ibsen, Henrik. *Ibsen: The Complete Major Prose Plays*, trans. by Rolf Fjelde, Plume, 1978.

———. *Letters and Speeches*, trans. by Evert Sprinchorn. Hill and Wang, 1964.

———. *Når vi døde vågner: En dramatisk epilog i tre akter*, 1. utg. 1899. Henrik Ibsens skrifter, Historisk-kritisk utgave, elektronisk versjon. www.ibsen.uio.no/DRVIT_NV|NVht.xhtml.PDF

———. *John Gabriel Borkman: skuespil i fire akter*, 1. utg. 1896. Henrik Ibsens skrifter, Historisk-kritisk utgave, elektronisk versjon. www.ibsen.uio.no/DRVIT_JG%7CJGht.xhtml.PDF

———. *Lille Eyolf: skuespil i tre akter*, 1. utg. 1894. Henrik Ibsens skrifter, Historisk-kritisk utgave, elektronisk versjon. www.ibsen.uio.no/DRVIT_LE|LEht.xhtml.PDF

———. *Bygmester Solness: Skuespil i tre akter*. 1. utg. 1892. Henrik Ibsens skrifter, Historisk-kritisk utgave, elektronisk versjon. www.ibsen.uio.no/DRVIT_BS|BSht.xhtml.PDF

———. *Hedda Gabler*, Hovedtekst, 1. utg. 1890 Henrik Ibsens skrifter, Historisk-kritisk utgave, elektronisk versjon. www.ibsen.uio.no/DRVIT_HG%7CHGht.xhtml.PDF

———. *Et dukkehjem*, Hovedtekst, 1. utg. 1879. Henrik Ibsens skrifter, Historisk-kritisk utgave, elektronisk versjon. www.ibsen.uio.no/VERK_Du.xhtml.PDF

Jarcho, Julia. "Cold Theory, Cruel Theater. Staging the Death Drive with Lee Edelman and Hedda Gabler." *Critical Inquiry*, vol. 44, no. 1, 2017, pp. 1–16.

Kafer, Alison. *Feminist, Queer, Crip*. Indiana University Press, 2013.

Kanagawa, Hiro. *Indian Arm*. Canada Playwrights Press, 2016.

Kerans, James E. "Kindermord and Will in Little Eyolf." *Modern Drama: Essays in Criticism*. Oxford University Press, 1965, pp. 192–208.

Key, Ellen. *Barnets århundrade*. A. Bonnier, 1911–12.

Kincaid, James R. *Erotic Innocence: The Culture of Child Molesting*. Duke University Press, 1998.

———. *Child-Loving: The Erotic Child and Victorian Culture*. Routledge, 1992.

Lesnik-Oberstein, Karín. "Childhood, Queer Theory, and Feminism." *Feminist Theory*, vol. 11, no. 3, 2010, pp. 309–321.

Lesnik-Oberstein, Karín and Stephen Thomson. "What Is Queer Theory Doing with the Child?" *Parallax*, vol. 8, no. 1, 2016, pp. 35–46, *ProQuest*, Web, 26 Apr. 2016.

Lisi, Leonardo F. "Nihilism and Boredom in *Hedda Gabler*." *Ibsen's Hedda Gabler: Philosophical Perspectives*, edited by Kristin Gjesdal. Oxford University Press, 2018.

Løken, Olaug. *Barnestel: en liden bog for unge mødre*. Det norske Aktieforlag, 1903 https://urn.nb.no/URN:NBN:no-nb_digibok_2018042548015

Løken, Olaug and Dr. L. W. Schibbye. *For barnepiger og mødre, veiledning i barnestel*. Aschehoug, 1905. https://urn.nb.no/URN:NBN:no-nb_digibok_2014021908119

Marder, Elissa. *The Mother in the Age of Mechanical Reproduction: Psychoanalysis, Photography, Deconstruction*. Fordham University Press, 2012.

Mavor, Carol. *Reading Boyishly: Roland Barthes, J.M. Barrie, Jacques Henri Lartigue, Marcel Proust, and D.W. Winnicott*. Duke University Press, 2007.

Melby, Kari. "Hanna Winsnes og Stadsinteresse." *KvinneMinneBok: til Ida Blom: på 60-årsdagen, 20. Februar, 1991*, edited by Bente Gullveig and Lisbeth Mikaelsson. Senter for humanistisk kvinneforskning, UiB, 1991. pp. 51–56. https://urn.nb.no/URN:NBN:no-nb_digibok_2007082201032

Miller, J. Hillis. *For Derrida*. Fordham University Press, 2009.

Moi, Toril. "Hedda's Silences: Beauty and Despair in Hedda Gabler." *Modern Drama*, vol. 56, no. 4, 2013, pp. 434–456.

———. *Henrik Ibsen and the Birth of Modernism: Art, Theater, Philosophy*. Oxford University Press, 2006.

Moretti, Franco. *The Bourgeois: Between History and Literature*. Verso, 2013.

Mortensen, Ellen. "Feminine Floker i Ibsens Hedda Gabler." *Edda*, no. 4, 2006, pp. 388–434.

Muñoz, José Esteban. *Cruising Utopia: the Then and There of Queer Futurity*. New York University Press, 2009.

Muriel, Bradbrook. "Ibsen and the Past Imperfect." *Literature in Action: Studies in Continental and Commonwealth Society*. Barnes & Noble, 1972.

Myhre, Jan Eivind. "The Middle Classes of Norway, 1840–1940." *The Scandinavian Middle Classes 1840–1940*, edited by Tom Ericsson, Jørgen Fink and Jan Eivind Myhre. Fagbokforlaget, 2004. pp. 103–145.

Naas, Michael. "To Reckon with the Dead: Jacques Derrida's Politics of Mourning." *The Work of Mourning* by Jacques Derrida, edited by Pascale-Anne Brault and Michael Nass. The University of Chicago Press, 2001. pp. 1–30.

Når man skal sætte bo. A. L. B. Cammermeyers Forlag, 1892. http://urn.nb.no/URN:NBN:no-nb_digibok_2016042848047.

Nordau, Max Simon. *Degeneration*, trans. by George L. Mosse. University of Nebraska Press, 1993.

Neubauer, John. *The Fin-de-siècle Culture of Adolescence.* Yale University Press, 1992.

Otten, Terry. "Ibsen's Paradoxical Attitudes toward Kindermord." *Mosaic: A Journal for the Interdisciplinary Study of Literature*, vol. 22, no. 3, 1989, pp. 117–131.

Parvulescu, Anca. "Reproduction and Queer Theory: Between Lee Edelman's 'No Future' and J.M. Coetzee's 'Slow Man'." *PMLA*, vol. 132, no. 1, 2017, pp. 86–100.

———. *The Traffic in Women's Work: East European Migration and the Making of Europe.* The University of Chicago Press, 2014.

Phelan, Peggy. *Unmarked: The Politics of Performance.* Routledge, 1993.

Prins, Yopie. "Greek Maenads, Victorian Spinsters." *Victorian Sexual Dissidence*, edited by Richard Dellamora. University of Chicago Press, 1999, pp. 43–81.

Rees, Ellen. "Problems of Landscape and Representation in Ibsen's *Når vi døde vågner.*" *Ibsen Studies*, vol. 10, no. 1, 2010, pp. 37–61.

Reynolds, Kimberley and Paul Yates, "Gone Too Soon: Representations of Childhood Death in Literature for Children." *Children in Culture: Approaches to Childhood*, edited by Karín Lesnik-Oberstein. St. Martin's, 1998. pp. 151–177.

Rich, Adrienne. "When We Dead Awaken: Writing as Re-Vision." *On Lies, Secrecy and Silence: Selected Prose 1966–1978.* W. W. Norton & Company, 1979. pp. 33–49.

Rose, Jacqueline. *The Case of Peter Pan, or, the Impossibility of Children's Fiction.* University of Pennsylvania, 1993.

Sandberg, Mark B. *Ibsen's Houses: Architectural Metaphor and the Modern Uncanny.* Cambridge University Press, 2015.

———. *Living Pictures, Missing Persons: Mannequins, Museums, and Modernity.* Princeton University Press, 2003.

S. B. "Hvor skal børnene være?" *Hjemmet*, no. 17 14, 1911. http://urn.nb.no/URN:NBN:no-nb_digitidsskrift_2015092280003_017

Schneider, Rebecca. *Performing Remains: Art and War in Times of Theatrical Reenactment.* Routledge, 2011.

Schwab, Gabriele. "Replacement Children: The Transgenerational Transmission of Traumatic Loss." *American Imago*, vol. 66, no. 3, 2009, pp. 277–310.

Sedgwick, Eve Kosofsky. "Tales of the Avunculate: The Importance of Being Earnest." *Tendencies.* Duke University Press, 1993, pp. 52–72.

Selmer, Ågot Gjems. *Vore børns sedelige opdragelse: et foredrag.* Aschehoug, 1902. https://urn.nb.no/URN:NBN:no-nb_digibok_2014052308068

Shaw, George Bernard. *Shaw and Ibsen: Bernard Shaw's The Quintessence of Ibsenism and Related Writings*, edited by J. L. Wisenthal, University of Toronto Press, 1979.

Shetelig, Haakon. "Lykkens dager." *Sigurd Pedersens ungdomserindringer.* Tanum, 1959, pp. 193–231 https://urn.nb.no/URN:NBN:no-nb_digibok_2012011608119

Sogner, Sølvi. *I gode og vonde dagar: familieliv i Noreg frå reformasjonen til vår tid*, edited by Hilde Sandvik, Kari Telste, Hanne Marie Johansen, and Beate Homlong. Det Norske Samlaget, 2003.

Sogner, Sølvi and Kari Telste. *Ut å søkje teneste: Historia om tenestejentene.* Det norske samlaget, 2005.

Steedman, Carolyn. *Strange Dislocations: Childhood and the Idea of Human Interiority, 1780–1930*. Harvard University Press, 1995.

Stenport, Anna Westerståhl. "The Sexonomics of Et Dukkehjem: Money, the Domestic Sphere and Prostitution." *Edda*, vol. 106, no. 4, 2006, pp. 339–433.

Stockton, Kathryn Bond. "The Queer Child Now and Its Paradoxical Global Effects." *GLQ: A Journal of Lesbian and Gay Studies*, vol. 22, no. 4. 2016, pp. 505–539.

———. *The Queer Child, or Growing Sideways in the Twentieth Century*. Duke University Press, 2009.

Stutfield, H.E.M. "The Psychology of Feminism." *Blackwood's Magazine*, 1897, p. 12.

Sverdrup Ugelstad, Janike. "Lerkefugl og pomponger." *Forstenet Tid. By og Bygd*, vol. 42, pp. 128–142. https://norskfolkemuseum.no/bb-42.PDF

Templeton, Joan. *Shaw's Ibsen: A Re-Appraisal*. Palgrave Macmillan, 2017.

———. *Ibsen's Women*. Cambridge University Press, 1997.

Telste, Kari. "'Familieklenodiet': tjenestejenta Ingeborg Gulbrandsen fra Ringerike og familien Sommerfelt." *Hringariki. Medlemsblad for Ringerike slektshistorielag*, no. 1, 2013, n.p.

———. "Tjenestepiken i hverdag og fritid." *Museumsbulletinen*, no. 4, 2006, pp. 14–19. https://docplayer.me/2341369-Tjenestejenter-og-hushjelper-i-wessels-gate-15.html.PDF

Vammen, Tinne. *Rent Og Urent: Hovedstadens Piger Og Fruer 1880–1920*. Gyldendals Bogklub, 1988.

Voronina, Olga. "The Tale of Enchanted Hunters: Lolita in Victorian Context." *Nabokov Studies*, vol. 10, no. 1, 2006, pp. 147–174.

Wegener, Hans. *Slægten som kommer: en bog for forældre og for dem, som vil blive det: det seksuelle problem i barne opdragelse*. Cammermeyers Forlag, 1913. https://urn.nb.no/URN:NBN:no-nb_digibok_2016091508027

Weinstein, Arnold. "My Life Had Stood, a Loaded Gun": Agency and Writing in *Hedda Gabler*." *Ibsen's Hedda Gabler: Philosophical Perspectives*, edited by Kristin Gjesdal, University Press, 2018, pp. 112–131.

———. "Metamorphosis in Ibsen's *Little Eyolf*." *Scandinavian Studies*, vol. 62, no. 3, 1990, pp. 293–318.

Winsnes, Hanna. *For tjenestepiger*. Wulfsberg, 1851. http://urn.nb.no/URN:NBN:no-nb_digibok_2009111110003

Young, Robin. *Time's Disinherited Children: Childhood, Regression, and Sacrifice in the Plays of Henrik Ibsen*. Norvik Press, 1989.

Index

Note: Page numbers followed by "n" denote endnotes.